NONPROFIT REPERTORY THEATRE IN NORTH AMERICA, 1958~1975

NONPROFIT REPERTORY THEATRE IN NORTH AMERICA, 1958~1975

A Bibliography and Indexes to the Playbill Collection of the Theatre Communications Group

Edited and Compiled by Laura J. Kaminsky

 GREENWOOD PRESS

WESTPORT, CONNECTICUT • LONDON, ENGLAND

Library of Congress Cataloging in Publication Data

Kaminsky, Laura J
  Nonprofit repertory theatre in North America, 1958-1975.
  1. Theatre programs—North Americas—Catalogs.
2. Theatre Communications Group. I. Title.
PN2093.K3   792'.097   77-71869
ISBN 0-8371-9536-5

Library of Congress Catalog Card Number: 77-71869
ISBN: 0-8371-9536-5

First published in 1977

Greenwood Press, Inc.
51 Riverside Avenue, Westport, Connecticut 06880

Printed in the United States of America

CONTENTS

PREFACE

Theatre, like any live performance, has a necessarily short life. When the final curtain falls, the set has been struck, and the company disbanded, only memories remain of what might, in another medium, have been considered an "immortal" artistic accomplishment. One tangible artifact, however, is the production's program or "playbill," giving not only the artists' names and duties, but very often a real sense of the production itself.

The *Theatre Communications Group Program Collection* is the most extensive collection available of programs from America's resident theatres.

A movement scarcely twenty years old, the nonprofit, professional theatre is now the most active source of new plays, revivals and classics, the greatest employer of theatre talent, and one of the most pervasive influences in the country today. The theatres exist in many forms, and their artistic impulses are as varied as their number. They do, however, share a common characteristic which differentiates them from the commercial, educational and avocational theatre: they all are continuing, professional organizations, committed to producing a body of work rather than a single play. Through myriad programs, moreover (workshops, training programs, touring programs and residencies on college campuses, in public schools, in prisons and in neighboring communities), these organizations touch the lives of many more people than those who make up their nightly audience. It is this quality of continued service, made possible through continued operation, which accounts for the astounding growth and development of these theatres over the past two decades. Their programs are an invaluable tool in monitoring, from the beginning, the advancement of this fastest-growing segment of American theatrical tradition.

Collected over the years from the theatres themselves and from The Ford Foundation, 2,500 programs are cataloged by theatre and indexed by play title. They give cast and staff lists, actors' biographies, and theatre histories for such nonprofit professional theatres as Washington's Arena Stage, San Francisco's American Conservatory Theatre, and The Guthrie Theater of Minneapolis, such major New York Groups as Circle in the Square and Chelsea Theater Center, and a number of landmark companies which, although now defunct, played a major role in providing the profession with acting, directorial and playwriting talent.

The program collection represents an invaluable resource to those involved in casting plays, musicals, movies and television productions. It includes the most extensive single source of information regarding the history of funding sources of theatres, including names of public and private agencies, corporations and individuals who have supported the profession. A majority of the programs also include biographical information on every actor, designer, director, playwright and producer involved in the more than 2,500 productions represented. Many theatres over the years have devoted considerable energy, moreover, to researching the history of their and other theatre organizations for articles included in their programs.

In all, the collection provides an unequaled fund of information on the nonprofit professional theatre in the United States and Canada, information of interest to students, teachers, theatre artists, producers and administrators, authors, playwrights, and historians.

JAMES COPELAND

INTRODUCTION

The information presented in this publication was drawn from the extensive collection of playbills of the Theatre Communications Group of New York. Greenwood Press has also made this collection available in microfiche form.

The bibliography has been arranged alphabetically by city. The theatres are listed under the heading for each city, and within each theatre entry the plays are listed alphabetically, under the appropriate season. All citations have been numbered sequentially; these numbers identify the play for indexing purposes.

Within each citation we have attempted to provide the reader with, at the very least, the names of the dramatist and the director of the play. (In rare instances, one of these names may not have been available.) Whenever possible, we have also endeavored to include the names of translators, adaptors, composers, lyricists, musical directors, and other pertinent information about the plays or the programs.

The seven indexes appended to this bibliography are: Titles, Dramatists, Directors, Translators, Adaptors, Composers-Lyricists-Musical Directors, and Theatres. The entries in each index appear in alphabetical order and are followed by the bibliographic citation number(s) to which the reader is referred.

The bibliography and indexes may be used as a reference source in itself, or in conjunction with the Greenwood Press microfiche collection, *Playbills: North American Nonprofit Repertory Theatres, 1958-1975*. The microfiche have not been numbered, but their organization parallels that of the bibliography, with the exception of the playbills within each seasonal category. An attempt was made to film the playbills in chronological sequence, although some programs were found to be undated. Full-page advertisements and other irrelevant material were omitted during the filming process.

The header on the microfiche contains the program title, city, name of theatre, chronology, and number of fiche for that theatre.

We wish to express our gratitude to The Theatre Communications Group for allowing us to borrow their fine playbill collection, and to James Copeland, Program Director of The Group, for his cooperation and assistance on this project.

BIBLIOGRAPHY TO
PLAYBILL COLLECTION

Abingdon, VA

BARTER THEATRE

1959

0001   AUNTIE MAME
(based on the novel by Patrick Dennis) by Jerome Lawrence and
Robert E. Lee; directed by Don Weightman

0002   CYRANO DE BERGERAC
by Edmond Rostand, translated by Brian Hooker; directed by Don
Weightman

0003   GIGI
(adapted from the novel by Colette) by Anita Loos; directed by
John Sillings

0004   RUMPELSTILTSKIN
by Charlotte B. Chorpenning; directed by Robert Porterfield

0005   THE SOLID GOLD CADILLAC
by Howard Teichman and George S. Kaufman; directed by Don
Weightman

0006   VOICE OF THE WHIRLWIND
by Pat Hale; directed by Graham Jarvis. World premiere

1960

0007   THE BOY FRIEND
by Sandy Wilson; directed by Don Weightman; musical director,
Kip Bruce Cohen

0008   THE DARK AT THE TOP OF THE STAIRS
by William Inge; directed by Don Weightman

0009   THE DISENCHANTED
(based on the novel by Budd Schulberg) by Budd Schulberg and
Harvey Breit; directed by Don Weightman

0010   FALLEN ANGELS
by Noel Coward; directed by Robert Porterfield

0011   THE GOLDEN FLEECING
by Lorenzo Semple, Jr.; directed by William Hammond

0012   REGIONS OF NOON
by R.G. Vliet; directed by Robert Porterfield

0013   THE SKIN OF OUR TEETH
by Thornton Wilder; directed by Don Weightman

0014   TWO FOR THE SEESAW
            by William Gibson; directed by Don Weightman

                                    1961

0015   DON JUAN IN HELL
            by George Bernard Shaw; directed by Ned Beatty

0016   THE LAND OF THE DRAGON
            by Madge Miller; directed by Don Weightman

0017   THE MARRIAGE-GO-ROUND
            by Leslie Stevens; directed by Ned Beatty

0018   THE PLEASURE OF HIS COMPANY
            by Sam Taylor; directed by Pat Miller

0019   RAIN
            (adapted from the short story by W. Somerset Maugham) by John
            Colton and Clemence Randolf; directed by Rocco Bufano

0020   THE TEAHOUSE OF THE AUGUST MOON
            (adapted from the novel by Vern Sneider) by John Patrick;
            directed by Pat Miller

0021   TO GOD IN ITALIAN
            by Jasper (Jerry) Oddo; directed by Pat Miller

0022   UNDER MILK WOOD
            by Dylan Thomas; directed by Rocco Bufano

0023   THE WARM PENINSULA
            by Joe Masteroff; directed by Rocco Bufano

0024   WHERE'S CHARLEY?
            by Brandon Thomas, book by George Abbott, music and lyrics by
            Frank Loesser; directed by Rocco Bufano

                                    1962

0025   THE BALD SOPRANO
            by Eugene Ionesco, translated by Donald M. Allen; directed by
            Rocco Bufano. Performed the same evening as *No Exit*

0026   NO EXIT
            by Jean Paul Sartre, adapted by Paul Bowles; directed by Rocco
            Bufano. Performed the same evening as *The Bald Soprano*

                                 1962-1963

0027   ACT WITHOUT WORDS
            by Samuel Beckett; directed by Jerry Hardin

0028   THE FANTASTICKS
            words by Tom Jones, music by Harvey Schmidt; directed by Rocco
            Bufano

0029   FIVE FINGER EXERCISE
        by Peter Shaffer, Rusti Moon, and Robert Pastene; directed by
        Jerry Hardin

0030   JANUS
        by Carolyn Green; directed by Robert Pastene

0031   THE LADY OF LARKSPUR LOTION
        by Tennessee Williams; directed by John Ritchey. Performed the
        same evening as *This Property is Condemned* and *27 Wagons Full
        of Cotton*, under the title of *An Evening of Tennessee Williams*

0032   LONG DAY'S JOURNEY INTO NIGHT
        by Eugene O'Neill; directed by Don Weightman

0033   THE MIRACLE WORKER
        by William Gibson; directed by Paul Melton

0034   MISALLIANCE
        by George Bernard Shaw; directed by Walter Beakel

0035   NIGHT OF THE AUK
        by Arch Oboler; directed by Robert Pastene

0036   PERIOD OF ADJUSTMENT
        by Tennessee Williams; directed by Owen Phillips

0037   RING AROUND THE MOON
        by Jean Anouilh, translated by Christopher Fry; directed by
        Jerry Hardin

0038   THE TAMING OF THE SHREW
        by William Shakespeare; directed by Edward Payson Call

0039   THIS PROPERTY IS CONDEMNED
        by Tennessee Williams; directed by John Ritchey. Performed the
        same evening as *The Lady of Larkspur Lotion* and *27 Wagons Full
        of Cotton*, under the title of *An Evening of Tennessee Williams*

0040   UNCLE VANYA
        by Anton Chekhov; directed by Hal George

0041   UNDER THE YUM-YUM TREE
        by Lawrence Roman; directed by Milt Commons

0042   THE WALTZ OF THE TOREADORS
        by Jean Anouilh; directed by Rocco Bufano. Performed the same
        evening as *The Zoo Story*

0043   WHERE'S CHARLEY?
        by Brandon Thomas, book by George Abbott, music and lyrics by
        Frank Loesser; directed by Don Weightman

0044   WRITE ME A MURDER
        by Frederick Knott; directed by Gordon Davidson

0045   THE ZOO STORY
        by Edward Albee; directed by Jerry Hardin. Performed the same
        evening as *The Waltz of the Toreadors*; also performed with
        27 Wagons Full of Cotton

0046   THE 13 CLOCKS
        by James Thurber, adapted by Frank Lowe; directed by Frank Lowe

0047   27 WAGONS FULL OF COTTON
        by Tennessee Williams; directed by John Ritchey. Performed the
        same evening as *The Zoo Story*; also performed the same evening
        as *The Lady of Larkspur Lotion* and *This Property is Condemned*,
        under the title of *An Evening of Tennessee Williams*

                            1963-1964

0048   BYE BYE BIRDIE
        book by Michael Stewart, music by Charles Strouse, lyrics by
        Lee Adams; directed by Owen Phillips

0049   COME BLOW YOUR HORN
        by Neil Simon; directed by Owen Phillips

0050   GEORGE WASHINGTON SLEPT HERE
        by Moss Hart and George S. Kaufman; directed by Owen Phillips

0051   THE GUARDSMAN
        by Franz Molnar, translated by Grace I. Colbron and Hans
        Bartsh, acting version by Philip Moeller; directed by Owen
        Phillips

0052   INVITATION TO A MARCH
        by Arthur Laurents; directed by Owen Phillips

0053   LOOK HOMEWARD, ANGEL
        (based on the novel by Thomas Wolfe) by Ketti Frings; directed
        by Don Weightman

0054   MAKE A MILLION
        by Norman Barasch and Carroll Moore; directed by Owen Phillips

0055   A MIDSUMMER NIGHT'S DREAM
        by William Shakespeare; directed by Hal George

0056   THE MILK TRAIN DOESN'T STOP HERE ANYMORE
        by Tennessee Williams; directed by Adrian Hall

0057   PERIOD OF ADJUSTMENT
        by Tennessee Williams; directed by Owen Phillips

0058   THE QUEEN AND THE REBELS
        by Ugo Betti; directed by Edwin Wilson

0059   A SHOT IN THE DARK
        by Marcel Archard, adapted by Harry Kurnitz; directed by
        Edwin Wilson

0060   SUNDAY IN NEW YORK
          by Norman Krasna; directed by Owen Phillips

1964-1965

0061   BY GEORGE BERNARD SHAW
          by George Bernard Shaw; directed by Peter W. Culman

0062   PICTURES IN THE HALLWAY
          by Sean O'Casey; directed by Jack Cowles

0063a   THE PRIVATE EAR
          by Peter Shaffer; directed by Lamont Palmer. Performed the
          same evening as *The Public Eye*

0063b   THE PUBLIC EYE
          by Peter Shaffer; directed by Lamont Palmer. Performed the
          same evening as *The Private Ear*

0064   WAITING FOR GODOT
          by Samuel Beckett; directed by Jerry Chase

0065   WHO'S AFRAID OF VIRGINIA WOOLF?
          by Edward Albee; directed by Clinton Atkinson

1965-1966

0066   THE ABSENCE OF A CELLO
          by Ira Wallach; directed by Ronald L. Hufham

0067   THE BAT
          by Mary Roberts Rinehart and Avery Hopwood; directed by
          William Woodman

0068   THE CAVE DWELLERS
          by William Saroyan; directed by Peter W. Culman

0069   THE HAPPIEST MILLIONAIRE
          by Kyle Crichton; directed by Clinton Atkinson

0070   HAY FEVER
          by Noel Coward; directed by Robert Porterfield

0071   JULIUS CAESAR
          by William Shakespeare; directed by Clinton Atkinson. Special
          performance

0072   A MAN FOR ALL SEASONS
          by Robert Bolt; directed by Clinton Atkinson

0073   MARY, MARY
          by Jean Kerr; directed by Clinton Atkinson

0074   TARTUFFE
          by Moliere, English translation by Richard Wilbur; directed by
          Clinton Atkinson

0075   THE THREEPENNY OPERA
        text and lyrics by Bertolt Brecht, music by Kurt Weill, English
        adaptation by Marc Blitzstein; directed by Clinton Atkinson

0076   TWELFTH NIGHT
        by William Shakespeare; directed by Ira Zuckerman

0077   YOU CAN'T TAKE IT WITH YOU
        by Moss Hart and George S. Kaufman; directed by Ira Zuckerman

                            1966-1967

0078   BAREFOOT IN THE PARK
        by Neil Simon; directed by Gordon Greene

0079   BLITHE SPIRIT
        by Noel Coward; directed by Kent Paul

0080   CHARLEY'S AUNT
        by Brandon Thomas; directed by Ned Beatty

0081   FIVE IN THE AFTERNOON
        by Elizabeth Blake; directed by Miranda d'Ancona

0082   HAMLET
        by William Shakespeare; directed by Larry Gates

0083   LOOK BACK IN ANGER
        by John Osborne; directed by Paul Emerson

0084   LUV
        by Murray Schisgal; directed by Robert Brink

0085   THE ODD COUPLE
        by Neil Simon; directed by Robert Brink

0086   ROMEO AND JULIET
        by William Shakespeare; directed by Robert Brink

0087   STOP THE WORLD - I WANT TO GET OFF
        by Leslie Bricusse and Anthony Newley; directed by Jay Lundy

0088   WHO'S AFRAID OF VIRGINIA WOOLF?
        by Edward Albee; directed by Paul Emerson

                            1969-1970

0089   ARMS AND THE MAN
        by George Bernard Shaw; directed by Owen Phillips

0090   THE HASTY HEART
        by John Patrick; directed by Jerry Hardin

0091   HERE TODAY
        by George Oppenheimer; directed by Owen Phillips

0092   THE INCOMPARABLE MAX
        by Jerome Lawrence and Robert E. Lee; directed by Jerome
        Lawrence

0093   THE LION IN WINTER
        by James Goldman; directed by Owen Phillips

0094   MERTON OF THE MOVIES
        (based on the story by Harry Leon) by George S. Kaufman and
        Marc Connelly; directed by Owen Phillips

0095   MONEY
        book and lyrics by David Axelrod and Tom Whedon, music by Sam
        Pottle; directed by Owen Phillips

0096   PLAZA SUITE
        by Neil Simon; directed by William Camp

0097   SEE HOW THEY RUN
        by Philip King; directed by Owen Phillips

0098   THE SHOW-OFF
        by George Kelly; directed by Owen Phillips

0099   THERE'S A GIRL IN MY SOUP
        by Terence Frisby; directed by Owen Phillips

0100   U.S.A.
        (based on the novel by John Dos Passos) by Paul Shyre and John
        Dos Passos; directed by Owen Phillips

0101   THE WINSLOW BOY
        by Terrence Rattigan; directed by Owen Phillips

0102   THE WORLD OF CARL SANDBERG
        by Norman Corwin; directed by Owen Phillips

                              1970-1971

0103   ANGEL STREET
        by Patrick Hamilton; directed by Owen Phillips

0104   ARSENIC AND OLD LACE
        by Joseph Kesselring; directed by Owen Phillips. Program con-
        tains background notes about the play

0105   DON'T DRINK THE WATER
        by Woody Allen; directed by Owen Phillips

0106   FORTY CARATS
        by Pierre Barillet and Jean-Pierre Gredy, adapted by Jay Allen;
        directed by Michael Norell

0107   THE GLASS MENAGERIE
        by Tennessee Williams; directed by Owen Phillips

0108   I DO! I DO!
           (based on *Fourposter* by Jan de Hartog) book and lyrics by Tom
           Jones, music by Harvey Schmidt; directed by Owen Phillips

0109   MUCH ADO ABOUT NOTHING
           by William Shakespeare; directed by Owen Phillips. Program
           contains background notes about the play

0110   THE RIVALRY
           by Norman Corwin; directed by Michael Norell

0111   SPOON RIVER ANTHOLOGY
           by Edgar Lee Masters, conceived, adapted, and arranged by
           Charles Aidman; directed by Michael Norell

0112   A STAND IN THE MOUNTAINS
           by Peter Taylor; directed by Michael Norell

0113   TOO YOUNG FOR SPRING
           by Jasper Oddo; directed by Owen Phillips. Program contains
           background notes about the playwright

1971-1972

0114   BUTTERFLIES ARE FREE
           by Leonard Gershe; directed by Kristina Callahan. Program con-
           tains background notes about the play

0115   THE COUNTRY GIRL
           by Clifford Odets; directed by Rae Allen. Program contains
           background notes about the author

0116   DEAR LIAR
           (based on correspondence of George Bernard Shaw and Mrs.
           Patricia Campbell) by Jerome Kilty; directed by Owen Phillips

0117   DRACULA
           (adapted from the novel by Bram Stoker) by Hamilton Dean and
           John L. Balderson; directed by Kenneth Frankel

0118   HARVEY
           by Mary Chase; directed by Owen Phillips

0119   THE LAST OF THE RED HOT LOVERS
           by Neil Simon; directed by Owen Phillips. Program contains
           background notes about the author

0120   MUCH ADO ABOUT NOTHING
           by William Shakespeare; directed by Owen Phillips. Program
           contains background notes about the play

0121   OUR TOWN
           by Thornton Wilder; directed by Owen Phillips. Program contains
           background notes about the play

0122   SUMMER AND SMOKE
           by Tennessee Williams; directed by George Touliatos

0123   YOU KNOW I CAN'T HEAR YOU WHEN THE WATER'S RUNNING
        by Robert Anderson; directed by John Going

                            1973

0124   CANDLE LIGHT
        by Sigfried Geyer, adapted by P.G. Wodehouse; directed by Rex
        Partington

0125   COCKTAILS WITH MIMI
        by Mary Chase; directed by Owen Phillips. World premiere

0126   THE COMEDY OF ERRORS
        by William Shakespeare; directed by Owen Phillips

0127   THE HOSTAGE
        by Brendan Behan; directed by Kenneth Costigan

0128   THE IMAGINARY INVALID
        by Moliere, adapted by Allen Lorensen; directed by John Olon

0129   LIFE WITH FATHER
        (based on the book by Clarence Day, Jr.) by Howard Lindsay and
        Russel Crouse; directed by Laurence Hugo

0130   THE MARRIAGE-GO-ROUND
        by Leslie Stevens; directed by Kenneth Frankel

0131   NIGHT MUST FALL
        by Emlyn Williams; directed by Kenneth Frankel

0132   SPOON RIVER ANTHOLOGY
        by Edgar Lee Masters, conceived, adapted, and arranged by
        Charles Aidman; directed by Rex Partington

0133   THE SUBJECT WAS ROSES
        by Frank D. Gilroy; directed by Kenneth Costigan

0134   THE VOICE OF THE TURTLE
        by John van Druten; directed by Owen Phillips

                            1974

0135   CANDIDA
        by George Bernard Shaw; directed by George Touliatos

0136   CHAMPAGNE COMPLEX
        by Leslie Stevens; directed by John Olon

0137   THE ODD COUPLE
        by Neil Simon; directed by Kenneth Frankel

0138   PRIVATE LIVES
        by Noel Coward; directed by Rae Allen

0139   SCAPIN
        by Moliere; directed by Rex Partington

0140   SILENT NIGHT, LONELY NIGHT
          by Robert Anderson; directed by Owen Phillips

0141   STRAIGHTJACKET
          by Howard Koch; directed by Kenneth Frankel. World premiere

0142   TEN NIGHTS IN A BARROOM
          (musical comedy version of the famous temperance drama) by
          William W. Pratt, adapted by Fred Carmichael; directed by
          John Olon

0143   THE TORCH-BEARERS
          by George Kelly; directed by Owen Phillips

                              1974-1975

0144   THE AMERICA EXPERIMENT
          by Peggity Price; directed by Peggity Price

0145   THE BEAUX' STRATAGEM
          by George Farquhar; directed by George Black

0146   BIOGRAPHY
          by S.N. Behrman; directed by John Going

0147   BROADWAY
          by Philip Dunning and George Abbott; directed by Charles Maryan

0148   THE DEVIL'S DISCIPLE
          by George Bernard Shaw; directed by Kenneth Frankel. Fiche
          collection contains two programs; one for the regular season's
          performances and one for the touring company, which contains
          pictures of the cast

0149   THE DIARY OF ANNE FRANK
          by Frances Goodrich and Albert Hackett; directed by Owen
          Phillips

0150   LA RONDE
          by Arthur Schnitzler; directed by Eric Davis

0151   LIGHT UP THE SKY
          by Moss Hart; directed by Owen Phillips

0152   THE MALE ANIMAL
          by James Thurber and Elliott Nugent; directed by Charles Maryan

0153   SLEUTH
          by Anthony Shaffer; directed by Kenneth Frankel

0154   SUBREAL
          conceived and directed by the Barter Intern Company

0155   TWO ON AN ISLAND
          by Elmer Rice; directed by Owen Phillips. Performed by the
          Barter Intern Company

Ann Arbor, MI

ASSOCIATION OF PRODUCING ARTISTS

1962-1963

0156   GHOSTS
        by Henrik Ibsen, translated by Eva Le Gallienne; directed by
        Eva Le Gallienne

0157   THE MERCHANT OF VENICE
        by William Shakespeare; directed by Richard Baldridge

0158   A MIDSUMMER NIGHT'S DREAM
        by William Shakespeare; directed by Ellis Rabb

0159   A PENNY FOR A SONG
        by John Whiting; directed by Ellis Rabb

0160   THE SCHOOL FOR SCANDAL
        by Richard Brinsley Sheridan; directed by Ellis Rabb

0161   THE TAVERN
        by George M. Cohan; directed by Ellis Rabb

0162   THE TRAGICAL HISTORY OF KING RICHARD THE SECOND
        by William Shakespeare; directed by Ellis Rabb

0163   WE, COMRADES THREE
        (adapted from the works of Walt Whitman) by Richard Baldridge;
        directed by Ellis Rabb

1963-1964

0164   IMPROMPTU AT VERSAILLES
        Moliere, translated by Stephen Porter; directed by Stephen
        Porter. Performed at the Phoenix Theatre of New York

0165   THE LOWER DEPTHS
        by Maxim Gorki; directed by Richard Baldridge. Performed in
        Fall '63 and Spring '64

0166   THE LOWER DEPTHS
        by Maxim Gorki, new translation by Alex Szogyi; directed by
        Ellis Rabb. Performed in Fall '63 and Spring '64 at the Phoenix
        Theatre of New York

0167   MUCH ADO ABOUT NOTHING
        by William Shakespeare; directed by Richard Baldridge

0168   A PHOENIX TOO FREQUENT
        by Christopher Fry; directed by Stephen Porter. Performed the
        same evening as *Scapin*, in Fall '63 and Spring '64

0169   RIGHT YOU ARE (IF YOU THINK YOU ARE)
            by Luigi Pirandello, English translation by Eric Bentley;
            directed by Stephen Porter. Performed in Fall '63 and Spring '64
            at the Phoenix Theatre of New York

0170   RIGHT YOU ARE (IF YOU THINK YOU ARE)
            by Luigi Pirandello, translated by Arthur Livingston; directed
            by Stephen Porter. Performed in Fall '63 and Spring '64

0171   SCAPIN
            by Moliere, translated by Stephen Porter and Ellis Rabb;
            directed by Stephen Porter. Performed the same evening as
            A Phoenix Too Frequent, in Fall '63 and Spring '64; fiche
            collection also includes program for Fall '63 and Spring '64
            performances at the Phoenix Theatre of New York

0172   THE TAVERN
            by George M. Cohan; directed by Ellis Rabb. Performed at the
            Phoenix Theatre of New York

                              1964-1965

0173   JUDITH
            by Jean Giraudoux, English version by John K. Savacool; directed
            by Ellis Rabb. Performed at the Phoenix Theatre of New York

0174   MAN AND SUPERMAN
            by George Bernard Shaw; directed by Stephen Porter. Performed
            at the Phoenix Theatre of New York

0175   WAR AND PEACE
            (adapted from the novel by Leo Tolstoy) adapted by Alfred
            Neumann, Erwin Piscator, and Guntram Prufer, English version
            by Robert David MacDonald; directed by Ellis Rabb. Performed
            at the Phoenix Theatre of New York

                              1965-1966

0176   HERAKLES
            by Archibald MacLeish; directed by Alan Schneider

0177   KRAPP'S LAST TAPE
            by Samuel Beckett; directed by Stephen Porter

0178   THE WILD DUCK
            by Henrik Ibsen, translated by Eva Le Gallienne; directed by
            Stephen Porter

0179   YOU CAN'T TAKE IT WITH YOU
            by Moss Hart and George S. Kaufman; directed by Ellis Rabb

                              1966-1967

0180   THE CAT AND THE MOON
            by W.B. Yeats; directed by Donald Moffat. Performed the same
            evening as *Escurial* and *Sweet of You to Say So*

0181   ESCURIAL
            by Michel de Ghelderode, English translation by Lionel Abel;
            directed by Hal George and John Houseman. Performed the same
            evening as *The Cat and the Moon* and *Sweet of You to Say So*

0182   RIGHT YOU ARE (IF YOU THINK YOU ARE)
            by Luigi Pirandello, English translation by Eric Bentley;
            directed by Stephen Porter. Also performed at the Lyceum
            Theatre of New York and the Huntington Hartford Theatre of
            Hollywood, CA

0183   THE SCHOOL FOR SCANDAL
            by Richard Brinsley Sheridan; directed by Ellis Rabb. Also
            performed at the Lyceum Theatre of New York and the Huntington
            Hartford Theatre of Hollywood, CA

0184   SWEET OF YOU TO SAY SO
            by Page Johnson; directed by Keene Curtis. Performed the same
            evening as *The Cat and the Moon* and *Escurial*

0185   WAR AND PEACE
            (adapted from the novel by Leo Tolstoy) adapted by Alfred
            Neumann, Erwin Piscator, and Guntram Prufer, English version
            by Robert David MacDonald; directed by Ellis Rabb. Performed
            at the Lyceum Theatre of New York

0186   WE, COMRADES THREE
            (adapted from the works of Walt Whitman) by Richard Baldridge;
            directed by Hal George and Ellis Rabb. Also performed at the
            Lyceum Theatre of New York

0187   THE WILD DUCK
            by Henrik Ibsen, translated by Eva Le Gallienne; directed by
            Stephen Porter. Performed at the Lyceum Theatre of New York

0188   YOU CAN'T TAKE IT WITH YOU
            by Moss Hart and George S. Kaufman; directed by Ellis Rabb.
            Performed at the Lyceum Theatre of New York and the Huntington
            Hartford Theatre of Hollywood, CA

Ashland, OR

OREGON SHAKESPEAREAN FESTIVAL

1953

0189   CORIOLANUS
            by William Shakespeare; directed by Allen Fletcher

0190   KING HENRY VI (PART 1)
            by William Shakespeare; directed by James Sandoe

0191   THE MERCHANT OF VENICE
            by William Shakespeare; directed by Richard Graham

0192   THE TAMING OF THE SHREW
          by William Shakespeare; directed by Philip Hanson

1954

0193   HAMLET
          by William Shakespeare; directed by Angus L. Bowmer

0194   HENRY VI (PART 2)
          by William Shakespeare; directed by James Sandoe

0195   THE MERRY WIVES OF WINDSOR
          by William Shakespeare; directed by Allen Fletcher

0196   THE WINTER'S TALE
          by William Shakespeare; directed by H. Paul Kliss

1955

0197   ALL'S WELL THAT ENDS WELL
          by William Shakespeare; directed by Robert B. Loper

0198   HENRY VI (PART 3)
          by William Shakespeare; directed by James Sandoe

0199   · THE LIFE OF TIMON OF ATHENS
          by William Shakespeare; directed by Robert B. Loper

0200   MACBETH
          by William Shakespeare; directed by H. Paul Kliss

0201   A MIDSUMMER NIGHT'S DREAM
          by William Shakespeare; directed by James Sandoe

1956

0202   LOVE'S LABOUR'S LOST
          by William Shakespeare; directed by Allen Fletcher

0203   RICHARD III
          by William Shakespeare; directed by Allen Fletcher

0204   ROMEO AND JULIET
          by William Shakespeare; directed by Hal J. Todd

0205   TITUS ANDRONICUS
          by William Shakespeare; directed by Hal J. Todd

0206   THE TRAGEDY OF CYMBELINE
          by William Shakespeare; directed by B. Iden Payne

1957

0207   AS YOU LIKE IT
          by William Shakespeare; directed by Angus L. Bowmer

0208   HENRY VIII
          by William Shakespeare; directed by Robert B. Loper

0209   OTHELLO
          by William Shakespeare; directed by James Sandoe

0210   PERICLES, PRINCE OF TYRE
          by William Shakespeare; directed by Robert B. Loper

0211   THE TWO GENTLEMEN OF VERONA
          by William Shakespeare; directed by James Sandoe

1958

0212   KING LEAR
          by William Shakespeare; directed by Robert B. Loper

0213   THE MERCHANT OF VENICE
          by William Shakespeare; directed by James Sandoe

0214   MUCH ADO ABOUT NOTHING
          by William Shakespeare; directed by Robert B. Loper

0215   TROILUS AND CRESSIDA
          by William Shakespeare; directed by James Sandoe

1959

0216   ANTONY AND CLEOPATRA
          by William Shakespeare; directed by James Sandoe

0217   THE LIFE AND DEATH OF KING JOHN
          by William Shakespeare; directed by Richard D. Risso

0218   THE MASKE OF THE NEW WORLD
          by William Shakespeare; directed by Jerry Turner. Performed
          the same evening as *Twelfth Night*

0219   MEASURE FOR MEASURE
          by William Shakespeare; directed by James Sandoe

0220   TWELFTH NIGHT
          by William Shakespeare; directed by Angus L. Bowmer. Performed
          the same evening as *The Maske of the New World*

1963

0221   THE LIFE OF KING HENRY V
          by William Shakespeare; directed by Jerry Turner

0222   LOVE'S LABOUR'S LOST
          by William Shakespeare; directed by Rod Alexander

0223   THE MERRY WIVES OF WINDSOR
          by William Shakespeare; directed by Edward S. Bruebaker

0224   ROMEO AND JULIET
          by William Shakespeare; directed by Robert B. Loper

                                    1964

0225   KING HENRY VI (PART 1)
          by William Shakespeare; directed by Jerry Turner

0226   KING LEAR
          by William Shakespeare; directed by Angus L. Bowmer

0227   THE MERCHANT OF VENICE
          by William Shakespeare; directed by Rod Alexander

0228   TWELFTH NIGHT
          by William Shakespeare; directed by Robert B. Loper

                                    1965

0229   KING HENRY VI (PART 2)
          by William Shakespeare; directed by Edward S. Bruebaker

0230   MACBETH
          by William Shakespeare; directed by Richard D. Risso

0231   MUCH ADO ABOUT NOTHING
          by William Shakespeare; directed by James Moll

0232   VOLPONE
          by Ben Jonson; directed by Nagle Jackson

0233   THE WINTER'S TALE
          by William Shakespeare; directed by Hugh C. Evans

                                    1966

0234   THE BEGGAR'S OPERA
          by John Gay; directed by Carl Ritchie and W. Bernard Winat

0235   HENRY VI (PART 3)
          by William Shakespeare; directed by Jerry Turner

0236   A MIDSUMMER NIGHT'S DREAM
          by William Shakespeare; directed by Hugh C. Evans

0237   OTHELLO
          by William Shakespeare; directed by Richard D. Risso

0238   THE TWO GENTLEMEN OF VERONA
          by William Shakespeare; directed by Nagle Jackson

                                    1970

0239   ANTIGONE
          by Jean Anouilh, translated by Kitty Black; directed by Larry
          Oliver. A Stage II production

0240   THE FANTASTICKS
        words by Tom Jones, music by Harvey Schmidt; directed by Peter
        Nyberg. A Stage II production

0241   ROSENCRANTZ AND GUILDENSTERN ARE DEAD
        by Tom Stoppard; directed by Angus L. Bowmer. A Stage II
        production

0242   YOU CAN'T TAKE IT WITH YOU
        by Moss Hart and George S. Kaufman; directed by Pat Patton. A
        Stage II production

                            1973

0243   THE ALCHEMIST
        by Ben Johnson; directed by Laird Williamson. A Stage II
        production

0244   AS YOU LIKE IT
        by William Shakespeare; directed by Pat Patton

0245   THE DANCE OF DEATH
        by August Strindberg; directed by Jerry Turner

0246   HENRY V
        by William Shakespeare; directed by Laird Williamson

0247   THE IMPORTANCE OF BEING EARNEST
        by Oscar Wilde; directed by Jim Edmondson. A Stage II pro-
        duction

0248   THE MERRY WIVES OF WINDSOR
        by William Shakespeare; directed by Thomas B. Markus

0249   OTHELLO
        by William Shakespeare; directed by Jerry Turner. A Stage II
        production

0250   OUR TOWN
        by Thornton Wilder; directed by Pat Patton. A Stage II pro-
        duction

                        1974 (Spring)

0251   A FUNNY THING HAPPENED ON THE WAY TO THE FORUM
        book by Burt Shevelove and Larry Gelbart, music and lyrics by
        Stephen Sondheim; directed by Jerry Turner. A Stage II pro-
        duction

0252   HEDDA GABLER
        by Henrik Ibsen; directed by Margaret Booker. A Stage II
        production

0253   THE TIME OF YOUR LIFE
        by William Saroyan; directed by Pat Patton. A Stage II pro-
        duction

0254   THE TWO GENTLEMEN OF VERONA
        by William Shakespeare; directed by Laird Williamson. A
        Stage II production

                            1974 (Summer)

0255   HAMLET
        by William Shakespeare; directed by Jerry Turner

0256   THE TIME OF YOUR LIFE
        by William Saroyan; directed by Pat Patton

0257   TITUS ANDRONICUS
        by William Shakespeare; directed by Laird Williamson

0258   TWELFTH NIGHT
        by William Shakespeare; directed by Jim Edmondson

0259   THE TWO GENTLEMEN OF VERONA
        by William Shakespeare; directed by Laird Williamson

0260   WAITING FOR GODOT
        by Samuel Beckett; directed by Andrew J. Traister

                                1975

0261   CHARLEY'S AUNT
        by Brandon Thomas; directed by Pat Patton. A Stage II pro-
        duction

0262   OEDIPUS THE KING
        by Sophocles, translated by Donald Sutherland; directed by
        Robert B. Loper. A Stage II production

0263   THE PETRIFIED FOREST
        by Robert Sherwood; directed by Jerry Turner. A Stage II
        production

0264   THE WINTER'S TALE
        by William Shakespeare; directed by Audrey Stanley. A Stage II
        production

                            1975 (Summer)

0265   ALL'S WELL THAT ENDS WELL
        by William Shakespeare; directed by Jon Jory

0266   CHARLEY'S AUNT
        by Brandon Thomas; directed by Pat Patton

0267   HENRY VI (PART 1)
        by William Shakespeare; directed by Will Huddleston

0268   LONG DAY'S JOURNEY INTO NIGHT
        by Eugene O'Neill; directed by Jerry Turner

0269   ROMEO AND JULIET
        by William Shakespeare; directed by Jim Edmondson

0270   THE WINTER'S TALE
        by William Shakespeare; directed by Audrey Stanley

Atlanta, GA

THE ALLIANCE THEATRE COMPANY

1970-1971

0271   A DELICATE BALANCE
        by Edward Albee; directed by John O'Shaughnessy

0272   LIFE WITH FATHER
        (based on the book by Clarence Day, Jr.) by Howard Lindsay
        and Russel Crouse; directed by John O'Shaughnessy

0273   LIGHT UP THE SKY
        by Moss Hart; directed by Harry Ellerbe

0274   THE NIGHT THOREAU SPENT IN JAIL
        by Jerome Lawrence and Robert E. Lee; directed by Anthony J.
        Stimac

0275   THE PRICE
        by Arthur Miller; directed by John O'Shaughnessy

0276   THE TAMING OF THE SHREW
        by William Shakespeare; directed by John Fernald

0277   THE THREE SISTERS
        by Anton Chekhov; directed by John Fernald

0278   A THURBER CARNIVAL
        by James Thurber; directed by Chuck Doughty

1971-1972

0279   AH, WILDERNESS!
        by Eugene O'Neill; directed by Harry Ellerbe. January program
        contains bibliographic material about Scott Joplin's *Treemonisha*

0280   ANTHONY BURNS
        by Pat Freni; directed by Anthony J. Stimac

0281   BROWN PELICAN
        by George Sklar; directed by Anthony J. Stimac. Program con-
        tains photograph of Preservation Jazz Band

0282   HAMLET
        by William Shakespeare; directed by Douglas Seale

0283   THE PRIME OF MISS JEAN BRODIE
        (adapted from the novel by Muriel Spark) by Jay Presson Allen;
        directed by Robert J. Farley

0284   PYGMALION
        by George Bernard Shaw; directed by John Fernald

0285   SOMETHING'S AFOOT
        by James McDonald, David Vos, and Robert Gerlach; directed by
        Anthony J. Stimac

0286   THIS WAY TO THE ROSE GARDEN
        by Don Tucker and Roger Cornish; directed by Anthony J. Stimac

                            1972-1973

0287   THE COMEDY OF ERRORS
        by William Shakespeare; directed by Jim Way

0288   THE GLASS MENAGERIE
        by Tennessee Williams; directed by Delbert Mann

0289   THE HOUSE OF BLUE LEAVES
        by John Guare; directed by Robert J. Farley

0290   JABBERWOCK
        by Jerome Lawrence and Robert E. Lee; directed by Leland Ball

0291   JACQUES BREL IS ALIVE AND WELL AND LIVING IN PARIS
        (based on Brel's lyrics and commentary) production conception,
        English lyrics, and additional material by Eric Blau and Mort
        Shuman; directed by Fred Chappell

0292   TOBACCO ROAD
        (adapted from the novel by Erskine Caldwell) by Jack Kirkland;
        directed by Fred Chappell

                            1973-1974

0293   CAT ON A HOT TIN ROOF
        by Tennessee Williams; directed by Fred Chappell

0294   COUNT DRACULA
        (based on the novel by Bram Stoker) by Ted Tiller; directed by
        Robert J. Farley

0295   THE HOT L BALTIMORE
        by Lanford Wilson, directed by Robert J. Farley

0296   OH COWARD!
        by Noel Coward, devised by Roderick Cook; directed by Fred
        Chappell

0297   OUR TOWN
        by Thornton Wilder; directed by Robert J. Farley

Baltimore, MD

CENTER STAGE

1962-1963

0298   AMPHITRYON 38
        by Jean Giraudoux, adapted by S.N. Behrman; directed by
        Edward J. Golden, Jr.

0299   ARMS AND THE MAN
        by George Bernard Shaw; directed by Edward J. Golden, Jr.

0300   BEYOND THE HORIZON
        by Eugene O'Neill; directed by Edward J. Golden, Jr.

0301   LA RONDE
        by Arthur Schnitzler, English translation by Eric Bentley;
        directed by Edward J. Golden, Jr.

0302   THE MAIDS
        by Jean Genet; directed by Edward J. Golden, Jr. Performed the
        same evening as *The Zoo Story*

0303   THE MOUSETRAP
        by Agatha Christie; directed by Edward J. Golden, Jr.

0304   YOU TOUCHED ME!
        (suggested by the short story of D.H. Lawrence) by Tennessee
        Williams and Donald Windham; directed by Edward J. Golden, Jr.

0305   THE ZOO STORY
        by Edward Albee; directed by Edward J. Golden, Jr. Performed
        the same evening as *The Maids*

1963-1964

0306   BEDTIME STORY
        by Sean O'Casey; directed by Kenneth Costigan

0307   THE IMPORTANCE OF BEING EARNEST
        by Oscar Wilde; directed by Edward J. Golden, Jr.

0308   LIGHT UP THE SKY
        by Moss Hart; directed by Edward J. Golden, Jr.

0309   THE ROOM
        by Harold Pinter; directed by Edward J. Golden, Jr. World
        premiere; performed the same evening as *The Sketches*

0310   THE SHADOW OF A GUNMAN
        by Sean O'Casey; directed by Kenneth Costigan. Performed the
        same evening as *U.S.A.*

0311   SILENT NIGHT, LONELY NIGHT
        by Robert Anderson; directed by Edward J. Golden, Jr.

0312   THE SKETCHES
        by Harold Pinter; directed by Edward J. Golden, Jr. World
        premiere; performed the same evening as *The Room*

0313   SUMMER OF THE SEVENTEENTH DOLL
        by Ray Lawler; directed by Edward J. Golden, Jr.

0314   TWELFTH NIGHT
        by William Shakespeare; staged by Bernard Hiatt

0315   U.S.A.
        (based on the novel by John Dos Passos) by Paul Shyre and
        John Dos Passos; directed by Edward J. Golden, Jr. Performed
        the same evening as *The Shadow of a Gunman*

                            1964-1965

0316   THE COUNTRY WIFE
        by William Wycherly; directed by Edward J. Golden, Jr.
        Programme contains background notes about the author

0317   THE DOCTOR'S DILEMMA
        by George Bernard Shaw; directed by John Olon

0318   GALILEO
        by Bertolt Brecht; directed by John Marley

0319   THE HOSTAGE
        by Brendan Behan; directed by Mesrop Kesdekian. Program con-
        tains background notes about the author

0320   THE LADY'S NOT FOR BURNING
        by Christopher Fry; directed by Edward J. Golden, Jr.

0321   THE PHYSICISTS
        by Friedrich Duerrenmatt; directed by Edward J. Golden, Jr.

0322   SIX CHARACTERS IN SEARCH OF AN AUTHOR
        by Luigi Pirandello; directed by John Olon

0323   A TOUCH OF THE POET
        by Eugene O'Neill; directed by Edward J. Golden, Jr.

                            1965-1966

0324   ARDELE
        by Jean Anouilh, translated by Lucienne Hill; directed by
        Douglas Seale

0325   AS YOU LIKE IT
        by William Shakespeare; directed by Douglas Seale

0326   THE BIRTHDAY PARTY
        by Harold Pinter; directed by Brooks Jones

0327   CAESAR AND CLEOPATRA
         by George Bernard Shaw; directed by Douglas Seale

0328   THE CHINESE WALL
         by Max Frisch, translated by James L. Rosenberg; directed by
         Douglas Seale

0329   THE DAYS BETWEEN
         by Robert Anderson; directed by Douglas Seale

0330   THE TAVERN
         by George M. Cohan; directed by John Marley

1966-1967

0331   THE BALCONY
         by Jean Genet, translated by Bernard Frechtman; directed by
         Brooks Jones

0332   BENITO CERENO
         by Robert Lowell; directed by Patrick Tovatt. Performed the
         same evening as *The Death of Bessie Smith*

0333   THE DEATH OF BESSIE SMITH
         by Edward Albee; directed by Richard Gillespie. Performed the
         same evening as *Benito Cereno*

0334   LADY AUDLEY'S SECRET
         (adapted from the novel by Mary Elizabeth Bradden) by Douglas
         Seale, music by George Goehring, lyrics by John Kuntz; directed
         by Douglas Seale

0335   THE MISER
         by Moliere; directed by Rod Alexander

0336   NOAH
         by Andre Obey, translated by Arthur Wilmurt; directed by
         Douglas Seale

0337   A PENNY FOR A SONG
         by John Whiting; directed by Douglas Seale. Centerfold con-
         tains a listing of all plays performed from 1963-1968, with
         countries of origin

0338   TITUS ANDRONICUS
         by William Shakespeare; directed by Douglas Seale

1967-1968

0339   THE DEVIL'S DISCIPLE
         by George Bernard Shaw; directed by Douglas Seale

0340   AN ENEMY OF THE PEOPLE
         by Henrik Ibsen, adapted by Arthur Miller; directed by
         Leonardo Cimino

0341   HAMLET
         by William Shakespeare; directed by Douglas Seale

0342   THE MEMBER OF THE WEDDING
         by Carson McCullers; directed by John Olon

0343   THE ROYAL FAMILY
         by George S. Kaufman and Edna Ferber; directed by Douglas Seale

0344   WAITING FOR GODOT
         by Samuel Beckett; directed by Ronald L. Hufham

                          1968-1969

0345   BOY MEETS GIRL
         by Bella and Sam Spewack; directed by Ruth White

0346   A DOLL'S HOUSE
         by Henrik Ibsen; directed by John Stix

0347   THE JOURNEY OF THE FIFTH HORSE
         by Ronald Ribman; directed by John Stix

0348   THE MERCHANT OF VENICE
         by William Shakespeare; directed by John Olon

                          1969-1970

0349   FIRE IN THE MINDHOUSE
         words by Arnold Borget, music by Lance Mulcahy; directed by
         Peter Culman and John Stix. World premiere

0350   THE KNACK
         by Ann Jellicoe; directed by Dennis Rosa

0351   LONG DAY'S JOURNEY INTO NIGHT
         by Eugene O'Neill; directed by Ben Piazza

0352   PARK
         book and lyrics by Paul Cherry, music by Lance Mulcahy;
         directed by John Stix

0353   SLOW DANCE ON THE KILLING GROUND
         by William Hanley; directed by John Stix

0354   THE TEMPEST
         by William Shakespeare; directed by Dennis Rosa

0355   WHO'S GOT HIS OWN
         by Ronald Miller; directed by Nathan George

                          1970-1971

0356   A CRY OF PLAYERS
         by William Gibson; directed by John Stix

0357   MARAT/SADE
by Peter Weiss, English translation by Geoffrey Skelton, verse adaptation by Adrian Mitchell; directed by Peter W. Culman

1971-1972*

0358   ANDORRA
by Max Frisch; directed by John Stix

0359   THE BEAUX' STRATAGEM
by George Farquhar; directed by John Lithgow

0360   DEATH OF A SALESMAN
by Arthur Miller; directed by Lee D. Sankowich. Performed by a Black cast

0361   THE SEA GULL
by Anton Chekhov, translated by Stark Young; directed by Robert Lewis

0362   STAIRCASE
by Charles Dyer; directed by Alfred Ryder

0363   THE TRIAL OF THE CATONSVILLE NINE
by Daniel Berrigan, S.J.; directed by John Stix

1972-1973

0364   DANDY DICK
by Sir Arthur Wing Pinero; directed by John Stix

0365   GIMPEL THE FOOL
(based on a story by Isaac Bashevis Singer) adapted by Larry Arrick, lyrics by Barbara Damasnek; directed by Larry Arrick. Performed the same evening as *St. Julian the Hospitalier*, under the title of *Two Saints*

0366   JULIUS CAESAR
by William Shakespeare; directed by Mitchell Nestor

0367   THE ME NOBODY KNOWS
(based on the book edited by Stephen M. Joseph) adapted by Robert H. Livingston and Herb Shapiro, music by Gary William Friedman, lyrics by Will Holt; directed by Robert H. Livingston

0368   ONE FLEW OVER THE CUCKOO'S NEST
(based on the novel by Ken Kesey) by Dale Wasserman; directed by John Stix

0369a   THE PETRIFIED FOREST
by Robert Sherwood; directed by John Stix

---

* Programs for this season contain interesting sketches, photographs, and articles.

0369b   ST. JULIAN THE HOSPITALIER
           (based on a story by Gustave Flaubert) adaptation and lyrics
           by Kenneth Cavander; directed by Larry Arrick. Performed the
           same evening as *Gimpel the Fool*, under the title of *Two Saints*

                                    1973-1974

0370   HAPPY BIRTHDAY, WANDA JUNE
           by Kurt Vonnegut, Jr.; directed by Carl Schurr

0371   HAY FEVER
           by Noel Coward; directed by Jacques Cartier

0372   THE HOT L BALTIMORE
           by Lanford Wilson; directed by John Stix

0373   UNCLE VANYA
           by Anton Chekhov; directed by Jacques Cartier

0374   A VIEW FROM THE BRIDGE
           by Arthur Miller; directed by Michael Murray

0375   WHO'S AFRAID OF VIRGINIA WOOLF
           by Edward Albee; directed by John Stix

Berkeley, CA

BERKELEY REPERTORY THEATRE*

                                       1969

0376   THE PLAYBOY OF THE WESTERN WORLD
           J.M. Synge; directed by Michael Leibert

                                       1970

0377   ANTIGONE
           by Jean Anouilh; directed by Robert Mooney. Program contains
           history of *Antigone*

0378   TOO GOOD TO BE TRUE
           by George Bernard Shaw; directed by William Douglas

                                       1971

0379   DEVILS
           (based on *The Devils* by John Whiting and *The Devils of Loudon*
           by Aldous Huxley) adapted by Peter Donat; directed by Peter
           Donat

---

* Unfortunately only a very limited number of programs were available
  for this theatre. All that were available have been filmed.

1973

0380   ARMS AND THE MAN
        by George Bernard Shaw; directed by Jean-Bernard Bucky

0381   THE COMEDY OF ERRORS
        by William Shakespeare; directed by Douglas Johnson

0382   THE SCHOOL FOR SCANDAL
        by Richard Brinsley Sheridan; directed by George House

1973-1974

0383   BORN YESTERDAY
        by Garson Kanin; directed by Michael Leibert

0384   CHARLEY'S AUNT
        by Brandon Thomas; directed by Douglas Johnson

0385   DRACULA: A MUSICAL NIGHTMARE
        (adapted from the novel by Bram Stoker) by Douglas Johnson;
        directed by Douglas Johnson

0386   THE FRONT PAGE
        by Ben Hecht and Charles MacArthur; directed by Michael Leibert

0387   HEARTBREAK HOUSE
        by George Bernard Shaw; directed by Angela Paton

0388   LONDON ASSURANCE
        by Dion Boucicault; directed by Douglas Johnson

0389   THE MASTER BUILDER
        by Henrik Ibsen; directed by Philip Larson

0390   THE MISANTHROPE
        by Moliere; directed by Jean-Bernard Bucky

0391   THE PETRIFIED FOREST
        by Robert Sherwood; directed by Michael Leibert

1974-1975

0392   BLITHE SPIRIT
        by Noel Coward; directed by Angela Paton

0393   THE LITTLE FOXES
        by Lillian Hellman; directed by William I. Oliver

Boston, MA

Charles Playhouse*

1963-1964

0394   THE GLASS MENAGERIE
        by Tennessee Williams; directed by Michael Murray.

1964-1965

0395   THE COLLECTION
        by Harold Pinter; directed by Michael Murray. Performed the
        same evening as *The Lover*

0396   THE LOVER
        by Harold Pinter; directed by Michael Murray. Performed the
        same evening as *The Collection*

0397   THE MADWOMAN OF CHAILLOT
        by Jean Giraudoux, adapted by Maurice Valency; directed by
        Michael Murray

0398   THE PLOUGH AND THE STARS
        by Sean O'Casey; directed by Michael Murray

0399   THE RIVALS
        by Richard Brinsley Sheridan; directed by Michael Murray

0400   SHE LOVES ME
        (based on the play by Miklos Laszlo) by Joe Masteroff, music
        by Jerry Bock, lyrics by Sheldon Harnick; directed by Ben
        Shaktman

0401   A TOUCH OF THE POET
        by Eugene O'Neill; directed by Michael Murray

1965-1966

0402   GALILEO
        by Bertolt Brecht, English version by Charles Laughton;
        directed by Michael Murray

0403   THE INSPECTOR GENERAL
        by Nikolai Gogol, new translation by Thomas J. Butler;
        directed by Michael Murray

---

* In general, the programs contain brief articles on various non-acting
  aspects of the theatre, such as costume designers, prompters, posters,
  etc.

0404   MAJOR BARBARA
by George Bernard Shaw; directed by Louis Criss

0405   THE MISER
by Moliere; new translation by Peggy Lamson; directed by
Michael Murray

0406   POOR BITOS
by Jean Anouilh, translated by Lucienne Hill; directed by
Michael Murray

0407   THE TIGER
by Murray Schisgal; directed by Michael Murray. Performed the
same evening as *The Typists*

0408   THE TYPISTS
by Murray Schisgal; directed by Michael Murray. Performed the
same evening as *The Tiger*

1966-1967

0409   THE BALCONY
by Jean Genet; directed by Ben Shaktman

0410   HAMLET
by William Shakespeare; directed by Michael Murray

0411   INADMISSIBLE EVIDENCE
by John Osborne; directed by Michael Murray

0412   LOVE FOR LOVE
by William Congreve; directed by Michael Murray

0413   MACBIRD!
by Barbara Garson; directed by Michael Murray

0414   MOTHER COURAGE AND ALL HER CHILDREN
by Bertolt Brecht, English version by Eric Bentley; directed
by Michael Murray

0415   OH! WHAT A LOVELY WAR
by Joan Littlewood and Charles Chilton; directed by Eric House;
musical director, Newton Wayland

1967-1968

0416   AMERICA HURRAH
by Jean-Claude van Itallie; directed by Thomas Bissinger

0417   AWAKE AND SING
by Clifford Odets; directed by Michael Murray

0418   DUTCHMAN
by LeRoi Jones; directed by Ted Kazanoff. Performed the same
evening as *Madness of Lady Bright* and *Nine O'Clock Mail*

0419   MADNESS OF LADY BRIGHT
          by Lanford Wilson; directed by Michael Murray. Performed the
          same evening as *Dutchman* and *Nine O'Clock Mail*

0420   NINE O'CLOCK MAIL
          by Howard Sackler; directed by Michael Murray. Performed the
          same evening as *Dutchman* and *Madness of Lady Bright*

0421   ROOM SERVICE
          by Allen Boretz and John Murray; directed by Michael Murray

0422   A VIEW FROM THE BRIDGE
          by Arthur Miller; directed by Mitchell Nestor

                                1968-1969

0423   THE BACCHAE OF EURIPIDES
          adaptation based on translation by William Arrowsmith; directed
          by Timothy S. Mayer

0424   EVERYTHING IN THE GARDEN
          by Edward Albee; directed by Louis Criss

0425   LOOK BACK IN ANGER
          by John Osborne; directed by Jon Jory

0426   THE MILLIONAIRESS
          by George Bernard Shaw; directed by Philip Minor

                                1969-1970

0427   ANTIGONE
          by Jean Anouilh, translated by Lewis Galantiere; directed by
          John Wood

0428   A FLEA IN HER EAR
          by Georges Feydeau, translated by Barnett Shaw; directed by
          Paxton Whitehead

0429   THE ICEMAN COMETH
          by Eugene O'Neill; directed by Michael Murray

0430   JACQUES BREL IS ALIVE AND WELL AND LIVING IN PARIS
          (based on Brel's lyrics and commentary) production conception,
          English lyrics, and additional material by Eric Blau and Mort
          Shuman; directed by Moni Yakim

0431   JUNGLE OF CITIES
          by Bertolt Brecht, translated by Anselm Hollo; directed by
          Louis Criss

0432   NARROW ROAD TO THE DEEP NORTH
          by Edward Bond; directed by Louis Criss

1970-1971

0433   IN THREE ZONES
by Wilford Leach; directed by Louis Criss. World premiere

0434   JACQUES BREL IS ALIVE AND WELL AND LIVING IN PARIS
(based on Brel's lyrics and commentary) production conception,
English lyrics, and additional material by Eric Blau and Mort
Shuman; directed by Moni Yakim

THEATRE COMPANY OF BOSTON

1964-1965

0435   CALIGULA
by Albert Camus; by David Wheeler

0436   CHARLIE
by Slawomir Mrozek, translated by Nicholas Bethell; directed
by David Wheeler. Performed the same evening as *Funnyhouse
of a Negro*

0437   FUNNYHOUSE OF A NEGRO
by Adrienne Kennedy, with Barbara Ann Teer; directed by David
Wheeler. Performed the same evening as *Charlie*

0438   THE GOOD WOMAN OF SETZUAN
by Bertolt Brecht, English version by Eric Bentley; directed
by David Wheeler

0439   HIM
by E.E. Cummings; directed by David Wheeler

0440   LIVE LIKE PIGS
by John Arden; directed by David Wheeler. American premiere

0441   A SLIGHT ACHE
by Harold Pinter; directed by David Wheeler. Performed the
same evening as *Talking to You*

0442   TALKING TO YOU
by William Saroyan; directed by David Wheeler. Performed the
same evening as *A Slight Ache*

0443   WHEN WE DEAD AWAKEN
by Henrik Ibsen, translated by William Zavis; directed by
David Wheeler

1965-1966

0444   ACT WITHOUT WORDS
by Samuel Beckett; directed by David Wheeler. Performed the
same evening as *The Lunch Hour* and *Play*

0445   THE BIRTHDAY PARTY
by Harold Pinter; directed by David Wheeler

0446   THE FEAR AND MISERY OF THE THIRD REICH
        by Bertolt Brecht, translated by Kenneth Tigar and Clayton
        Koelb; directed by David Wheeler

0447   FRANK MERRIWELL'S LAST RACE
        by Geoffrey Bush; directed by Timothy Affleck. Festival of
        New American Plays; performed the same evening as *Icarus's
        Mother* and *Servants of the People*

0448   ICARUS'S MOTHER
        by Sam Shepard; directed by Paul Benedict. Festival of New
        American Plays; performed the same evening as *Frank Merriwell's
        Last Race* and *Servants of the People*

0449   THE INFANTRY
        by Andy and Dave Lewis; directed by Andy Lewis

0450   THE INVESTIGATION
        by Rosalyn Drexler; directed by Paul Benedict. Festival of
        New American Plays; performed the same evening as *The Wax
        Museum*

0451   THE LUNCH HOUR
        by John Mortimer; directed by David Wheeler. Performed the
        same evening as *Act Without Words* and *Play*

0452   MEASURE FOR MEASURE
        by William Shakespeare; directed by David Wheeler

0453   PLAY
        by Samuel Beckett; directed by David Wheeler. Performed the
        same evening as *Act Without Words* and *The Lunch Hour*

0454   SERVANTS OF THE PEOPLE
        by Lawrence Ferlinghetti; directed by Frank Cassidy. Festival
        of New American Plays; performed the same evening as *Frank
        Merriwell's Last Race* and *Icarus's Mother*

0455   THE WAX MUSEUM
        by John Hawkes; directed by David Wheeler. Festival of New
        American Plays; performed the same evening as *The Investigation*

0456   YES IS FOR A VERY YOUNG MAN
        by Gertrude Stein; directed by David Wheeler

                                1966-1967

0457   ARMSTRONG'S LAST GOODNIGHT
        by John Arden; directed by David Wheeler. American premiere

0458   CANDAULES, COMMISSIONER
        by Daniel C. Gerould; directed by Ralph Waite. Festival of
        New American Plays; performed the same evening as *So Proudly
        We Hail*

0459 THE CAUCASIAN CHALK CIRCLE
by Bertolt Brecht, English version by Eric Bentley; directed
by David Wheeler

0460 KRAPP'S LAST TAPE
by Samuel Beckett; directed by David Wheeler. Performed the
same evening as *The Undertaker*

0461 MARAT/SADE
by Peter Weiss, English version by Geoffrey Skelton, verse
adaptation by Adrian Mitchell; directed by David Wheeler

0462 SO PROUDLY WE HAIL: A MEMORIAL SERVICE FOR WILLIAM JENNINGS
BRYAN
by Geoffrey Bush; directed by David Wheeler. Festival of New
American Plays; performed the same evening as *Candaules,
Commissioner*

0463 TINY ALICE
by Edward Albee; directed by David Wheeler

0464 THE UNDERTAKER
by John Hawkes; directed by David Wheeler. Performed the same
evening as *Krapp's Last Tape*

1967-1968

0465 LEFT-HANDED LIBERTY
by John Arden; directed by David Wheeler. American premiere

0466 WHO'S AFRAID OF VIRGINIA WOOLF?
by Edward Albee; directed by David Wheeler

1968-1969

0467 BENITO CERENO
by Robert Lowell; directed by David Wheeler and Frank Cassidy

0468 MORE STATELY MANSIONS
by Eugene O'Neill; directed by David Wheeler

1969-1970

0469 ADAPTATION
by Elaine May; directed by Elaine May. Performed the same
evening as *Next*

0470 NEXT
by Terrence McNally; directed by Elaine May. Performed the
same evening as *Adaptation*

1970-1971

0471 THE BASIC TRAINING OF PAVLO HUMMEL
by David Rabe; directed by David Wheeler

0472   THE BURGHERS OF CALAIS
            by Edgar White; directed by Paul Benedict

0473   SUBJECT TO FITS (A RESPONSE TO DOSTOYEVSKI'S *THE IDIOT*)
            by Robert Montgomery; directed by David Chambers

                              1972-1973

0474   OLD TIMES
            by Harold Pinter; directed by David Wheeler and William Young

0475   PLAY STRINDBERG
            choreography by Friedrich Duerrenmatt, translated by James
            Kirkup; directed by F.M. Kimball

0476   RICHARD III
            by William Shakespeare; directed by David Wheeler

Brooklyn, NY

CHELSEA THEATER CENTER

                              1966-1967

0477   JUNEBERG GRADUATES TONIGHT!
            by Archie Shepp; directed by Robert Kalfin

                              1968-1969

0478   CHRISTOPHE
            by John Gay; directed by Robert Kalfin

0479   THE GENTLEMAN CALLER
            by Ed Bullins; directed by Allie Woods. Performed the same
            evening as *Great Goodness of Life*, *Prayer Meeting*, and *The
            Warning*, under the title of *A Black Quartet*

0480   GREAT GOODNESS OF LIFE (A COONSHOW)
            by LeRoi Jones; directed by Irving Vincent. Performed the
            same evening as *The Gentleman Caller*, *Prayer Meeting*, and *The
            Warning*, under the title of *A Black Quartet*

0481   PRAYER MEETING, OR THE FIRST MILITANT
            by Minister Ben Caldwell; directed by Irving Vincent. Performed
            the same evening as *The Gentleman Caller*, *Great Goodness of
            Life*, and *The Warning*, under the title of *A Black Quartet*

0482   THE WARNING - A THEME FOR LINDA
            by Ronald Milner; directed by Woodie King. Performed the same
            evening as *The Gentleman Caller*, *Great Goodness of Life*, and
            Prayer Meeting, under the title of *A Black Quartet*

0483   THE WATCH-PIT
            by Kit Jones; directed by Robert Bonnard

1969-1970

0484   SLAVE SHIP
         by LeRoi Jones; directed by Gilbert Moses

1970-1971

0485   SAVED
         by Edward Bond; by Alan Schneider

1971-1972

0486   THE BEGGAR'S OPERA
         by John Gay, musical score by Ryan Edwards; directed by Gene
         Lesser

0487   KADDISH
         poem by Allen Ginsberg; directed by Robert Kalfin

0488   THE SCREENS
         by Jean Genet; directed by Minos Volanakis

1972-1973

0489   LADY DAY: A MUSICAL TRAGEDY
         by Aishah Rahman, music by Archie Shepp; directed by Paul
         Carter Harrison

0490   SUNSET
         by Isaac Babel, translated by Mirra Ginsburg and Raymond
         Rosenthal; directed by Robert Kalfin

1973-1974

0491   CANDIDE
         (adapted from the book by Voltaire) by Hugh Wheeler, music by
         Leonard Bernstein, lyrics by Richard Wilbur; directed by
         Harold Prince

0492   THE CONTRACTOR
         by David Storey; directed by Barry Davis

0493   TOTAL ECLIPSE
         by Christopher Hampton; directed by Robert Kalfin

1974-1975

0494   THE FAMILY 1-2-3-4
         by Lodewijk de Boer, translated by Albert Maurits; directed by
         Barry Davis

0495   HOTHOUSE
         by Megan Terry; directed by Rae Allen

0496   POLLY (A SEQUEL TO *THE BEGGAR'S OPERA*)
         by John Gay, adapted by Robert Kalfin, music by Mel Marvin;
         directed by Robert Kalfin

0497   SANTA ANITA '42
          by Allan Knee; directed by Steven Robman

0498   YENTL THE YESHIVA BOY
          by Isaac Bashevis Singer, adapted by Leah Napolin and Isaac
          Bashevis Singer; directed by Robert Kalfin

Buffalo, NY

STUDIO ARENA THEATRE

1965-1966

0499   THE FANTASTICKS
          words by Tom Jones, music by Harvey Schmidt; directed by
          Allan Leicht; musical director, William Cox

0500   THE FIREBUGS
          by Max Frisch; directed by Kim Swados

0501   IRMA LA DOUCE
          by Alexandre Breffort and Marguerite Monnet, English book and
          lyrics by Julian More, David Heneker, and Monty Norman;
          directed by Neal DuBrock; musical director, William Cox

0502   THE LITTLE FOXES
          by Lillian Hellman; directed by Edward Parone

0503   A MAN FOR ALL SEASONS
          by Robert Bolt; directed by Hy Kalus

0504   OH! WHAT A LOVELY WAR
          by Joan Littlewood and Charles Chilton; directed by Edward
          Parone; musical director, William Cox

0505   THE ROAR OF THE GREASEPAINT - THE SMELL OF THE CROWD
          by Leslie Bricusse and Anthony Newley; directed by Neal DuBrock.
          Produced for Broadway stage by David Merrick

0506   THE ROSE TATTOO
          by Tennessee Williams; directed by Milton Katselas

0507   YOU CAN'T TAKE IT WITH YOU
          by Moss Hart and George S. Kaufman; directed by Hy Kalus

1966-1967

0508   AFTER THE FALL
          by Arthur Miller; directed by Tom Gruenewald

0509   ANTIGONE
          by Jean Anouilh; directed by Allan Leicht. Performed the same
          evening as *The Lesson*

0510   CYRANO DE BERGERAC
        by Edmond Rostand; directed by Cyril Simon and Rocco Bufano

0511   THE IMPORTANCE OF BEING EARNEST
        by Oscar Wilde; directed by Tom Gruenewald

0512   THE LESSON
        by Eugene Ionesco; directed by Allan Leicht. Performed the
        same evening as *Antigone*

0513   THE MIKADO
        by W.S. Gilbert and Arthur Sullivan; directed by Allan Leicht;
        musical director, William Cox

0514   OH, KAY!
        by George and Ira Gershwin, book by Guy Bolton and P.G.
        Wodehouse; directed by Allan Leicht

                        1967-1968

0515   CHARLEY'S AUNT
        by Brandon Thomas; directed by Paxton Whitehead

0516   A DELICATE BALANCE
        by Edward Albee; directed by Warren Enters

0517   THE EMPEROR (ENRICO IV)
        by Luigi Pirandello, English version by Eric Bentley; directed
        by Stephen Porter

0518   H.M.S. PINAFORE
        by W.S. Gilbert and Arthur Sullivan; directed by Allan Leicht;
        musical director, Stuart Hamilton

0519   THE IMAGINARY INVALID
        by Moliere, original score by T.V. Figenshu; directed by
        Donald Davis

0520   THE KNACK
        by Ann Jellicoe; directed by Maurice Breslow

0521   THE THREEPENNY OPERA
        text and lyrics by Bertolt Brecht, music by Kurt Weill, English
        adaptation by Marc Blitzstein; directed by Tom Gruenewald;
        musical director, Philip Saltz

                        1968-1969

0522   THE LION IN WINTER
        by James Goldman; directed by Nikos Psacharopoulos

0523   YOU'RE A GOOD MAN, CHARLIE BROWN
        (based on *Peanuts* by Charles M. Schulz) by Arthur Whitelaw and
        Gene Persson; directed by Joseph Hardy

1969-1970

0524   DON'T DRINK THE WATER
        by Woody Allen; directed by Warren Enters

0525   EPISODE IN THE LIFE OF AN AUTHOR
        by Jean Anouilh, translated by Miriam John; directed by Jose
        Quintero. Performed the same evening as *The Orchestra*

0526   A FUNNY THING HAPPENED ON THE WAY TO THE FORUM
        book by Burt Shevlove and Larry Gelbart, music and lyrics by
        Stephen Sondheim; directed by Marvin Gordon; musical director,
        Stuart Hamilton

0527   LEMON SKY
        by Lanford Wilson; directed by Warren Enters

0528   THE ONLY GAME IN TOWN
        by Frank D. Gilroy; directed by Warren Enters

0529   THE ORCHESTRA
        by Jean Anouilh, translated by Miriam John; directed by Jose
        Quintero. Performed the same evening as *Episode in the Life
        of an Author*

0530   STOP THE WORLD - I WANT TO GET OFF
        by Leslie Bricusse and Anthony Newley; directed by Neal DuBrock;
        musical director, Stuart Hamilton

0531   TINY ALICE
        by Edward Albee; directed by Warren Enters

0532   UNCLE VANYA
        by Anton Chekhov; directed by Warren Enters

1970-1971

0533   DAMES AT SEA
        by George Haimsohn and Robin Miller; directed by Don Price

0534   THE EFFECT OF GAMMA RAYS ON MAN-IN-THE-MOON MARIGOLDS
        by Paul Zindel; directed by Warren Enters

0535   INDIANS
        by Arthur Kopit; directed by Neal DuBrock

0536   JACQUES BREL IS ALIVE AND WELL AND LIVING IN PARIS
        (based on Brel's lyrics and commentary) production conception,
        English lyrics, and additional material by Eric Blau and Mort
        Shuman; directed by Moni Yakim; musical director, Mort Shuman

0537   OTHELLO
        by William Shakespeare; directed by Louis Criss

0538   THE PRICE
        by Arthur Miller; directed by Warren Enters

0539   SCENES FROM AMERICAN LIFE
        by A.R. Gurney, Jr.; directed by Warren Enters. World premiere

0540   SCUBA DUBA
        by Bruce Jay Friedman; directed by Clarke Gordon

0541   THE SURVIVAL OF ST. JOAN
        by James Lineberger; directed by Chuck Gnys; musical
        coordination by Stephen Schwartz. World premiere

                            1971-1972

0542   BUYING OUT
        by Lawrence Roman; directed by Warren Enters

0543   THE GINGERBREAD LADY
        by Neil Simon; directed by Arthur Storch

0544   MAMA
        by Neal DuBrock; directed by Warren Enters. A new musical

0545   MAN OF LA MANCHA
        by Dale Wasserman, music by Mitch Leigh, lyrics by Joe Darian;
        directed by Antony de Vecchi

0546   THE ME NOBODY KNOWS
        (based on the book edited by Stephen M. Joseph) adapted by
        Robert H. Livingston and Herb Shapiro, music by Gary William
        Friedman, lyrics by Will Holt; directed by Gerri Dean; musical
        director, Neal Tate

0547   ROMEO AND JULIET
        by William Shakespeare; directed by Warren Enters

0548   THE TRIAL OF THE CATONSVILLE NINE
        by Daniel Berrigan, S.J.; directed by Robert W. Tolan

                            1972-1973

0549   BERLIN TO BROADWAY WITH KURT WEILL
        music by Kurt Weill; musical director, Robert Rogers

0550   BUTTERFLIES ARE FREE
        by Leonard Gershe; directed by Elizabeth Caldwell

0551   CHILD'S PLAY
        by Robert Marasco; directed by Warren Enters

0552   PETER PAN
        by Sir James M. Barrie; directed by Bick Goss

0553   RING-A-LEVIO
        by Donald Ross; directed by Paul Aaron. World premiere

0554   ROBERTA
        (adapted from the story by Alice Duer Miller) by Otto Harbach;
        directed by William Gile

0555   SAVING GRACE
        by John Tobias; directed by Leland Ball. World premiere;
        performed the same evening as *Sitting*

0556   SITTING
        by John Tobias; directed by Leland Ball. World premiere;
        performed the same evening as *Saving Grace*

0557   THE TAMING OF THE SHREW
        by William Shakespeare; directed by Warren Enters

                                1973-1974

0558   FLINT
        by David Mercer; directed by Warren Enters

0559   FUNNY FACE
        by George and Ira Gershwin; book by Fred Thompson and Paul
        Gerard Smith; directed by Neal DuBrock

0560   THE MISER
        by Moliere, translated by Wallace Fowlie; directed by Warren
        Enters

0561   OH COWARD!
        by Noel Coward, devised by Roderick Cook; directed by Roderick
        Cook

0562   OTHER VOICES, OTHER ROOMS
        (based on the novel by Truman Capote) by Anna Maria Barlow;
        directed by Melvin Bernhardt. World premiere

0563   A STREETCAR NAMED DESIRE
        by Tennessee Williams; directed by Jerome Guardino

0564   THAT CHAMPIONSHIP SEASON
        by Jason Miller; directed by Warren Enters

0565   THERE'S A GIRL IN MY SOUP
        by Terence Frisby; directed by Stuart Bishop

                                1974-1975

0566   BUTLEY
        by Simon Gray; directed by Richard Barr

0567   COME BACK, LITTLE SHEBA
        by William Inge; directed by Warren Enters

0568   DESIRE UNDER THE ELMS
        by Eugene O'Neill; directed by Warren Enters

0569   GABRIELLE
        book by Jose Quintero, original lyrics and adaptation by Jason
        Darrow, music by Gilbert Becaud; directed by Jose Quintero.
        World premiere

0570   GODSPELL
        (a musical based upon the Gospel according to *St. Matthew*)
        conceived by John-Michael Tebelak, music and lyrics by Stephen
        Schwartz; directed by John-Michael Tebelak

0571   I GOT A SONG
        by E.Y. Harburg; directed by Harold Stone

0572   THE LEGEND OF WU CHANG
        by Tisa Chang; directed by Tisa Chang

0573   P.S. YOUR CAT IS DEAD
        by James Kirkwood; directed by Richard Barr

0574   13 RUE DE L'AMOUR
        by Georges Feydeau, adapted by Mawley Greene and Ed Feilbert;
        directed by Donald Moffat

Burlington, VT

CHAMPLAIN SHAKESPEARE FESTIVAL

1974

0575   CYMBELINE, KING OF BRITAIN
        by William Shakespeare; directed by Nancy Haynes

0576   HAMLET, PRINCE OF DENMARK
        by William Shakespeare; directed by Michael Diamond

0577   THE TEMPEST
        by William Shakespeare; directed by Edward J. Feidner

Chicago, IL

GOODMAN THEATRE

1969-1970

0578   THE BASEMENT
        by Harold Pinter; directed by Joseph Slowik. Performed the
        same evening as *Tea Party*

0579   HEARTBREAK HOUSE
        by George Bernard Shaw; directed by Douglas Seale

0580   THE MAN IN THE GLASS BOOTH
        by Robert Shaw; directed by Douglas Seale

0581   TEA PARTY
            by Harold Pinter; directed by Patrick Henry. Performed the
            same evening as *The Basement*

                              1970-1971
                          Children's Theatre

0582   ALICE IN WONDERLAND
            (based on the novel by Lewis Carroll) by Thom Racina; directed
            by Thom Racina

0583   HOW THE FIRST LETTER WAS WRITTEN
            by Aurand Harris; directed by Joseph Slowik. Touring company
            production

0584   SACRAMENTO FIFTY MILES
            Eleanor and Ray Harder; directed by Jack Jones

0585   THE THWARTING OF BARON BOLLIGREW
            by Robert Bolt; directed by Joseph Slowik. Touring company
            production

                              1970-1971

0586   LADY AUDLEY'S SECRET
            (adapted from the novel by Mary Elizabeth Bradden) by Douglas
            Seale, music by George Goehring, lyrics by John Kuntz; directed
            by Douglas Seale

0587   MARCHING SONG
            by John Whiting; directed by Douglas Seale

0588   THE NIGHT THOREAU SPENT IN JAIL
            by Jerome Lawrence and Robert E. Lee; directed by Patrick Henry

0589   POOR BITOS
            by Jean Anouilh, translated by Lucienne Hill; directed by
            Douglas Campbell

0590   THE THREEPENNY OPERA
            text and lyrics by Bertolt Brecht, music by Kurt Weill, English
            adaptation by Marc Blitzstein; directed by Douglas Seale

0591   TWELFTH NIGHT
            by William Shakespeare; directed by Douglas Seale

                              1971-1972

0592   ASSASSINATION, 1865
            by Stuart Vaughan; directed by Stuart Vaughan. World premiere

0593   A PLACE WITHOUT DOORS
            by Marguerite Duras; directed by Brian Murray

0594   THE RULING CLASS
            by Peter Barnes; directed by Patrick Henry

1972-1973
Children's Theatre

0595   THE COMICAL TRAGEDY-OR-TRAGICAL COMEDY OF PUNCH AND JUDY
        by Aurand Harris; directed by Ned Schmidtke

0596   LITTLE RED RIDING HOOD
        by Eugene Schwartz, translated by George Shail; directed by
        Libby Appel

0597   SLEEPING BEAUTY, OR THE GREAT ROSE TABOO
        book and lyrics by Barbara Fried, music by Norman Sachs;
        directed by Kelly Danford

0598   THE THREE MUSKETEERS
        (based on the novel by Alexander Dumas) by Brian Way; directed
        by John Medici

1972-1973

0599   IN THE MATTER OF J. ROBERT OPPENHEIMER
        by Heinar Kipphardt, translated by Ruth Speirs; directed by
        Gene Lesser

0600   THE LADY'S NOT FOR BURNING
        by Christopher Fry; directed by Stephen Porter

0601   OLD TIMES
        by Harold Pinter; directed by Michael Kahn

0602   PAL JOEY
        by John O'Hara, music by Richard Rodgers, lyrics by Lorenz
        Hart; directed by Melvin Bernhardt

0603   SCENES FROM AMERICAN LIFE
        by A.R. Gurney, Jr.; directed by Harold Stone

0604   TWENTIETH CENTURY
        by Ben Hecht and Charles MacArthur; directed by William Woodman

1973-1974
Children's Theatre

0605   APPLESEED
        by Ed Graczyk, music and lyrics by Errol Pearlman; directed by
        Bella Itkin

0606   THE EMPEROR'S NEW CLOTHES
        by Hans Christian Anderson, adapted by Allen Lorenson; directed
        by Ned Schmidtke

0607   THE LION WHO WOULDN'T
        book and lyrics by Gifford W. Wingate, original music and
        additional lyrics by David Coleman; directed by Kelly Danford

0608   THE WIND IN THE WILLOWS
          by Kenneth Grahame, adapted by Joseph Baldwin; directed by
          Joseph Slowik

                              1973-1974

0609   A DOLL'S HOUSE
          by Henrik Ibsen, translated by Christopher Hampton; directed
          by Tormod Skagestad

0610   THE FREEDOM OF THE CITY
          by Brian Friel; directed by William Woodman

                              1974-1975
                           Children's Theatre

0611   MERTON OF THE MOVIES
          (based on the story by Harry Leon) by George S. Kaufman and
          Marc Connelly, adapted by Kelly Danford, music and lyrics by
          David Coleman; directed by Kelly Danford

0612   THE PRINCE, THE WOLF, AND THE FIREBIRD
          by Jackson Lacey; directed by Bella Itkin

0613   WINNEBAGO
          by Frank Galati; directed by Frank Galati

Cincinnati, OH

CINCINNATI PLAYHOUSE

                              1963

0614   ACT WITHOUT WORDS
          by Samuel Beckett; directed by Brooks Jones. Performed the
          same evening as *Cavalry* and *The Zoo Story*

0615   THE CARETAKER
          by Harold Pinter; directed by Mesrop Kesdekian

0616   CAVALRY
          by W.B. Yeats; directed by Brooks Jones. Performed the same
          evening as *Act Without Words* and *The Zoo Story*

0617   THE DEVIL'S DISCIPLE
          by George Bernard Shaw; directed by Stephen Porter

0618   THE EMPEROR (ENRICO IV)
          by Luigi Pirandello, translated by Eric Bentley; directed by
          Brooks Jones

0619   THE HOSTAGE
          by Brendan Behan; directed by Stephen Porter

0620   THE LADY'S NOT FOR BURNING
        by Christopher Fry; directed by Stephen Porter

0621   THE ZOO STORY
        by Edward Albee; directed by Brooks Jones. Performed the same
        evening as *Act Without Words* and *Cavalry*

1964

0622   ARMS AND THE MAN
        by George Bernard Shaw; directed by Donald Moffat

0623   THE BURNT FLOWER BED
        by Ugo Betti, translated by Eugene Lyon; directed by Stephen
        Porter

0624   THE DOCTOR IN SPITE OF HIMSELF
        by Moliere, translated by Morris Bishop; directed by Stephen
        Porter. Performed the same evening as *The Forced Marriage*

0625   THE FANTASTICKS
        words by Tom Jones, music by Harvey Schmidt; directed by Brooks
        Jones

0626   THE FORCED MARRIAGE
        by Moliere, translated by Albert Bermel; directed by Stephen
        Porter. Performed the same evening as *The Doctor in Spite of
        Himself*

0627   THE LOVE OF DON PERLIMPLIN
        by Federico Garcia Lorca, translated by Richard O'Connell and
        James E. Luhan; directed by Brooks Jones. Performed the same
        evening as *The Zoo Story*

0628   A MOON FOR THE MISBEGOTTEN
        by Eugene O'Neill; directed by David Hooks

0629   OH DAD, POOR DAD, MAMMA'S HUNG YOU IN THE CLOSET AND I'M
        FEELIN' SO SAD
        by Arthur Kopit; directed by Brooks Jones

0630   RHINOCEROS
        by Eugene Ionesco, translated by Derek Prouse; directed by
        Michael Murray

0631   THE THREEPENNY OPERA
        text and lyrics by Bertolt Brecht, music by Kurt Weill, English
        adaptation by Marc Blitzstein; directed by Brooks Jones

0632   THE ZOO STORY
        by Edward Albee; directed by Brooks Jones. Performed the same
        evening as *The Love of Don Perlimplin*

1965

0633   THE BLOOD KNOT
        by Athol Fugard; directed by Brooks Jones

0634   THE COLLECTION
            by Harold Pinter; directed by Brooks Jones. Performed the same
            evening as *The Lover*

0635   THE FANTASTICKS
            words by Tom Jones, music by Harvey Schmidt

0636   GHOSTS
            by Henrik Ibsen, translated by Eva Le Gallienne; directed by
            Lloyd Richards

0637   THE GLASS MENAGERIE
            by Tennessee Williams; directed by David Hooks

0638   THE LOVER
            by Harold Pinter; directed by Brooks Jones. Performed the same
            evening as *The Collection*

0639   MAJOR BARBARA
            by George Bernard Shaw; directed by Stephen Porter

0640   SHE STOOPS TO CONQUER
            by Oliver Goldsmith; directed by Douglas Seale

0641   SUMMER OF THE SEVENTEENTH DOLL
            by Ray Lawler; directed by David Hooks

                                1966

0642   THE AMERICAN DREAM
            by Edward Albee; directed by Brooks Jones. Performed the same
            evening as *Benito Cereno*

0643   BENITO CERENO
            by Robert Lowell; directed by Brooks Jones. Performed the same
            evening as *The American Dream*

0644   CHARLEY'S AUNT
            by Brandon Thomas; directed by David Hooks

0645   EH?
            by Henry Livings; directed by Melvin Bernhardt. U.S. premiere

0646   MAN AND SUPERMAN
            by George Bernard Shaw; directed by David Hooks

0647   THE SKIN OF OUR TEETH
            by Thornton Wilder; directed by Brooks Jones

0648   SODOM AND GOMORRAH
            by Jean Giraudoux, translated by Herma Briffault; directed by
            Stephen Porter

1967

0649   ANATOL
        (adapted from the book by Arthur Schnitzler) by Tom Jones;
        directed by David Hooks and Brooks Jones

0650   THE CAVERN
        by Jean Anouilh, translated by Lucienne Hill; directed by
        Michael Kahn. U.S. premiere

0651   ESCURIAL
        by Michel de Ghelderode, English translation by Lionel Abel;
        directed by Brooks Jones. Performed the same evening as
        The Lesson

0652   THE FANTASTICKS
        words by Tom Jones, music by Harvey Schmidt; directed by
        Ty McConnell

0653   THE LESSON
        by Eugene Ionesco, translated by Donald M. Allen; directed by
        David Hooks. Performed the same evening as *Escurial*

1968-1969

0654   THE COMEDY OF ERRORS
        by William Shakespeare; directed by David Hooks

0655   HONOR AND OFFER
        by Henry Livings; directed by Melvin Bernhardt

0656   MISALLIANCE
        by George Bernard Shaw; directed by David Hooks

0657   SAINT JOAN
        by George Bernard Shaw; directed by Brooks Jones

1970

0658   ARDELE
        by Jean Anouilh; directed by Jeff Bleckner

0659   COME BACK, LITTLE SHEBA
        by William Inge; directed by Gene Lesser

0660   THE FANTASTICKS
        words by Tom Jones, music by Harvey Schmidt; directed by
        Word Baker

0661   HENRY IV (PART 1)
        by William Shakespeare; directed by David Hooks

0662   MANY HAPPY RETURNS - A REVIEW OF REVUES
        sketches and lyrics by Howard Dietz, music by Arthur Schwartz;
        directed by Word Baker; musical director, Worth Gardner

0663   OLDENBERG
        by Barry Bermange; directed by Brian Murray. Performed the
        same evening as *A Slight Ache*; an Off-Off Broadway production

0664   PYGMALION
        by George Bernard Shaw; directed by Word Baker

0665   A SLIGHT ACHE
        by Harold Pinter; directed by Brian Murray. Performed the same
        evening as *Oldenberg*; an Off-Off Broadway production

0666   TOBACCO ROAD
        (based on the novel by Erskine Caldwell) by Jack Kirkland;
        directed by Word Baker and Dan Early

1971

0667   ANGEL STREET
        by Patrick Hamilton; directed by Anthony Perkins

0668   CARAVAGGIO
        by Michael Straight; directed by Word Baker

0669   HAMLET
        by William Shakespeare; directed by Word Baker and Dan Early

0670   JACQUES BREL IS ALIVE AND WELL AND LIVING IN PARIS
        (based on Brel's lyrics and commentary) production conception,
        English lyrics, and additional material by Eric Blau and Mort
        Shuman; directed by Moni Yakim

0671   THE LAST SWEET DAYS OF ISAAC
        book and lyrics by Gretchen Cryer, music by Nancy Ford;
        directed by Word Baker

0672   LIFE WITH FATHER
        (based on the book by Clarence Day, Jr.) by Howard Lindsay and
        Russel Crouse; directed by Michael Flanagan

0673   RAIN
        (adapted from the story by W. Somerset Maugham) by John Colton
        and Clemence Randolph; directed by Michael Flanagan

0674   SLOW DANCE ON THE KILLING GROUND
        by William Hanley; directed by Dan Early

0675   WHY HANNA'S SKIRT WON'T STAY DOWN
        by Tom Eyer; directed by Neil Flanagan

1972

0676   BABOON!!!
        by Word Baker, Dan Early, and Maria Irene Fornes; directed by
        Word Baker

0677   THE CRUCIBLE
          by Arthur Miller; directed by Word Baker

0678   THE INNOCENTS
          (based on *Turn of the Screw* by Henry James) by William
          Archibald; directed by Michael Flanagan

0679   THE PLAY'S THE THING
          by Ferenc Molnar; directed by Word Baker

0680   THE RIVALS
          by Richard Brinsley Sheridan; directed by Word Baker

0681   THE SCHOOL FOR WIVES
          by Moliere, English translation by Richard Wilbur; directed by
          Adrian Hall

0682   SENSATIONS OF THE BITTER PARTNER
          by Milburn Smith; directed by Word Baker. World premiere

0683   SHELTER
          book and lyrics by Gretchen Cryer, music by Nancy Ford;
          directed by Word Baker. World premiere

1973

0684   A DELICATE BALANCE
          by Edward Albee; directed by Harold Scott

0685   INCIDENT AT VICHY
          by Arthur Miller; directed by Harold Scott

0686   KISS ME, KATE
          book by Bella and Samuel Spewack, music and lyrics by Cole
          Porter; directed by Word Baker

0687   LONG DAY'S JOURNEY INTO NIGHT
          by Eugene O'Neill; directed by Harold Scott

0688   A MEMORY OF TWO MONDAYS
          by Arthur Miller; directed by Kent Paul

0689   A RAISIN IN THE SUN
          by Lorraine Hansberry; directed by Edmund Cambridge

0690   THE SEA PLAYS
          by Eugene O'Neill; directed by Kent Paul

0691   A STREETCAR NAMED DESIRE
          by Tennessee Williams; directed by Glenn Jordan

1973-1974

0692   HARVEY
          by Mary Chase; directed by John Going

0693   OLD TIMES
            by Harold Pinter; directed by Harold Scott

0694   THE TEMPEST
            by William Shakespeare; directed by Garland Wright

0695   TRAVELLERS
            book and lyrics by Corinne Jacker, music by Jonathan Tunick;
            directed by Tony Giordano

                              1974-1975

0696   ARSENIC AND OLD LACE
            by Joseph Kesselring; directed by Anthony Stimac

0697   THE HOT L BALTIMORE
            by Lanford Wilson; directed by Daniel Sullivan

0698   OH COWARD!
            by Noel Coward, devised by Roderick Cook; directed by Garland
            Wright

0699   TARTUFFE
            by Moliere, English translation by Richard Wilbur; directed by
            Daniel Sullivan

0700   THAT CHAMPIONSHIP SEASON
            by Jason Miller; directed by John Dillon

0701   WHO'S AFRAID OF VIRGINIA WOOLF?
            by Edward Albee; directed by Garland Wright

Cleveland, OH

CLEVELAND PLAYHOUSE

                              1958-1959

0702   THE CONFIDENTIAL CLERK
            by T.S. Eliot; directed by Bertram Tanswell

0703   THE DIARY OF ANNE FRANK
            by Frances Goodrich and Albert Hackett; directed by Bertram
            Tanswell

0704   FAIR GAME
            by Sam Locke; directed by Kirk Willis

0705   THE HAPPIEST MILLIONAIRE
            by Kyle Crichton; directed by Kirk Willis

0706   HEAVEN COME WEDNESDAY
            by Reginald Lawrence; directed by Thomas Hill

0707   JOB
by Thomas Hill and Alan Alda; directed by Thomas Hill

0708   MACBETH
by William Shakespeare; directed by Frederic McConnell

0709   THE MAGNIFICENT YANKEE
by Emmet Lavery; directed by Bertram Tanswell

0710   MONIQUE
by Dorothy and Michael Blankfort; directed by Kirk Willis

0711   MOTHER COURAGE
by Bertolt Brecht, English translation by Eric Bentley;
directed by Benno Frank

0712   THE MOUSETRAP
by Agatha Christie; directed by Bertram Tanswell

0713   NO TIME FOR SERGEANTS
(based on the book by Mac Hyman) by Ira Levin; directed by
Kirk Willis

0714   OEDIPUS REX
by Sophocles, translated by Albert Cook; directed by Frederic
McConnell

0715   THE PERFECT ALIBI
by A.A. Milne; directed by Frederic McConnell

0716   PICTURES IN THE HALLWAY
by Sean O'Casey; directed by Frederic McConnell

0717   PURPLE DUST
by Sean O'Casey; directed by Bertram Tanswell

0718   THE SONG OF BERNADETTE
(based on the novel by Franz Werfel) by Jean and Walter Kerr;
directed by Kirk Willis

0719   SPIDER'S WEB
by Agatha Christie; directed by Bertram Tanswell

0720   A STREETCAR NAMED DESIRE
by Tennessee Williams; directed by Bertram Tanswell

0721   TO DOROTHY, A SON
by Roger MacDougall; directed by Bertram Tanswell

0722   WHO WAS THAT LADY I SAW YOU WITH?
by Norman Krasna; directed by K. Elmo Lowe

1960-1961

0723   J.B.
by Archibald MacLeish; directed by Frederic McConnell

0724   LOOK HOMEWARD, ANGEL
           (based on the novel by Thomas Wolfe) by Ketti Frings; directed
           by David Hager

0725   TWO FOR THE SEESAW
           by William Gibson; directed by Michael McGuire and David Hager

                                   1961-1962

0726   THE ANDERSONVILLE TRIAL
           by Saul Levitt; directed by Frederic McConnell

0727   ARMS AND THE MAN
           by George Bernard Shaw; directed by Bertram Tanswell

0728   BIG FISH, LITTLE FISH
           by High Wheeler; directed by Kirk Willis

0729   BUILD ME A BRIDGE
           by Mary Drayton; directed by Mary Drayton

0730   A COOK FOR MR. GENERAL
           by Steven Gethers; directed by Kirk Willis

0731   ENRICO IV
           by Luigi Pirandello, adapted by John Reich; directed by
           Frederic McConnell

0732   ERNEST IN LOVE
           (based on a novel by Oscar Wilde) book and lyrics by Anne
           Croswell, music by Lee Pockriss; directed by Bertram Tanswell

0733   FIVE FINGER EXERCISE
           by Peter Shaffer; directed by Bertram Tanswell

0734   HEDDA GABLER
           by Henrik Ibsen; directed by David Hager

0735   A MAJORITY OF ONE
           by Leonard Spigelgass; directed by Bertram Tanswell

0736   NOT IN THE BOOK
           by Arthur Watkyn; directed by Bertram Tanswell

0737   PERIOD OF ADJUSTMENT
           by Tennessee Williams; directed by Thomas Hill

0738   PICTURES IN THE HALLWAY
           by Sean O'Casey, adapted by Paul Shyre; directed by Michael
           McGuire

0739   THE PLEASURE OF HIS COMPANY
           by Samuel Taylor and Cornelia Otis Skinner; directed by Kirk
           Willis

0740   ROMAN CANDLE
           by Sidney Sheldon; directed by Kirk Willis

0741   SIMONE
            (adapted from *Visions of Simone Machard* by Bertolt Brecht and
            Lion Feuchtwanger) by Ben Hecht; directed by Harold Stone

0742a   SISTER WAS A SPORT
            by John Josef Wolf; directed by Bertram Tanswell

0742b   THE SOUND OF MURDER
            by William Fairchild; directed by Kirk Willis

0743   THE TEMPEST
            by William Shakespeare; directed by Kirk Willis

0744   UNDER THE YUM-YUM TREE
            by Lawrence Roman; directed by David Hager

                            1962-1963

0745   THE ALCHEMIST
            by Ben Jonson; directed by Thomas Hill

0746   THE AMERICAN DREAM
            by Edward Albee; directed by Thomas Hill

0747   THE ASPERN PAPERS
            by Henry James, adapted by Michael Redgrave; directed by John
            Cromwell

0748   THE BALD SOPRANO
            by Eugene Ionesco; directed by Thomas Hill

0749   BREATH OF SPRING
            by Peter Coke; directed by Bertram Tanswell

0750   THE CARETAKER
            by Harold Pinter; directed by Thomas Hill

0751   COME BLOW YOUR HORN
            by Neil Simon; directed by Kirk Willis

0752   A COOK FOR MR. GENERAL
            by Steven Gethers; directed by Kirk Willis

0753   CRITIC'S CHOICE
            by Ira Levin; directed by Kirk Willis

0754   THE FANTASTICKS
            words by Tom Jones, music by Harvey Schmidt; directed by Kirk
            Willis

0755   GHOSTS
            by Henrik Ibsen, translated by R. Farquharson Sharp; directed
            by David Hager

0756   GIDEON
            by Paddy Chayefsky; directed by Kirk Willis

0757   I KNOCK AT THE DOOR
        by Sean O'Casey, adapted by Paul Shyre; directed by David Hager

0758   THE IMPORTANCE OF BEING EARNEST
        by Oscar Wilde; directed by Bertram Tanswell

0759   LONG DAY'S JOURNEY INTO NIGHT
        by Eugene O'Neill; directed by Thomas Hill

0760   THE MIRACLE WORKER
        by William Gibson; directed by Bertram Tanswell

0761   MUCH ADO ABOUT NOTHING
        by William Shakespeare; directed by Kirk Willis

0762   RHINOCEROS
        by Eugene Ionesco, translated by Derek Prouse; directed by
        Thomas Hill

0763   SUNDAY IN NEW YORK
        by Norman Krasna; directed by David Hager

0764   THE TAVERN
        by George M. Cohan; directed by Kirk Willis

0765   A THURBER CARNIVAL
        by James Thurber; directed by Kirk Willis

0766   UNDER THE YUM-YUM TREE
        by Lawrence Roman; directed by David Hager

1963-1964

0767   THE APOLLO OF BELLAC
        by Jean Giraudoux, adapted by Maurice Valency; directed by
        David Hager. Performed the same evening as *A Phoenix Too
        Frequent*

0768   THE BANKER'S DAUGHTER
        book and lyrics by Edward Eliscu, music by Sol Kaplan; directed
        by Kirk Willis

0769   BECKET
        by Jean Anouilh, translated by Lucienne Hill; directed by
        William Woodman

0770   CALCULATED RISK
        by Joseph Hayes; directed by Kirk Willis

0771   COME BLOW YOUR HORN
        by Neil Simon; directed by Kirk Willis

0772   THE DOCK BRIEF
        by John Mortimer; directed by William Paterson. Performed the
        same evening as *Scapin*

0773   THE DOCTOR'S DILEMMA
       by George Bernard Shaw; directed by William Woodman

0774   JOHNNY
       by Dalton Trumbo, adapted by David Hager; directed by David
       Hager

0775   KING HENRY IV (PART 1)
       by William Shakespeare; directed by Kirk Willis

0776   THE MADWOMAN OF CHAILLOT
       by Jean Giraudoux, adapted by Maurice Valency; directed by
       John Cromwell

0777   THE NIGHT OF THE IGUANA
       by Tennessee Williams; directed by William Woodman

0778   OH DAD, POOR DAD, MAMMA'S HUNG YOU IN THE CLOSET AND I'M
       FEELIN' SO SAD
       by Arthur Kopit; directed by Paul Rodgers

0779   A PHOENIX TOO FREQUENT
       by Christopher Fry; directed by David Hager. Performed the
       same evening as *The Apollo of Bellac*

0780   THE RIVALRY
       by Norman Corwin; directed by David Hager

0781   RIVERWIND
       by John Jennings; directed by Kirk Willis

0782   SCAPIN
       by Moliere; directed by Kirk Willis. Performed the same evening
       as *The Dock Brief*

0783   TAKE HER, SHE'S MINE
       by Phoebe and Henry Ephron; directed by William Woodman

0784   THE TAVERN
       by George M. Cohan; directed by Kirk Willis

0785   THE TIGER
       by Murray Schisgal; directed by William Paterson. Performed the
       same evening as *The Typists*

0786   THE TYPISTS
       by Murray Schisgal; directed by William Paterson. Performed the
       same evening as *The Tiger*

1964-1965

0787   ALL THE KING'S MEN
       by Robert Penn Warren; directed by David Hager

0788   THE CHALK GARDEN
       by Enid Bagnold; directed by Robert Henderson

0789   ENTER LAUGHING
          (adapted from the book by Carl Reiner) by Joseph Stein; directed
          by Kirk Willis

0790   GALILEO
          by Bertolt Brecht, translated by Charles Laughton; directed by
          K. Elmo Lowe

0791   THE MADWOMAN OF CHAILLOT
          by Jean Giraudoux, adapted by Maurice Valency; directed by
          David Hager

0792   MAJOR BARBARA
          by George Bernard Shaw; directed by Robert Henderson

0793   MARY, MARY
          by Jean Kerr; directed by Kirk Willis

0794   A MIDSUMMER NIGHT'S DREAM
          by William Shakespeare; directed by Kirk Willis

0795   THE PHYSICISTS
          by Friedrich Duerrenmatt, translated by James Kirkup; directed
          by David Hager

0796a   THE PRIVATE EAR
          by Peter Shaffer; directed by Robert Henderson. Performed the
          same evening as *The Public Eye*

0796b   THE PUBLIC EYE
          by Peter Shaffer; directed by Robert Henderson. Performed the
          same evening as *The Private Ear*

0797   RATTLE OF A SIMPLE MAN
          by Charles Dyer; directed by Kirk Willis

0798   TAKE HER, SHE'S MINE
          by Phoebe and Henry Ephron; directed by David Hager

0799   A THOUSAND CLOWNS
          by Herb Gardner; directed by Kirk Willis

0800   TWELVE ANGRY MEN
          by Reginald Rose; directed by Kirk Willis

0801   THE WALTZ OF THE TOREADORS
          by Jean Anouilh, translated by Lucienne Hill; directed by
          David Hager

                              1965-1966

0802   THE ABSENCE OF A CELLO
          by Ira Wallach; directed by Robert Snook

0803   THE AMOROUS FLEA
          by Moliere, book by Jerry Devine, music and lyrics by Bruce
          Montgomery; directed by Kirk Willis

0804   ANTIGONE
            by Jean Anouilh, adapted by Lewis Galantiere; directed by
            Robert Snook

0805   THE BALLAD OF THE SAD CAFE
            (adapted from the novel by Carson McCullers) by Edward Albee;
            directed by William Woodman

0806   CARVED IN SNOW
            by Milton Geiger; directed by William Woodman

0807   DYLAN
            by Sidney Michaels; directed by William Woodman

0808   MARY, MARY
            by Jean Kerr; directed by Kirk Willis

0809   NEVER TOO LATE
            by Sumner Arthur Long; directed by Kirk Willis

0810   OUR TOWN
            by Thornton Wilder; directed by Kirk Willis

0811   POOR RICHARD
            by Jean Kerr; directed by Kirk Willis

0812   SLOW DANCE ON THE KILLING GROUND
            by William Hanley; directed by Kirk Willis

0813   TARTUFFE
            by Moliere, translated by Richard Wilbur; directed by William
            Woodman

0814   TWELFTH NIGHT
            by William Shakespeare; directed by Kirk Willis

0815   UNCLE VANYA
            by Anton Chekhov, adapted by Robert Snook; directed by Robert
            Snook

0816   WHO'S AFRAID OF VIRGINIA WOOLF?
            by Edward Albee; directed by Kirk Willis

0817   YOU CAN'T TAKE IT WITH YOU
            by Moss Hart and George S. Kaufman; directed by Kirk Willis

0818   YOU NEVER CAN TELL
            by George Bernard Shaw; directed by William Woodman

1966-1967

0819   ANY WEDNESDAY
            by Muriel Resnik; directed by Raphael Kelly

0820   BAREFOOT IN THE PARK
            by Neil Simon; directed by Richard Oberlin

0821   BLITHE SPIRIT
            by Noel Coward; directed by William Paterson

0822   BRECHT ON BRECHT
            by Bertolt Brecht, translated by George Tabori; directed by
            Robert Snook

0823   A CASE OF LIBEL
            (based on the book by Louis Nizer) by Henry Denker; directed
            by Tom Brennan

0824   THE HOSTAGE
            by Brendan Behan; directed by Richard Oberlin

0825   LIFE WITH FATHER
            (based on the book by Clarence Day, Jr.) by Howard Lindsay and
            Russel Crouse; directed by Stuart Levin

0826   THE MISER
            by Moliere, adapted by Miles Malleson; directed by William
            Woodman

0827   A PROFILE OF BENJAMIN FRANKLIN
            by William Paterson; directed by William Paterson. A one-man
            show

0828   A PROFILE OF HOLMES
            by William Paterson; directed by William Paterson. A one-man
            show

0829   THE SKIN OF OUR TEETH
            by Thornton Wilder; directed by William Woodman

0830   THE SUBJECT WAS ROSES
            by Frank D. Gilroy; directed by Kirk Willis

0831   THE TEMPEST
            by William Shakespeare; directed by Robert Snook

0832   U.S.A.
            (based on the novel by John Dos Passos) by Paul Shyre and John
            Dos Passos; directed by Stuart Levin

                                    1967-1968

0833   BAREFOOT IN THE PARK
            by Neil Simon; directed by Richard Oberlin

0834   CHARLEY'S AUNT
            by Brandon Thomas; directed by Mario Siletti

0835   THE COLLECTION
            by Harold Pinter; directed by Tom Brennan. Performed the same
            evening as *The Dumb Waiter*, under the title of *The Pinter Plays*

0836   DEAR LIAR
        (based on correspondence of George Bernard Shaw and Mrs.
        Patricia Campbell) by Jerome Kilty; directed by Richard Oberlin

0837   THE DUMB WAITER
        by Harold Pinter; directed by Tom Brennan. Performed the same
        evening as *The Collection*, under the title of *The Pinter Plays*

0838   GENERATION
        by William Goodhart; directed by Richard Oberlin

0839   THE GOVERNMENT INSPECTOR
        by Nikolai Gogol; directed by Richard Oberlin

0840   LUV
        by Murray Schisgal; directed by Henry Butler

0841   MORNING'S AT SEVEN
        by Paul Osborn; directed by Jonathan Bolt

0842   THE ODD COUPLE
        by Neil Simon; directed by Tom Brennan

0843   THE ROSE TATTOO
        by Tennessee Williams; directed by Mario Siletti

0844   THE STRONG ARE LONELY
        by Fritz Hochwaelder, adapted by Eva Le Gallienne; directed by
        John Marley

0845   THE TEMPEST
        by William Shakespeare; directed by Robert Snook

                          1968-1969

0846   AFTER THE RAIN
        by John Bowen; directed by William Greene

0847   AH, WILDERNESS!
        by Eugene O'Neill; directed by Robert Snook

0848   THE BIRTHDAY PARTY
        by Harold Pinter; directed by Richard Oberlin

0849   THE DAY OF THE LION
        by Joel Wyman, adapted by Dan Jacobson; directed by John Marley

0850   DEAR LIAR
        (based on correspondence of George Bernard Shaw and Mrs.
        Patricia Campbell) by Jerome Kilty; directed by Richard Oberlin

0851   THE DOCTOR IN SPITE OF HIMSELF
        by Moliere; directed by William Greene. Performed the same
        evening as *The Jealous Husband*

0852   A FLEA IN HER EAR
        by Georges Feydeau, translated by John Mortimer; directed by
        William Greene

0853   IPHIGENIA IN AULIS
        by Euripides; directed by Mario Siletti

0854   THE JEALOUS HUSBAND
        by Moliere; directed by William Greene. Performed the same
        evening as *The Doctor in Spite of Himself*

0855   THE MALE ANIMAL
        by James Thurber and Elliot Nugent; directed by William Greene

0856   MONEY
        book and lyrics by David Axelrod and Tom Whedon, music by Sam
        Pottle; directed by Richard Oberlin

0857   MRS. LINCOLN
        by Thomas Cullinan; directed by Robert Snook

0858   THE PLAY'S THE THING
        by Ferenc Molnar, adapted by P.G. Wodehouse; directed by Mario
        Siletti

0859   SUMMERTREE
        by Ron Cowen; directed by Mario Siletti

0860   THIEVES' CARNIVAL
        by Jean Anouilh, English translation by Lucienne Hill; directed
        by Mario Siletti

0861   THE UNITED STATES VS. JULIUS AND ETHEL ROSENBERG
        by Donald Freed; directed by Larry Tarrant

                            1969-1970*

0862   ALL THE WAY HOME
        (based on *A Death in the Family* by James Agee) by Tad Mosel;
        directed by Robert Snook

0863   BEA, FRANK, RICHIE AND JOAN
        (adapted from *Lovers and Other Strangers* by Renee Taylor and
        Joseph Bologna) by Renee Taylor and Joseph Bologna; directed
        by Richard Oberlin. Performed the same evening as *Black Comedy*

0864   BLACK COMEDY
        by Peter Shaffer; directed by Richard Oberlin. Performed the
        same evening as *Bea, Frank, Richie and Joan*

0865   THE COUNTRY WIFE
        by William Wycherley; directed by John Going

_____

* Programs for this season contain a series of articles on conversations
  with critics.

0866   DON JUAN IN HELL
        by George Bernard Shaw; directed by Stuart Levin

0867   THE EFFECT OF GAMMA RAYS ON MAN-IN-THE-MOON MARIGOLDS
        by Paul Zindel; directed by Jonathan Bolt

0868   HARVEY
        by Mary Chase; directed by John Going

0869   THE HUF AND THE PUF
        by Norman Wexler; directed by Robert Snook. Performed the same
        evening as *Whatever Happened to Hugging and Kissing?*

0870   JOE EGG
        by Peter Nichols; directed by Larry Tarrant

0871   LOOT
        by Joe Orton; directed by Richard Oberlin

0872   RED'S MY COLOR, WHAT'S YOURS
        by Norman Wexler; directed by John Going

0873   THE ROYAL HUNT OF THE SUN
        by Peter Shaffer, music by Marc Wilkinson; directed by Robert
        Snook

0874   THE TAMING OF THE SHREW
        by William Shakespeare; directed by John Going

0875   THE UNITED STATES VS. JULIUS AND ETHEL ROSENBERG
        by Donald Freed; directed by Larry Tarrant. Program contains
        background information on the Rosenberg case

0876   WHATEVER HAPPENED TO HUGGING AND KISSING?
        by Norman Wexler; directed by Robert Snook. Performed the same
        evening as *The Huf and the Puf*

1970-1971

0877   ENDGAME
        by Samuel Beckett; directed by Larry Tarrant

0878   FALLEN ANGELS
        by Noel Coward; directed by Richard Oberlin

0879   GALLOWS HUMOR
        by Jack Richardson; directed by Jonathan Bolt

0880   THE THREEPENNY OPERA
        text and lyrics by Bertolt Brecht, music by Kurt Weill, English
        adaptation by Marc Blitzstein; directed by John Going

1971-1972

0881   THE ANNIVERSARY
        by Anton Chekhov; directed by Bjorn Pernvik. Performed the same
        evening as *On the Harmfulness of Tobacco*, *The Proposal*, and
        The Reluctant Tragedian, under the title of *The Portable Chekhov*

0882   THE BIRDS
        by Aristophanes; directed by J.J. Garry, Jr.

0883   CHILD'S PLAY
        by Robert Marasco; directed by Bertram Tanswell

0884   DARK OF THE MOON
        by Howard Richardson and William Berney; directed by J.J.
        Garry, Jr.

0885   A DOLL'S HOUSE
        by Henrik Ibsen, translated by Eva Le Gallienne; directed by
        Douglas Seale

0886   FORTY CARATS
        by Pierre Barillet and Jean-Pierre Gredy, adapted by Jay Allen;
        directed by Jonathan Bolt

0887   FRANK MERRIWELL (OR HONOR CHALLENGED)
        book by Skip Redwine, Larry Frank, and Heywood Gould, music and
        lyrics by Skip Redwine and Larry Frank; directed by George
        Touliatos

0888   THE HOUSE OF BLUE LEAVES
        by John Guare; directed by Bob Moak

0889   THE LIAR
        by Carlo Goldoni, translated by Tunc Yalman; directed by Tunc
        Yalman

0890   MOBY DICK, REHEARSED
        (adapted from the novel by Herman Melville) by Orson Welles;
        directed by Eric Conger

0891   ON THE HARMFULNESS OF TOBACCO
        by Anton Chekhov; directed by Jon Beryl. Performed the same
        evening as *The Anniversary*, *The Proposal*, and *The Reluctant
        Tragedian*, under the title of *The Portable Chekhov*

0892   PLAZA SUITE
        by Neil Simon; directed by Jonathan Bolt

0893   THE PRICE
        by Arthur Miller; directed by Jonathan Bolt

0894   THE PRIME OF MISS JEAN BRODIE
        (adapted from the novel by Muriel Spark) by Jay Presson Allen;
        directed by Bertram Tanswell

0895   THE PROPOSAL
          by Anton Chekhov; directed by Bob Moak. Performed the same
          evening as *The Anniversary*, *On the Harmfulness of Tobacco*, and
          The Reluctant Tragedian, under the title of *The Portable
          Chekhov*

0896   THE RELUCTANT TRAGEDIAN
          by Anton Chekhov; directed by Eric Conger. Performed the same
          evening as *The Anniversary*, *On the Harmfulness of Tobacco*, and
          The Proposal, under the title of *The Portable Chekhov*

0897   WHAT THE BUTLER SAW
          by Joe Orton; directed by Andrew Lack

0898   WOMAN IN THE DUNES
          (adapted from the novel by Kobo Abe) by Peter Coe; directed by
          Peter Coe

                              1972-1973

0899   SHERLOCK HOLMES
          (based on the novels by Sir Arthur Conan Doyle) by William
          Gillette, adapted by Dennis Rosa; directed by Dennis Rosa

0900   A YARD OF SUN
          by Christopher Fry; directed by Jose Ferrer

                              1973-1974*

0901   BORN YESTERDAY
          by Garson Kanin; directed by Edmund Lyndeck

0902   COUNT DRACULA
          (based on the novel by Bram Stoker) by Ted Tiller; directed by
          Larry Tarrant. Program contains an article about Transylvania

0903   THE FRONT PAGE
          by Ben Hecht and Charles MacArthur; directed by Tom Gruenewald

0904   HAMLET, PRINCE OF DENMARK
          by William Shakespeare; directed by J. Ranelli. Program con-
          tains an article about past performances of *Hamlet*

0905   IN FASHION
          book by Jon Jory, music by Jerry Blatt, lyrics by Lonnie
          Burstein; directed by Dennis Rosa

0906   LOOK BACK IN ANGER
          by John Osborne; directed by Douglas Seale

0907   THE MORGAN YARD
          by Kevin O'Morrison; directed by Jonathan Farwell

---

* Programs for this season contain articles about either the playwright
  or the play.

0908   PRIVATE LIVES
            by Noel Coward; directed by Paul Lee

0909   THE REMOVALISTS
            by David Williamson; directed by Larry Tarrant

0910   ROSENCRANTZ AND GUILDENSTERN ARE DEAD
            by Tom Stoppard; directed by J. Ranelli

0911   SCHOOL FOR WIVES
            by Moliere, translated by Richard Wilbur; directed by Dennis
            Rosa

0912   A TOUCH OF THE POET
            by Eugene O'Neill; directed by Paul Lee

                          1974-1975*

0913   CAT ON A HOT TIN ROOF
            by Tennessee Williams; directed by Jonathan Bolt

0914   COLETTE
            (based on *Earthly Paradise*, the collection on Colette's auto-
            biographical writings by Robert Phelps) by Elinor Jones, lyrics
            by Tom Jones, music by Harvey Schmidt; directed by Fran Soeder

0915   CONFESSIONS AT NIGHT
            by Aleksei Arbuzov, translated by Ariadne Nicolaeff; directed
            by Larry Tarrant

0916   COUNT DRACULA
            (based on the novel by Bram Stoker) by Ted Tiller; directed by
            Larry Tarrant

0917   THE COUNT OF MONTE CRISTO
            (based on the novel by Alexandre Dumas) by Marshall Borden;
            directed by William Rhys

0918   THE FREEDOM OF THE CITY
            by Brian Friel; directed by Larry Tarrant

0919   HAPPY END
            lyrics by Bertolt Brecht, music by Kurt Weill, adaptation and
            new lyrics by Michael Feingold; directed by Dennis Rosa

0920   HAY FEVER
            by Noel Coward; directed by Paul Lee

0921   THE HOT L BALTIMORE
            by Lanford Wilson; directed by Jonathan Bolt

0922   THE PRISONER OF SECOND AVENUE
            by Neil Simon; directed by Richard Halverson

* Programs for this season contain biographical sketches and chronology
  of life events of authors.

0923   RICHARD III
by William Shakespeare, music by Frederick Koch; directed by
William Francisco

0924   THE RIVALS
by Richard Brinsley Sheridan; directed by Paul Lee

0925   THE SEA HORSE
by Edward J. Moore; directed by Paul Lee

1975-1976

0926   FIRST MONDAY IN OCTOBER
by Jerome Lawrence and Robert E. Lee; directed by Jerome
Lawrence

Costa Mesa, CA

SOUTH COAST REPERTORY

1973-1974

0927   GODSPELL
(a musical based upon the Gospel according to *St. Matthew*)
conceived by John-Michael Tebelak, music and lyrics by Stephen
Schwartz; directed by John-David Keller

0928   THE HOUSE OF BLUE LEAVES
by John Guare; directed by Martin Benson

0929   THE PHILANTHROPIST
by Christopher Hampton; directed by David Emmes

0930   STICKS AND BONES
by David Rabe; directed by Martin Benson

0931   THE TAMING OF THE SHREW
by William Shakespeare; directed by Dan Sullivan

0932   THE TAVERN
by George M. Cohan; directed by Robert Bonaventura

0933   THE WOULD-BE GENTLEMAN
by Moliere; directed by David Emmes

1974-1975

0934   AFTER MAGRITTE
by Tom Stoppard; directed by John-David Keller. Performed the
same evening as *The Real Inspector Hound*

0935   THE CAVE DWELLERS
by William Saroyan; directed by Martin Benson

0936   THE REAL INSPECTOR HOUND
         by Tom Stoppard; directed by John-David Keller. Performed the
         same evening as *After Magritte*

0937   SUBJECT TO FITS
         by Robert Montgomery; directed by David Emmes

0938   THAT CHAMPIONSHIP SEASON
         by Jason Miller; directed by David Emmes

                              1975-1976

0939   JUMPERS
         by Tom Stoppard; directed by David Emmes

.0940   A MIDSUMMER NIGHT'S DREAM
         by William Shakespeare; directed by Dan Sullivan

0941   SCENES FROM AMERICAN LIFE
         by A.R. Gurney, Jr.; directed by Asaad Kelada

Hartford, CT

HARTFORD STAGE COMPANY

                               1964

0942   THE COUNTRY WIFE
         by William Wycherley; directed by Jacques Cartier

0943   OTHELLO
         by William Shakespeare; directed by Jacques Cartier

                            1964-1965

0944   BEDTIME STORY
         by Sean O'Casey; directed by Charles Kimbrough. Performed the
         same evening as *Putting on the Agony*

0945   DEATH OF A SALESMAN
         by Arthur Miller; directed by Jacques Cartier

0946   THE ENTERTAINER
         by John Osborne; directed by Jacques Cartier

0947   THE IMAGINARY INVALID
         by Moliere, adapted by Miles Malleson; directed by William
         Woodman

0948   PUTTING ON THE AGONY
         by Joel Oliansky; directed by Jacques Cartier. Performed the
         same evening as *Bedtime Story*

0949   SHE STOOPS TO CONQUER
         by Oliver Goldsmith; directed by William Francisco

0950   THE TEMPEST
         by William Shakespeare; directed by Jacques Cartier

0951   UNCLE VANYA
         by Anton Chekhov; directed by Jacques Cartier

0952   WAITING FOR GODOT
         by Samuel Beckett; directed by William Francisco

1965-1966

0953   THE BALCONY
         by Jean Genet; directed by Jacques Cartier

0954   CAT ON A HOT TIN ROOF
         by Tennessee Williams; directed by Jacques Cartier

0955   HEDDA GABLER
         by Henrik Ibsen, translated by William Archer; directed by
         Jacques Cartier

0956   THE IMPORTANCE OF BEING EARNEST
         by Oscar Wilde; directed by Mel Shapiro

0957   MAJOR BARBARA
         by George Bernard Shaw; directed by Jacques Cartier

0958   TARTUFFE
         by Moliere, translated by Richard Wilbur; directed by Paul
         Weidner

0959   TWELFTH NIGHT
         by William Shakespeare; directed by Paul Weidner

0960   WHO'S AFRAID OF VIRGINIA WOOLF?
         by Edward Albee; directed by Jacques Cartier

1966-1967

0961   ACT WITHOUT WORDS
         by Samuel Beckett; directed by Paul Weidner. Performed the
         same evening as *Endgame*

0962   ENDGAME
         by Samuel Beckett; directed by Paul Weidner and Jacques Cartier.
         Performed the same evening as *Act Without Words*

0963   ENRICO IV
         by Luigi Pirandello, translated by John Reich; directed by
         Jacques Cartier

0964   THE FANTASTICKS
         words by Tom Jones, music by Harvey Schmidt; directed by
         Peter Hunt

0965   POOR BITOS
            by Jean Anouilh; directed by Jacques Cartier

0966   THE SERVANT OF TWO MASTERS
            by Carlo Goldoni, translated by Paul Weidner; directed by
            Paul Weidner

0967   UNDER THE GASLIGHT
            by Augustin Daly; directed by Gordon Hunt

                                1967-1968

0968   ANTIGONE
            by Sophocles; directed by Michael Murray

0969   THE FIREBUGS
            by Max Frisch, translated by Mordecai Gorelik; directed by
            Jacques Cartier

0970   HAY FEVER
            by Noel Coward; directed by Jacques Cartier

0971   THE HOSTAGE
            by Brendan Behan; directed by Louis Beachner

0972   SKINFLINT OUT WEST
            (based on *The Miser* by Moliere) by Jacques Cartier; directed
            by Jacques Cartier

0973   THE THREEPENNY OPERA
            text and lyrics by Bertolt Brecht, music by Kurt Weill, English
            adaptation by Marc Blitzstein; directed by Peter Hunt

0974   A VIEW FROM THE BRIDGE
            by Arthur Miller; directed by Melvin Bernhardt

                                1968-1969

0975   THE HOMECOMING
            by Harold Pinter; by Melvin Bernhardt

0976   LIFE WITH FATHER
            (based on the book by Clarence Day, Jr.) by Howard Lindsay and
            Russel Crouse; directed by Louis Beachner

0977   THE ROSE TATTOO
            by Tennessee Williams; directed by Arthur Storch

0978   THE SEA GULL
            by Anton Chekhov, translated by Eva LeGallienne; directed by
            Paul Weidner

0979   THE TRIAL
            (based on the novel by Franz Kafka) by Andre Gide and Jean-Louis
            Barrault, translated by Leon Katz and Joseph Katz; directed by
            Paul Weidner

0980   THE WALTZ INVENTION
         by Vladimir Nabokov; directed by Paul Weidner

                            1969-1970

0981   ANYTHING GOES
         book by P.G. Wodehouse, Guy Bolton, Howard Lindsay, and Russel
         Crouse, music and lyrics by Cole Porter; directed by Don Price

0982   A DELICATE BALANCE
         by Edward Albee; directed by Paul Weidner

0983   JOE EGG
         by Peter Nichols; directed by Charles Maryan

0984   MISALLIANCE
         by George Bernard Shaw; directed by Tom Gruenewald

0985   SCAPIN
         by Moliere, translated by Paul Weidner; directed by Paul Weidner

0986   THE TRIAL OF ABE LINCOLN
         by James Daminco; directed by Paul Weidner

                            1970-1971

0987   BLITHE SPIRIT
         by Noel Coward; directed by Nagle Jackson

0988   THE BOYS IN THE BAND
         by Mart Crowley; directed by Paul Weidner

0989   A GUN PLAY
         by Yale M. Udoff; directed by Paul Weidner

0990   LONG DAY'S JOURNEY INTO NIGHT
         by Eugene O'Neill; directed by Jacques Cartier

0991   RING AROUND THE MOON
         by Jean Anouilh, translated by Christopher Fry; directed by
         Philip Minor

0992   ROSENCRANTZ AND GUILDENSTERN ARE DEAD
         by Tom Stoppard; directed by Paul Weidner

                            1971-1972

0993   CHARLEY'S AUNT
         by Brandon Thomas; directed by Jeremiah Sullivan

0994   HENRY V
         by William Shakespeare; directed by Paul Weidner

0995   NO PLACE TO BE SOMEBODY
         by Charles Gordone; directed by Richard Ward

0996   ROOTED
        by Alexander Buzo; directed by Paul Weidner. American premiere

0997   TINY ALICE
        by Edward Albee; directed by Paul Weidner

                                1972-1973

0998   THE MISANTHROPE
        by Moliere, translated by Richard Wilbur; directed by Paul
        Weidner

0999   NIGHTLIGHT
        by Kenneth H. Brown; directed by Paul Weidner. World premiere;
        program contains a list of all plays performed by the Hartford
        Stage Co. from 1964-1973

1000   OLD TIMES
        by Harold Pinter; directed by Paul Weidner

1001   A STREETCAR NAMED DESIRE
        by Tennessee Williams; directed by Jacques Cartier

1002   YOU CAN'T TAKE IT WITH YOU
        by Moss Hart and George S. Kaufman; directed by Paul Weidner

                                1973-1974

1003   ARSENIC AND OLD LACE
        by Joseph Kesselring; directed by Eve Collyer

1004   GETTING MARRIED
        by George Bernard Shaw; directed by Douglas Seale

1005   THE SCHOOL FOR SCANDAL
        by Richard Brinsley Sheridan; directed by Paul Weidner

1006   A TOUCH OF THE POET
        by Eugene O'Neill; directed by Paul Weidner

1007   UBU-ROI
        by Alfred Jarry, translated by Paul Weidner; directed by Paul
        Weidner

                                1974-1975

1008   AFTERNOON TEA
        by Harvey Perr; directed by Paul Weidner

1009   ANNELIES MARIE FRANK: WITNESS
        compiled and adapted by Irene Lewis; directed by Irene Lewis.
        Performed by the Hartford Stage Touring Co.

1010   THE CHERRY ORCHARD
        by Anton Chekhov; directed by Paul Weidner

1011   THE HOT L BALTOMORE
by Lanford Wilson; directed by Paul Weidner

1012   A RAISIN IN THE SUN
by Lorraine Hansberry; directed by Irene Lewis

1013   ROOM SERVICE
by John Murray and Allen Boretz; directed by Paul Weidner

1014   SHORT EYES
by Miguel Pinero; directed by Marvin Felix Camillo

1975-1976

1015   ALL OVER
by Edward Albee; directed by Paul Weidner

1016   AWAKE AND SING
by Clifford Odets; directed by Paul Weidner. Performed in Yiddish

Houston, TX

ALLEY THEATRE

1947-1948

1017   A SOUND OF HUNTING
by Harry Brown; directed by Nina Vance

1958-1959

1018   THE MADWOMAN OF CHAILLOT
by Jean Giraudoux; directed by Nina Vance

1959-1960

1019   THE CAINE MUTINY COURT-MARTIAL
by Herman Wouk; directed by John Wylie

1020   THE CAVE DWELLERS
by William Saroyan; directed by Eugenie Leontovich

1021   HOLIDAY FOR LOVERS
by Ronald Alexander; directed by John Wylie

1022   THE ICEMAN COMETH
by Eugene O'Neill; directed by Nina Vance

1023   A MOON FOR THE MISBEGOTTEN
by Eugene O'Neill; directed by Nina Vance

1024   NUDE WITH VIOLIN
by Noel Coward; directed by John Wylie

1025   ONCE MORE WITH FEELING
        by Harry Kurnitz; directed by William Ball

1026   ORPHEUS DESCENDING
        by Tennessee Williams; directed by Nina Vance

1027   RASHOMON
        (based on stories by Ryunosuke Akutagawa) by Fay and Michael
        Kanin; directed by Nina Vance

1028   SUNRISE AT CAMPOBELLO
        by Dore Schary; directed by John Wylie

1029   WAITING FOR GODOT
        by Samuel Beckett; directed by Alan Schneider

1030   THE WALTZ OF THE TOREADORS
        by Jean Anouilh; directed by Nina Vance

1031   WHO WAS THAT LADY I SAW YOU WITH?
        by Norman Krasna; directed by John Wylie

                              1960-1961

1032   BOUND EAST FOR CARDIFF
        by Eugene O'Neill; directed by Nina Vance and John Wylie.
        Performed the same evening as *The End of the Beginning*, *In the
        Zone*, and *The Proposal*, under the title of *Friends and Lovers
        (Four Plays in Three Acts)*

1033   THE END OF THE BEGINNING
        by Sean O'Casey; directed by Nina Vance and John Wylie. Per-
        formed the same evening as *Bound East for Cardiff*, *In the Zone*,
        and *The Proposal*, under the title of *Friends and Lovers (Four
        Plays in Three Acts)*

1034   AN ENEMY OF THE PEOPLE
        by Henrik Ibsen; directed by Nina Vance

1035   IN THE ZONE
        by Eugene O'Neill; directed by Nina Vance and John Wylie.
        Performed the same evening as *Bound East for Cardiff*, *The End
        of the Beginning*, and *The Proposal*, under the title of *Friends
        and Lovers (Four Plays in Three Acts)*

1036   JANE
        (based on the story by W. Somerset Maugham) by S.N. Behrman;
        directed by Nina Vance

1037   THE LIBRARY RAID
        by Frank Gagliano; directed by Nina Vance

1038   THE LITTLE FOXES
        by Lillian Hellman; directed by John Wylie

1039   MAKE A MILLION
        by Norman Barasch and Carroll Moore; directed by John Wylie

1040 ONDINE
   by Jean Giraudoux, adapted by Maurice Valency; directed by
   Nina Vance

1041 THE PROPOSAL
   by Anton Chekhov; directed by Nina Vance and John Wylie. Performed the same evening as *Bound East for Cardiff*, *The End of
   the Beginning*, and *In the Zone*, under the title of *Friends and
   Lovers (Four Plays in Three Acts)*

1042 SIX CHARACTERS IN SEARCH OF AN AUTHOR
   by Luigi Pirandello, adapted by Paul Avila Mayer; directed by
   Nina Vance

1961-1962

1043 COME BACK, LITTLE SHEBA
   by William Inge; directed by John Wylie

1044 GARDEN SPOT, U.S.A.
   by George Garrett; directed by Nina Vance

1045 HAMLET
   by William Shakespeare; directed by John Wylie

1046 JOHN BROWN'S BODY
   by Stephen Vincent Benet; directed by Angela Wood

1047 THE MIRACLE WORKER
   by William Gibson; directed by Nina Vance

1048 MISALLIANCE
   by George Bernard Shaw; directed by Nina Vance

1049 PERIOD OF ADJUSTMENT
   by Tennessee Williams; directed by John Wylie

1050 VOLPONE
   by Ben Jonson; directed by Nina Vance

1962-1963

1051 AMPHITRYON 38
   (based on the comedy by Jean Giraudoux) by S.N. Behrman;
   directed by John Wylie

1052 BECKET (OR THE HONOR OF GOD)
   by Jean Anouilh, translated by Lucienne Hill; directed by Nina
   Vance

1053 THE HOSTAGE
   by Brendan Behan; directed by John Wylie

1054 AN INSPECTOR CALLS
   by J.B. Priestly; directed by Joyce Randall

1055   LIFE WITH FATHER
        (based on the book by Clarence Day, Jr.) by Howard Lindsay and
        Russel Crouse; directed by Joyce Randall

1056   LONG DAY'S JOURNEY INTO NIGHT
        by Eugene O'Neill; directed by Nina Vance

1057   THE PONDER HEART
        (adapted from the book by Eudora Welty) by Joseph Fields and
        Jerome Chodorov; directed by Joyce Randall

1058   THE TAMING OF THE SHREW
        by William Shakespeare; directed by John Wylie

1059   TOYS IN THE ATTIC
        by Lillian Hellman; directed by John Wylie

                            1963-1964

1060   BERNARDINE
        by Mary Chase; directed by Joyce Randall

1061   THE BEST MAN
        by Gore Vidal; directed by John Wylie

1062   HARVEY
        by Mary Chase; directed by Joyce Randall

1063   OH DAD, POOR DAD, MAMMA'S HUNG YOU IN THE CLOSET AND I'M
        FEELIN' SO SAD
        by Arthur Kopit; directed by John Wylie

1064   THE QUEEN AND THE REBELS
        by Ugo Betti; directed by Nina Vance

1065   THE THREE SISTERS
        by Anton Chekhov; directed by Nina Vance

                            1964-1965

1066   THE EFFECT OF GAMMA RAYS ON MAN-IN-THE-MOON MARIGOLDS
        by Paul Zindel; directed by Nina Vance

1067   THE KNACK
        by Ann Jellicoe; directed by John Wylie

1068   A SOUND OF HUNTING
        by Harry Brown; directed by John Wylie

1069   THE TENTH MAN
        by Paddy Chayefsky; directed by Nina Vance

1070   THE TROJAN WOMEN
        by Euripides, adapted by Nina Vance and Samuel Rosen; directed
        by Nina Vance

1965-1966

1071   AH, WILDERNESS!
        by Eugene O'Neill; directed by Joseph Ruskin

1072   THE DEVIL'S DISCIPLE
        by George Bernard Shaw; directed by John Wylie

1073   DUEL OF ANGELS
        by Jean Giraudoux, translated by Christopher Fry, adapted by
        Nina Vance and John Wylie; directed by Nina Vance and John
        Wylie

1074   RIGHT YOU ARE (IF YOU THINK YOU ARE)
        by Luigi Pirandello, translated by Eric Bentley; directed by
        Nina Vance

1075   YOU CAN'T TAKE IT WITH YOU
        by Moss Hart and George S. Kaufman; directed by William Hardy

1966-1967

1076   THE CARETAKER
        by Harold Pinter; directed by Nina Vance

1077   THE DIARY OF A SCOUNDREL
        by Alexander Ostrovsky, adapted by Rodney Ackland; directed by
        Joseph Ruskin

1078   THE GREAT SEBASTIANS
        by Howard Lindsay and Russel Crouse; directed by William Hardy

1079   THE PHYSICISTS
        by Friedrich Duerrenmatt, translated by James Kirkup; directed
        by Louis Criss

1080   THE SEA GULL
        by Anton Chekhov; directed by Nina Vance

1081   THE WORLD OF SHOLEM ALEICHEM
        by Arnold Perl; directed by John Wylie

1968-1969

1082   ALL THE WAY HOME
        (based on *A Death in the Family* by James Agee) by Tad Mosel;
        directed by William Hardy

1083   BILLY LIAR
        by Keith Waterhouse and Willis Hall; directed by Beth Sanford

1084   CHARLIE
        by Slawomir Mrozek, translated by Nicholas Bethell; directed
        by Louis Criss. Performed the same evening as *Out at Sea*

1085   GALILEO
            by Bertolt Brecht, translated by Charles Laughton; directed by
            Nina Vance

1086   LIGHT UP THE SKY
            by Moss Hart; directed by Sherman Marks

1087   OUT AT SEA
            by Slawomir Mrozek, translated by Nicholas Bethell; directed
            by Louis Criss. Performed the same evening as *Charlie*

1088   SAINT JOAN
            by George Bernard Shaw; directed by Michael Meacham

1089   WAR AND PEACE
            (adapted from the novel by Leo Tolstoy) adapted by Alfred
            Neumann, Erwin Piscator, and Guntram Prufer, English version
            by Robert David MacDonald; directed by Robert David MacDonald

                            1969-1970

1090   THE ANDERSONVILLE TRIAL
            by Saul Levitt; directed by Pat Brown. Program contains
            interesting historical notes

1091   BLITHE SPIRIT
            by Noel Coward; directed by Milton Selzer

1092   CHARLEY'S AUNT
            by Brandon Thomas; directed by William Hardy

1093   DEAR LIAR
            (based on correspondence of George Bernard Shaw and Mrs.
            Patricia Campbell) by Jerome Kilty; directed by Jerome Kilty

1094   EVERYTHING IN THE GARDEN
            (based on a play by Giles Cooper) by Edward Albee; directed by
            Beth Sanford

1095   THE ROSE TATTOO
            by Tennessee Williams; directed by Philip Minor

1096   TARTUFFE
            by Moliere; directed by Kirk Denmark

1097   THE WORLD OF CARL SANDBURG
            by Norman Corwin; directed by R. Edward Leonard

                            1970-1971

1098   DIAL "M" FOR MURDER
            by Frederidk Knott; directed by Burry Fredrik

1099   MOURNING BECOMES ELECTRA
            by Eugene O'Neill; directed by Nina Vance and Beth Sanford

1100   THE NIGHT THOREAU SPENT IN JAIL
        by Jerome Lawrence and Robert E. Lee; directed by Beth Sanford

1101   OUR TOWN
        by Thornton Wilder; directed by R. Edward Leonard

1102   THE PRIME OF MISS JEAN BRODIE
        (adapted from the novel by Muriel Spark) by Jay Presson Allen;
        directed by R. Edward Leonard

1103   RING AROUND THE BATHTUB
        by Jane Trahey; directed by William Hardy

                          1971-1972*

1104   CAMINO REAL
        by Tennessee Williams; directed by Nina Vance

1105   CHILD'S PLAY
        by Robert Marasco; directed by Beth Sanford

1106   A FLEA IN HER EAR
        by Georges Feydeau; directed by R. Edward Leonard

1107   HADRIAN VII
        by Peter Luke; directed by William Trotman

1108   SPOON RIVER ANTHOLOGY
        by Edgar Lee Masters, conceived, adapted, and arranged by
        Charles Aidman; directed by William Trotman

1109   THE TAMING OF THE SHREW
        by William Shakespeare; directed by R. Edward Leonard

1110   WHAT THE BUTLER SAW
        by Joe Orton; directed by Beth Sanford

                          1972-1973

1111   ALL OVER
        by Edward Albee; directed by Nina Vance

1112   COLETTE
        (based on *Earthly Paradise*, the collection of Colette's auto-
        biographical writings by Robert Phelps) by Elinor Jones, lyrics
        by Tom Jones, music by Harvey Schmidt; directed by Nina Vance

1113   HAPPY BIRTHDAY, WANDA JUNE
        by Kurt Vonnegut, Jr.; directed by R. Edward Leonard

1114   THE HOSTAGE
        by Brendan Behan; directed by R. Edward Leonard

---

* Silver Anniversary Season

1115   JACQUES BREL IS ALIVE AND WELL AND LIVING IN PARIS
        (based on Brel's lyrics and commentary) production conception,
        English lyrics, and additional material by Eric Blau and Mort
        Shuman; directed by Beth Sanford

1116   LIFE WITH FATHER
        (based on the book by Clarence Day, Jr.) by Howard Lindsay and
        Russel Crouse; directed by Jack Westin

1117   PANTAGLEIZE
        by Michel de Ghelderode; directed by Nina Vance

1118   THE SCHOOL FOR WIVES
        by Moliere; directed by R. Edward Leonard

                            1973-1974

1119   AH, WILDERNESS!
        by Eugene O'Neill; directed by Beth Sanford

1120   COMEDY OF MARRIAGE
        by Friedrich Duerrenmatt; directed by Robert Symonds

1121   COUNT DRACULA
        (based on the novel by Bram Stoker) by Ted Tiller; directed
        by William Trotman. Program contains information and legends
        about Dracula

1122   THE DECLINE AND FALL OF THE ENTIRE WORLD AS SEEN THROUGH THE
        EYES OF COLE PORTER
        by Ben Bagley, words and music by Cole Porter; directed by
        Beth Sanford

1123   ENCORE!
        by Denise LeBrun, arranged by Paul Dupree; directed by Nina
        Vance. An evening of music

1124   INHERIT THE WIND
        by Jerome Lawrence and Robert E. Lee; directed by R. Edward
        Leonard

1125   A MIDSUMMER NIGHT'S DREAM
        by William Shakespeare; directed by R. Edward Leonard

1126   THE PURIFICATION
        by Tennessee Williams; directed by Nina Vance

                            1974-1975

1127   THE CONTEST
        by Shirley Mezvinsky Lauro; directed by Nina Vance

1128   THE MAN WHO CAME TO DINNER
        by Moss Hart and George S. Kaufman; directed by R. Edward
        Leonard

1129   A STREETCAR NAMED DESIRE
             by Tennessee Williams; directed by Beth Sanford

1130   TOBACCO ROAD
             (adapted from the novel by Erskine Caldwell) by Jack Kirkland;
             directed by William Trotman

1131   TWELFTH NIGHT
             by William Shakespeare; directed by R. Edward Leonard

1132   WIN WITH WILSON
             by George Greanias; directed by Nina Vance

Huntington, NY

PAF PLAYHOUSE

1972-1973

1133   BAREFOOT IN THE PARK
             by Neil Simon; directed by Clint Marantz

1134   THE GLASS MENAGERIE
             by Tennessee Williams; directed by Richard Jamieson

1135   HEDDA GABLER
             by Henrik Ibsen, translated by Arvid Paulson; directed by
             Richard Jamieson

1136   LITTLE MURDERS
             by Jules Feiffer; directed by Richard Jamieson

1137   PRIVATE LIVES
             by Noel Coward; directed by Richard Jamieson

1138   THE SHOW-OFF
             by George Kelly; directed by Thomas B. Markus

1139   TARTUFFE
             by Moliere, translated by Richard Wilbur; directed by Richard
             Jamieson

1140   WAITING FOR GODOT
             by Samuel Beckett; directed by Richard Jamieson

1973-1974

1141   CANDIDA
             by George Bernard Shaw; directed by Richard Jamieson

1142   OF MICE AND MEN
             by John Steinbeck; directed by Steven Robman

1974-1975

1143   BORN YESTERDAY
          by Garson Kanin; directed by Richard Jamieson

1144   THE CARETAKER
          by Harold Pinter; directed by Joseph Brockett

1145   THE INNOCENTS
          (based on *Turn of the Screw* by Henry James) by William
          Archibald; directed by Joseph Brockett

Indianapolis, IN

INDIANA REPERTORY THEATRE

1972-1973

1146   CHARLEY'S AUNT
          by Brandon Thomas; directed by Edward J. Stern

1147   COUNT DRACULA
          (adapted from the novel by Bram Stoker) by Ted Tiller; directed
          by Benjamin Mordecai

1148   FABLES HERE AND THEN
          by David Feldshuh; directed by Edward J. Stern and Benjamin
          Mordecai

1149   THE GLASS MENAGERIE
          by Tennessee Williams; directed by Edward J. Stern

1150   THE HOUSE OF BLUE LEAVES
          by John Guare; directed by Benjamin Mordecai

1151   THE SCAMP
          by Moliere; directed by Pierre LeFeure

1973-1974

1152   JACQUES BREL IS ALIVE AND WELL AND LIVING IN PARIS
          (based on Brel's lyrics and commentary) production conception,
          English lyrics, and additional material by Eric Blau and Mort
          Shuman; directed by Benjamin Mordecai

1153   OF MICE AND MEN
          by John Steinbeck; directed by Edward J. Stern

1154   OUR TOWN
          by Thornton Wilder; directed by Benjamin Mordecai

1155   THE SERVANT OF TWO MASTERS
          by Carlo Goldoni, translated by Paul Weidner; directed by
          John Going

1156   SHERLOCK HOLMES
        (based on the novels by Sir Arthur Conan Doyle) by William
        Gillette; directed by Edward J. Stern

1157   WHAT THE BUTLER SAW
        by Joe Orton; directed by Edward J. Stern

1974-1975

1158   A BIRD IN THE HAND
        by Georges Feydeau, translated and adapted by Edward and Anne
        Ward Stern; directed by Benjamin Mordecai

1159   THE CARETAKER
        by Harold Pinter; directed by Edward J. Stern

1160   HARVEY
        by Mary Chase; directed by Edward J. Stern

1161   THE LITTLE FOXES
        by Lillian Hellman; directed by John Going

1162   ONE FLEW OVER THE CUCKOO'S NEST
        (based on the novel by Ken Kesey) by Dale Wasserman; directed
        by Edward J. Stern

1163   THE RAINMAKER
        by N. Richard Nash; directed by Edward J. Stern

1164   THE TAMING OF THE SHREW
        by William Shakespeare; directed by Garland Wright

Lakewood, OH

GREAT LAKES SHAKESPEARE FESTIVAL

1965

1165   CORIOLANUS
        by William Shakespeare; directed by Arthur Lithgow

1166   MACBETH
        by William Shakespeare; directed by Arthur Lithgow

1167   THE MARRIAGE PROPOSAL
        by Anton Chekhov; directed by Arthur Lithgow. Performed the
        same evening as *The School for Wives*

1168   A MIDSUMMER NIGHT'S DREAM
        by William Shakespeare; directed by David Hooks

1169   THE RIVALS
        by Richard Brinsley Sheridan; directed by Mario Siletti

1170   THE SCHOOL FOR WIVES
         by Moliere, translated by Morris Bishop; directed by Larry
         Linville. Performed the same evening as *The Marriage Proposal*

                                   1973

1171   AN ITALIAN STRAW HAT
         by Eugene Labiche

1172   A MIDSUMMER NIGHT'S DREAM
         by William Shakespeare

1173   MUCH ADO ABOUT NOTHING
         by William Shakespeare

1174   TARTUFFE
         by Moliere; directed by John Beary

1175   TWELFTH NIGHT
         by William Shakespeare; directed by Lawrence Carra

                                   1974

1176   THE COMEDY OF ERRORS
         by William Shakespeare, lyrics by Mary Fournier Bill, music by
         Frederick Koch; directed by Lawrence Carra

1177   KING LEAR
         by William Shakespeare; directed by Lawrence Carra

1178   THE PLAYBOY OF THE WESTERN WORLD
         by J.M. Synge; directed by Lawrence Carra

1179   UNDER THE GASLIGHT
         by Augustin Daly; directed by Lawrence Carra

                                   1975

1180   THE MISER
         by Moliere; directed by Jean Gascon

Los Angeles, CA

CENTER THEATRE GROUP

                                1959-1960

1181   MOTHER COURAGE
         by Bertolt Brecht, English version by Eric Bentley; directed
         by Alan Cooke

1182   MURDER IN THE CATHEDRAL
         by T.S. Eliot; directed by John Houseman

1183   SODOM AND GOMORRAH
by Nikos Kazantzakis, translated by Kimon Friar; directed by
James S. Elliot

1184   UNDER MILK WOOD
by Dylan Thomas; directed by Lamont Johnson

1960-1961

1185   ACT WITHOUT WORDS
by Samuel Beckett; directed by Lamont Johnson. Performed the
same evening as *The Lesson*, *The Sandbox*, and *This Property is
Condemned*, under the title of *Four Comedies of Despair*

1186   I KNOCK AT THE DOOR
by Sean O'Casey, adapted by Paul Shyre; directed by Paul Shyre

1187   THE LESSON
by Eugene Ionesco; directed by Lamont Johnson. Performed the
same evening as *Act Without Words*, *The Sandbox*, and *This
Property is Condemned*, under the title of *Four Comedies of
Despair*

1188   PICTURES IN THE HALLWAY
by Sean O'Casey, adapted by Paul Shyre; directed by Paul Shyre

1189   THE PRODIGAL
by Jack Richardson; directed by Theodore Marcuse

1190   THE SANDBOX
by Edward Albee; directed by Lamont Johnson. Performed the same
evening as *Act Without Words*, *The Lesson*, and *This Property is
Condemned*, under the title of *Four Comedies of Despair*

1191   SIX CHARACTERS IN SEARCH OF AN AUTHOR
by Luigi Pirandello, adapted by Paul Avila Mayer; directed by
John Houseman

1192   THIS PROPERTY IS CONDEMNED
by Tennessee Williams; directed by Lamont Johnson. Performed
the same evening as *Act Without Words*, *The Lesson*, and *The
Sandbox*, under the title of *Four Comedies of Despair*

1193   THE THREE SISTERS
by Anton Chekhov, translated by Stark Young; directed by John
Houseman

1194   U.S.A.
(based on the novel by John Dos Passos) by Paul Shyre and John
Dos Passos; directed by Paul Shyre

1961-1962

1195   BETWEEN TWO THIEVES
(adapted from the play by Diego Fabbri) by Warner LeRoy;
directed by Joseph Sargent

1196   THE CHILD BUYER
            by John Hersey, adapted by Paul Shyre; directed by Paul Shyre

1197   CREDITORS
            by August Strindberg, adapted by Paul Shyre; directed by Paul
            Shyre

1198   THE EGG
            by Felicien Marceau, translated by Robert Schlitt; directed by
            Lamont Johnson

1199   THE ICEMAN COMETH
            by Eugene O'Neill; directed by John Houseman and Ralph Senesky

1200   MEASURE FOR MEASURE
            by William Shakespeare; directed by John Houseman

                                1962-1963

1201   ANTIGONE
            by Jean Anouilh; directed by John Houseman

1202   BURLESQUE
            by George Manker Watter and Arthur Hopkins; directed by Jack
            Albertson and John Houseman; musical director, Robin Frost

1203   THE CHINESE WALL
            by Max Frisch, translated by James L. Rosenberg; directed by
            Norman Corwin

1204   HEARTBREAK HOUSE
            by George Bernard Shaw; directed by Terence Kilburn

1205   PERIBANEZ
            by Lope De Vega, translated by Jill Booty; directed by Lamont
            Johnson. Performed the same evening as *'Tis Pity She's a Whore*,
            under the title of *A Summer of Repertory*

1206   ROCKET TO THE MOON
            by Clifford Odets; directed by Daniel Mann

1207   SPOON RIVER ANTHOLOGY
            by Edgar Lee Masters, conceived, adapted, and arranged by
            Charles Aidman; directed by Charles Aidman

1208   'TIS PITY SHE'S A WHORE
            by John Ford; directed by Lamont Johnson. Performed the same
            evening as *Peribanez*, under the title of *A Summer of Repertory*

                                1963-1964

1209   BRECHT ON BRECHT
            adapted by George Tabori; directed by William Allyn

1210   P.S. 193
            by David Rayfiel; directed by Sydney Pollack

1211   THE SEA GULL
         by Anton Chekhov, translated by Stark Young; directed by John
         Houseman

                              1964-1965

1212   THE BALD SOPRANO
         by Eugene Ionesco; directed by Joseph Sargent. Performed the
         same evening as *The Chairs*

1213   THE CHAIRS
         by Eugene Ionesco; directed by Joseph Sargent. Performed the
         same evening as *The Bald Soprano*

1214   KING LEAR
         by William Shakespeare; directed by John Houseman

1215   LADIES OF HANOVER TOWER
         by Carroll O'Connor; directed by Carroll O'Connor and Robert
         Brown

1216   NAKED
         by Luigi Pirandello, adapted by William Murray; directed by
         E.W. Swackhamer

1217   ROSMERSHOLM
         by Henrik Ibsen, translated by Michael Meyers; directed by
         Terence Kilburn

CENTER THEATRE GROUP/MARK TAPER FORUM

                              1965-1966

1218   THE DEPUTY
         by Rolf Hochhuth, adapted by Jerome Rothenberg; directed by
         Gordon Davidson

1219   I RISE IN FLAME, CRIED THE PHOENIX
         by Tennessee Williams; directed by Alfred Ryder. Performed the
         same evening as *The Lover* and *Windows*

1220   THE LOVER
         by Harold Pinter; directed by Alfred Ryder. Performed the same
         evening as *I Rise in Flame, Cried the Phoenix* and *Windows*

1221   OH! WHAT A LOVELY WAR
         by J. Littlewood and C. Chilton; directed by Edward Parone

1222   PURGATORY
         by W.B. Yeats, adapted by Paul Shyre; directed by Paul Shyre.
         Performed the same evening as *The Words Upon the Window Pane*,
         under the title of *Yeats and Company*; the prose, poetry, and
         plays of W.B. Yeats

1223   ROBERT FROST - PROMISES TO KEEP
         by Philip Abbott; directed by Philip Abbott and John McLiam

1224   WINDOWS
        by Murray Schisgal; directed by Alfred Ryder. Premiere; per-
        formed the same evening as *I Rise in Flame, Cried the Phoenix*
        and *The Lover*

1225   THE WORDS UPON THE WINDOW PANE
        by W.B. Yeats, adapted by Paul Shyre; directed by Paul Shyre.
        Performed the same evening as *Yeats and Company*; the prose,
        poetry, and plays of W.B. Yeats

                                1966

1226   THE BIRTHDAY PARTY
        by Harold Pinter; directed by Mel Shapiro

1227   CANDIDE
        (a comic operetta based on the satirical classic by Voltaire)
        book by Lillian Hellman, music by Leonard Bernstein, lyrics by
        Richard Wilbur, additional lyrics by John LaTouche, Dorothy
        Parker, Lillian Hellman, and Leonard Bernstein; directed by
        Gordon Davidson

1228   NEXT TIME I'LL SING TO YOU
        by James Saunders; directed by Malcolm Black

1229   POOR BITOS
        by Jean Anouilh, translated by Lucienne Hill; directed by
        Malcolm Black

                                1967

1230   THE DEVILS
        (based on the novel by Aldous Huxley) by John Whiting; directed
        by Gordon Davidson

1231   THE MARRIAGE OF MR. MISSISSIPPI
        by Friedrich Duerrenmatt, translated by Michael Bullock;
        directed by Malcolm Black

1232   MORE STATELY MANSIONS
        by Eugene O'Neill; directed by Jose Quintero. American premiere;
        performed at the Ahmanson Theatre

1233   THE SORROWS OF FREDERICK
        by Romulus Linney; directed by Elliot Martin

1234   WHO'S HAPPY NOW?
        by Oliver Hailey; directed by Gordon Davidson. World premiere

                                1968

1235   CAMINO REAL
        by Tennessee Williams; directed by Milton Katselas

1236   THE GOLDEN FLEECE
        by A.R. Gurney, Jr.; directed by Jered Barclay. Performed the
        same evening as *Muzeeka*

1237   IN THE MATTER OF J. ROBERT OPPENHEIMER
        (a play freely adapted on the basis of documents by Heinar
        Kipphardt) by Heinar Kipphardt, translated by Ruth Speirs;
        directed by Gordon Davidson

1238   THE MISER
        by Moliere, translated by George Gravely; directed by Douglas
        Campbell

1239   MUZEEKA
        by John Guare; directed by Edward Parone. Performed the same
        evening as *The Golden Fleece*

                                1969

1240   THE ADVENTURES OF THE BLACK GIRL IN HER SEARCH FOR GOD
        by George Bernard Shaw, adapted for stage by Christopher
        Isherwood; directed by Lamont Johnson

1241   CHEMIN DE FER
        by Georges Feydeau, translated and adapted by Suzanne Grossmann
        and Paxton Whitehead; directed by Stephen Porter

1242   HADRIAN VII
        by Peter Luke; directed by Jean Gascon. Performed by the
        Stratford National Company of Canada at the Ahmanson Theatre

1243   THE HOUSE OF ATREUS
        by Aeschylus, adapted by John Lewin; directed by Tyrone Guthrie.
        performed by the Minnesota Theatre Co.

1244   THE RESISTIBLE RISE OF ARTURO UI
        by Bertolt Brecht, translated by George Tabori; directed by
        Edward Payson Call. Performed by the Minnesota Theatre Co.

1245   UNCLE VANYA
        by Anton Chekhov, translated by Alex Szogyi; directed by Harold
        Clurman

                                1970

1246   THE BEAUX' STRATAGEM
        by George Farquhar; directed by William Gaskill. Performed by
        the National Theatre Company of Great Britain

1247   BLACK JUDAS
        by Robert Valine; directed by Alfred Rossi. Performed the same
        evening as *Cafeteria Style Lunch* and *Momsie and the Midnight
        Bride*

1248   CAFETERIA STYLE LUNCH
        by David Trainer; directed by Wallace Chappell. Performed the
        same evening as *Black Judas* and *Momsie and the Midnight Bride*

1249   CRYSTAL & FOX
        by Brian Friel; directed by Hilton Edwards

1250   DESIGN FOR LIVING
         by Noel Coward; directed by Peter Wood

1251   THE DREAM ON MONKEY MOUNTAIN
         by Derek Walcott; directed by Michael A. Schultz

1252   L.A. UNDER SIEGE
         by Mayo Simon; directed by Edward Parone

1253   MOMSIE AND THE MIDNIGHT BRIDE
         by Alan Ormsby; directed by Wallace Chappell. Performed the
         same evening as *Black Judas* and *Cafeteria Style Lunch*

1254   MURDEROUS ANGELS
         by Conor Cruise O'Brien; directed by Gordon Davidson

1255   ROSEBLOOM
         by Harvey Perr; directed by Gordon Davidson

1256.   STORY THEATRE
         devised by Paul Sills; directed by Paul Sills

1257   THE TRIAL OF THE CATONSVILLE NINE
         by Daniel Berrigan, S.J.; directed by Gordon Davidson

1258   THE THREE SISTERS
         by Anton Chekhov; directed by Laurence Olivier. Performed by
         the National Theatre Company of Great Britain

1259   A WORK-IN-PROGRESS
         by Oliver Hailey; directed by Michael Montel

                              1971

1260   AUBREY BEARDSLEY, THE NEOPHYTE
         by Jon Renn McDonald; directed by Michael Montel. New Theatre
         for Now production

1261   GODSPELL
         (a musical based upon the Gospel according to *St. Matthew*)
         conceived by John-Michael Tebelak, music and lyrics by Stephen
         Schwartz; directed by John-Michael Tebelak

1262   JADE FLOWER PALACE
         translated by Kenneth Rexroth; directed by Lou Harrison. An
         evening of Chinese music and verse; new Theatre for Now pro-
         duction

1263   MAJOR BARBARA
         by George Bernard Shaw; directed by Edward Parone

1264   THE METAMORPHASES
         by Ovid, translated, adapted with lyrics by Arnold Weinstein,
         music by Country Joe McDonald; directed by Paul Sills

1265   OTHELLO
         by William Shakespeare; directed by John Berry

1266   TEN COM. ZIP COM. ZIP
        by Matthew Silverman; directed by Edward Parone. New Theatre
        for Now production

1267   THE TRIAL OF THE CATONSVILLE NINE
        by Daniel Berrigan, S.J.; directed by Gordon Davidson

1268   WHO WANTS TO BE THE LONE RANGER
        by Lee Kalcheim; directed by Edward Parone

                            1972

1269   HENRY IV
        by William Shakespeare; directed by Gordon Davidson

1270   HERE ARE LADIES
        (based on the works of Irish writers) directed by Sean O'Riada.
        Performed the same evening as *The Works of Beckett*

1271   OLD TIMES
        by Harold Pinter; directed by Jeff Bleckner

1272   VOLPONE
        (an uninhibited adaptation of the Ben Jonson comedy) by Ben
        Jonson, music and lyrics by Jack Rowe, Timothy Near, Holly
        Near, and Cordis Langley; directed by Edward Parone

1273   THE WORKS OF BECKETT
        adapted by Jack MacGowran. Performed the same evening as *Here
        Are Ladies*

                            1973

1274   FORGET-ME-NOT LANE
        by Peter Nichols; directed by Arvin Brown

1275   THE HOT L BALTIMORE
        by Lanford Wilson; directed by Marshall W. Mason

1276   THE MAHAGONNY SONGPLAY
        by Bertolt Brecht, translated by Michael Feingold, music by
        Kurt Weill; directed by Edward Payson Call. Performed the same
        evening as *The Measures Taken*, under the title of *Brecht Sacred
        and Profane*

1277   MASS
        by Leonard Bernstein, texts from the liturgy of the Roman Mass,
        additional texts by Stephen Schwartz and Leonard Bernstein;
        directed by Gordon Davidson. A theatre piece for singers,
        players, and dancers

1278   THE MEASURES TAKEN
        by Bertolt Brecht, translated by Eric Bentley, music by Hans
        Eisler; directed by Edward Payson Call. Performed the same
        evening as *The Mahagonny Songplay*, under the title of *Brecht
        Sacred and Profane*

1279   THE MIND WITH THE DIRTY MAN
          by Jules Tasca; directed by Edward Parone

                              1974-1975

1280   THE CHARLATAN
          by Derek Walcott, music by Galt MacDermot; directed by Mel
          Shapiro

1281   THE DYBBUK
          by S. Ansky, adapted by John Hirsch; directed by John Hirsch.
          Superb program notes on the play

1282   HAMLET
          by William Shakespeare; directed by Gordon Davidson. Excellent
          program notes

1283   JUNO AND THE PAYCOCK
          by Sean O'Casey; directed by George Seaton

1284   ME AND BESSIE
          by Will Holt and Linda Hopkins; directed by Robert Greenwald

1285   SAVAGES
          by Christopher Hampton; directed by Gordon Davidson; Excellent
          program notes on the play

          MARK TAPER FORUM
          (*see CENTER THEATRE GROUP/MARK TAPER FORUM*)

Los Gatos, CA

CALIFORNIA ACTORS THEATRE

                              1974-1975

1286   DARLIN' BOY
          by Tom McCorry; directed by Peter Nyberg

1287   DETECTIVE STORY
          by Sidney Kingsley; directed by Peter Nyberg

1288   THE HAPPY HUNTER
          by Georges Feydeau, English adaptation by Barnett Shaw; directed
          by John Reich

1289   LADY AUDLEY'S SECRET
          (adapted from the novel by Mary Elizabeth Braddon) by Douglas
          Seale; directed by Milton Lyon

1290   OLD TIMES
          by Harold Pinter; directed by Peter Nyberg

1291   ROSES DON'T GROW HERE NO MORE
          by Tom McCorry; directed by Peter Nyberg

1292   THE SERVANT OF TWO MASTERS
          by Carlo Goldoni, adapted by Stuart and Anne Vaughan; directed
          by James Dunn. World premiere of a new adaptation

1975-1976

1293   ENRICO IV
          by Luigi Pirandello, translated by John Reich; directed by
          John Reich

Louisville, KY

ACTORS THEATRE OF LOUISVILLE

1964-1965

1294   AMPHITRYON
          by Titus Maccus Plautus, adapted by Richard Block; directed by
          Richard Block

1295   ARMS AND THE MAN
          by George Bernard Shaw; directed by Richard Block

1296   THE CARETAKER
          by Harold Pinter; directed by Richard Block

1297   THE GLASS MENAGERIE
          by Tennessee Williams; directed by Ewel Cornett

1298   JOHN BROWN'S BODY
          by Stephen Vincent Benet; directed by Ewel Cornett

1299   RASHOMON
          (based on stories by Ryunosuke Akutagawa) by Fay and Michael
          Kanin; directed by Ewel Cornett

1965-1966

1300   DEATH OF A SALESMAN
          by Arthur Miller; directed by Tom Gruenewald

1301   A DOLL'S HOUSE
          by Henrik Ibsen; directed by Richard Block

1302   THE IMPORTANCE OF BEING EARNEST
          by Oscar Wilde; directed by James Dyas

1303   NO EXIT
          by Jean Paul Sartre; directed by Kenneth Costigan. Performed
          the same evening as *The Public Eye*

1304   PRIVATE LIVES
            by Noel Coward; directed by James Dyas

1305   THE PUBLIC EYE
            by Peter Shaffer; directed by Kenneth Costigan. Performed the
            same evening as *No Exit*

1306   THE SCHOOL FOR WIVES
            by Moliere; directed by Richard Block

1307   THE TAVERN
            by George M. Cohan; directed by Richard Block

1308   WAITING FOR GODOT
            by Samuel Beckett; directed by Richard Block

                              1966-1967

1309   ALL MY SONS
            by Arthur Miller; directed by Richard Block

1310   CHARLEY'S AUNT
            by Brandon Thomas; directed by Jock Ferguson

1311   IN WHITE AMERICA
            by Martin Duberman; directed by Jordan Hott

1312   THE KNACK
            by Ann Jellicoe; directed by Richard Block

1313   MISS JULIE
            by August Strindberg; directed by Richard Block

1314   NATHAN WEINSTEIN'S DAUGHTER
            by David Rafiel; directed by Gennaro Montanino

1315   SLOW DANCE ON THE KILLING GROUND
            by William Hanley; directed by Richard Block

1316   A STREETCAR NAMED DESIRE
            by Tennessee Williams; directed by Philip Minor

                              1967-1968

1317   ALL THE KING'S MEN
            by Robert Penn Warren; directed by Richard Block

1318   ENDGAME
            by Samuel Beckett; directed by Richard Block

1319   THE FIREBUGS
            by Max Frisch, translated by Mordecai Gorelik; directed by
            Richard Block

1320   THE HOSTAGE
            by Brendan Behan; directed by Gerald Harte

1321   LONG DAY'S JOURNEY INTO NIGHT
     by Eugene O'Neill; directed by Gerald Harte

1322   MISALLIANCE
     by George Bernard Shaw; directed by Gordon Phillips

1323   A NIGHT OF THE DUNCE
     by Frank Gagliano; directed by William Woodman

1324   THIEVES' CARNIVAL
     by Jean Anouilh, translated by Lucienne Hill; directed by
     Richard Block

1968-1969

1325   AFTER THE FALL
     by Arthur Miller; directed by Richard Block

1326   THE BIRTHDAY PARTY
     by Harold Pinter; directed by Richard Block

1327   THE CRESTA RUN
     by N.F. Simpson; directed by Pirie MacDonald

1328   THE IMAGINARY INVALID
     by Moliere, adapted by Miles Malleson; directed by Richard Block

1329   THE MEMBER OF THE WEDDING
     by Carson McCullers; directed by Tom Gruenewald

1330   RHINOCEROS
     by Eugene Ionesco; directed by Jacques Cartier

1331   SUMMER AND SMOKE
     by Tennessee Williams; directed by Louis Criss

1332a   UNCLE VANYA
     by Anton Chekhov; directed by Richard Block

1969-1970

1332b   BEYOND THE FRINGE
     by Alan Bennett, Peter Cook, Jonathan Miller, and Dudley Moore;
     directed by Ken Jenkins

1333   CAT ON A HOT TIN ROOF
     by Tennessee Williams; directed by Victor Jory

1334   HAMLET
     by William Shakespeare; directed by Jon Jory

1335   THE KILLING OF SISTER GEORGE
     by Frank Marcus; directed by Christopher Murney

1336   SEE HOW THEY RUN
     by Philip King; directed by Jon Jory

1337   STAIRCASE
          by Charles Dyer; directed by Ken Jenkins

1338   THE STAR SPANGLED GIRL
          by Neil Simon; directed by Jon Jory

1339   A THOUSAND CLOWNS
          by Herb Gardner; directed by David Semonin

1340   TOBACCO ROAD
          (adapted from the novel by Erskine Caldwell) by Jack Kirkland;
          directed by Jon Jory

1341   UNDER MILK WOOD
          by Dylan Thomas; directed by Jon Jory

                              1970-1971

1342   DRACULA
          (adapted from the novel by Bram Stoker) by Hamilton Dean and
          John Balderson; directed by Christopher Murney

1343   JOE EGG
          by Peter Nichols; directed by Ken Jenkins

1344   MAJOR BARBARA
          by George Bernard Shaw; directed by Jon Jory

1345   OUR TOWN
          by Thornton Wilder; directed by Jon Jory

1346   THE TAMING OF THE SHREW
          by William Shakespeare; directed by Jon Jory

1347   THE TENTH MAN
          by Paddy Chayefsky; directed by Jon Jory

                              1971-1972

1348   ANGEL STREET
          by Patrick Hamilton; directed by Patrick Tovatt

1349   DEAR LIAR
          (based on the correspondence of George Bernard Shaw and Mrs.
          Patricia Campbell) by Jerome Kilty; directed by Christopher
          Murney

1350   HEDDA GABLER
          by Henrik Ibsen; directed by Jon Jory

1351   MARAT/SADE
          by Peter Weiss; directed by Jon Jory. Program contains
          historical background of play

1352   A MIDSUMMER NIGHT'S DREAM
          by William Shakespeare; directed by Jon Jory

1353   NIGHT MUST FALL
        by Emlyn Williams; directed by Christopher Murney

1354   TRICKS
        (a musical comedy based on *Scapin* by Moliere) book by Jon Jory,
        music by Jerry Blatt, lyrics by Lonnie Burstein; directed by
        Jon Jory

                        1972-1973

1355   ADAPTATION
        by Elaine May; directed by Charles Kerr. Off-Broadway series;
        performed the same evening as *Next*

1356   IN FASHION
        book by Jon Jory, music by Jerry Blatt, lyrics by Lonnie
        Burstein; directed by Jon Jory

1357   JUST BETWEEN US - AN EVENING WITH PEGGY COWLES
        adapted by Daniel Stein. Off-Broadway series

1358   KENTUCKY!
        by Daniel Stein; directed by Patrick Tovatt

1359   MACBETH
        by William Shakespeare; directed by Jon Jory

1360   A MAN FOR ALL SEASONS
        by Robert Bolt; directed by Jon Jory. Program contains
        historical background of play

1361   NEXT
        by Terrence McNally; directed by Charles Kerr. Off-Broadway
        series; performed the same evening as *Adaptation*

1362   THE PIRATES OF PENZANCE
        by W.S. Gilbert and Arthur Sullivan; directed by Frank Wicks;
        musical director, Alan Rafel

1363   WHAT THE BUTLER SAW
        by Joe Orton; directed by Jon Jory

1364   YOU CAN'T TAKE IT WITH YOU
        by Moss Hart and George S. Kaufman; directed by Victor Jory

                        1973-1974

1365   THE BOOR
        by Anton Chekhov; directed by Jon Jory. Off-Broadway series,
        Victor Jory Theatre; performed the same evening as *The Man of
        Destiny*, under the title of *Matching Wits*

1366   THE BOYS IN THE BAND
        by Mart Crowley; directed by Charles Kerr. Off-Broadway series,
        Victor Jory Theatre

1367   CHIPS 'N' ALE
         (adapted from *She Stoops to Conquer* by Oliver Goldsmith) by
         Jon Jory and Anne Croswell; directed by Jon Jory

1368   THE JOURNEY OF THE FIFTH HORSE
         by Ronald Ribman; directed by Jon Jory

1369   THE LAST OF THE RED HOT LOVERS
         by Neil Simon; directed by Vaughn McBride and Adale O'Brien.
         Off-Broadway series, Victor Jory Theatre

1370   LONG DAY'S JOURNEY INTO NIGHT
         by Eugene O'Neill; directed by Jon Jory

1371   THE MAN OF DESTINY
         by George Bernard Shaw; directed by Jon Jory. Off-Broadway
         series, Victor Jory Theatre; performed the same evening as
         The Boor, under the title of *Matching Wits*

1372   THE MIRACLE WORKER
         by William Gibson; directed by William Cain

1373   ONE FLEW OVER THE CUCKOO'S NEST
         (based on the book by Ken Kesey) by Dale Wasserman; directed
         by Jeffrey Tambor

1374   PLAY STRINDBERG
         by Friedrich Duerrenmatt; directed by Charles Kerr. Off-Broadway
         series, Victor Jory Theatre

1375   RENDEZVOUS
         by Georges Feydeau, new adaptation by Jon Jory; directed by
         Sue Lawless

1376   TARTUFFE
         by Moliere, translated by Richard Wilbur; directed by Jon Jory

                              1974-1975

1377   BALLAD OF THE SAD CAFE
         (based on the book by Carson McCullers) adapted by Edward
         Albee; directed by Jon Jory

1378   COUNTESS DRACULA
         by David Campton; directed by Charles Kerr. Performed the same
         evening as *Frankenstein*

1379   FEMALE TRANSPORT
         by Steve Gooch; directed by Jon Jory. Off-Broadway series

1380   A FLEA IN HER EAR
         by Georges Feydeau; directed by Jon Jory

1381   FRANKENSTEIN
         by David Campton; directed by Charles Kerr. Performed the same
         evening as *Countess Dracula*

1382   JACQUES BREL IS ALIVE AND WELL AND LIVING IN PARIS
(based on Brel's lyrics and commentary) production conception,
English lyrics, and additional material by Eric Blau and Mort
Shuman; directed by Teri Ralston. Off-Broadway series

1383   LUV
by Murray Schisgal; directed by Elizabeth Ives. Off-Broadway
series

1384   NOON
by Terrence McNally. Off-Broadway series, State Theatre of
Kentucky; performed the same evening as *Welcome to Andromeda*,
under the title of *Yanks*

1385   THE REAL INSPECTOR HOUND
by Tom Stoppard; directed by Jon Jory. Performed the same
evening as *Red Peppers* and *Swan Song*, under the title of
Stages - Three One-Act Plays

1386   RED PEPPERS
by Noel Coward; directed by Jon Jory. Performed the same
evening as *The Real Inspector Hound* and *Swan Song*, under the
title of *Stages - Three One-Act Plays*

1387   RELATIVELY SPEAKING
by Alan Ayckbourn; directed by Christopher Murney

1388   SLEUTH
by Anthony Shaffer; directed by Adale O'Brien

1389   SWAN SONG
by Anton Chekhov; directed by Jon Jory. Performed the same
evening as *The Real Inspector Hound* and *Red Peppers*, under the
title of *Stages - Three One-Act Plays*

1390   THAT CHAMPIONSHIP SEASON
by Jason Miller; directed by Israel Hicks

1391   THE THREEPENNY OPERA
text and lyrics by Bertolt Brecht, music by Kurt Weill, English
adaptation by Marc Blitzstein; directed by Jon Jory

1392   WELCOME TO ANDROMEDA
by Ron Whyte. Off-Broadway series, State Theatre of Kentucky;
performed the same evening as *Noon*, under the title of *Yanks*

Memphis, TN

FRONT STREET THEATRE

1962-1963

1393   OKLAHOMA!
(based on *Green Grow the Lilacs* by Linda Riggs) book and lyrics
by Oscar Hammerstein II, music by Richard Rodgers; directed by
George Touliatos

1394   THE STUDENT PRINCE
book and lyrics by Dorothy Donnelly, music by Sigmund Romberg;
directed by George Touliatos

1395   WHERE'S CHARLEY?
by Brandon Thomas, book by George Abbott, music and lyrics by
Frank Loesser; directed by George Touliatos

1963-1964

1396   ANNIE GET YOUR GUN
book by Dorothy Fields and Herbert Fields, music and lyrics by
Irving Berlin; directed by George Touliatos

1397   IRMA LA DOUCE
by Alexandre Breffort and Marguerite Monnot, English book and
lyrics by Julian More, David Heneker, and Monty Norman;
directed by George Touliatos

1398   KISMET
(based on the play by Edward Knoblock) book by Charles Lederer
and Luther Davis, music by Alexander Borodin, music adaptation
and lyrics by Robert Wright and George Forest; directed by
George Touliatos

1399   MISALLIANCE
by George Bernard Shaw; directed by George Touliatos

1400   MY THREE ANGELS
(based on the book by Albert Husson) by Sam and Bella Spewack;
directed by Peter Thompson

1401   THREE MEN ON A HORSE
by John Cecil Holm and George Abbott; directed by Peter Thompson

1402   THE THREEPENNY OPERA
text and lyrics by Bertolt Brecht, music by Kurt Weill, English
adaptation by Marc Blitzstein; directed by George Touliatos

1964 (Summer)

1403   THE COUNTRY WIFE
        by William Wycherley; directed by Carl M. Weber

1404   THE LITTLE HUT
        by Andre Raussin, adapted by Nancy Mitford; directed by Philip
        Wyeth

1405   THE SOUND OF MUSIC
        book by Howard Lindsay and Russel Crouse, music by Richard
        Rodgers, lyrics by Oscar Hammerstein II; directed by George
        Touliatos

1964-1965

1406   AH, WILDERNESS!
        by Eugene O'Neill; directed by George Touliatos

1407   DAMN YANKEES
        (based on the novel by Douglas Wallop) book by George Abbott
        and Douglas Wallop, words and music by Richard Adler and Jerry
        Ross; directed by George Touliatos

1408   MAJOR BARBARA
        by George Bernard Shaw; directed by James Dyas

1409   THE MUSIC MAN
        by Meredith Wilson; directed by Robert Baker

1410   MY FAIR LADY
        (based on *Pygmalion* by George Bernard Shaw) book and lyrics by
        Alan Jay Lerner, music by Frederick Loewe; directed by George
        Touliatos

1411   OH DAD, POOR DAD, MAMMA'S HUNG YOU IN THE CLOSET AND I'M
        FEELIN' SO SAD
        by Arthur Kopit; directed by Philip Wyeth

1412   ROBERTA
        by Jerome Kern and Otto Harbach; directed by Robert Baker

1965-1966

1413   ANTONY AND CLEOPATRA
        by William Shakespeare; directed by William Woodman

1414   THE BALLAD OF THE SAD CAFE
        (based on the book by Carson McCullers) adapted by Edward Albee;
        directed by Kurt Reis

1415   BECKET
        by Jean Anouilh, translated by Luciene Hill; directed by William
        Woodman

1416   THE COCKTAIL PARTY
        by T.S. Eliot; directed by George Touliatos

1417   THE GLASS MENAGERIE
        by Tennessee Williams; directed by George Touliatos

1418   GUYS AND DOLLS
        (based on stories by Damon Runyon) book by Joe Swerling and
        Abe Burrows, music and lyrics by Frank Loesser; directed by
        James Dyas

1419   THE KING AND I
        (based on *Anna and the King of Siam* by Margaret Landon) book
        and lyrics by Oscar Hammerstein II, music by Richard Rodgers;
        directed by George Touliatos

1420   THE TAVERN
        by George M. Cohan; directed by James Dyas

                            1966-1967

1421   A FUNNY THING HAPPENED ON THE WAY TO THE FORUM
        book by Burt Shevelove and Larry Gelbart, music and lyrics by
        Stephen Sondheim; directed by George Touliatos

1422   GYPSY
        book by Arthur Laurents, lyrics by Stephen Sondheim, music by
        Jules Styne; directed by George Touliatos

1423   THE LITTLE FOXES
        by Lillian Hellman; directed by Kurt Reis

1424   MACBETH
        by William Shakespeare; directed by Kurt Reis

1425   THE MISER
        by Moliere; directed by Carl Weber

1426   SIX CHARACTERS IN SEARCH OF AN AUTHOR
        by Luigi Pirandello, translated by Paul Avila Mayer; directed
        by George Touliatos

1427   A STREETCAR NAMED DESIRE
        by Tennessee Williams; directed by George Touliatos

1428   YOU NEVER CAN TELL
        by George Bernard Shaw; directed by Louis Criss

                            1967-1968

1429   THE KNACK
        by Ann Jellicoe; directed by Sarah Sanders

1430   LUV
        by Murray Schisgal; directed by Charles Maryan

1431   THE SUBJECT WAS ROSES
        by Frank D. Gilroy; directed by Keith Kennedy

1432   TWELFTH NIGHT
            by William Shakespeare; directed by Harvey Landa

Middletown, VA

WAYSIDE THEATRE

1974*

1433   BORN YESTERDAY
            by Garson Kanin; directed by Norman Gevanthor

1434   THE MISER
            by Moliere, adapted by Jerry Heymann; directed by Sue Lawless

1435   6 RMS RIV VU
            by Bob Randall; directed by Norman Gevanthor

Milwaukee, WI

MILWAUKEE REPERTORY THEATRE COMPANY

1962-1963

1436   AS YOU DESIRE ME
            by Luigi Pirandello, translated by Marta Abba; directed by
            Paul Shyre

1437   BEYOND THE HORIZON
            by Eugene O'Neill; directed by Paul Shyre

1438   THE COMEDY OF ERRORS
            by William Shakespeare; directed by Word Baker

1439   THE ELDER STATESMAN
            by T.S. Eliot; directed by Paul Shyre

1440   THE FANTASTICKS
            words by Tom Jones, music by Harvey Schmidt; directed by Gordon
            Duffey

1441   MAJOR BARBARA
            by George Bernard Shaw; directed by Edwin Sherin

1442   THE SHOW-OFF
            by George Kelly; directed by Charles Olsen

---

* These were the only programs available.

1443   U.S.A.
(based on the novel by John Dos Passos) by Paul Shyre and John Dos Passos; directed by Paul Shyre

1963-1964

1444   THE HOSTAGE
by Brendan Behan; directed by Adrian Hall

1445   LONG DAY'S JOURNEY INTO NIGHT
by Eugene O'Neill; directed by Byron Ringland

1446   THE MADWOMAN OF CHAILLOT
by Jean Giraudoux, English adaptation by Maurice Valency; directed by Patrick Hines

1447   RIGHT YOU ARE (IF YOU THINK YOU ARE)
by Luigi Pirandello, translated by Arthur Livingston; directed by Philip Minor

1448   A THURBER CARNIVAL
by James Thurber; directed by Rocco Bufano

1449   TWELFTH NIGHT
by William Shakespeare; directed by Philip Minor

1964-1965

1450   ANATOL
by Arthur Schnitzler, adapted by Tom Jones; directed by Jay Harnik

1451   OH DAD, POOR DAD, MAMMA'S HUNG YOU IN THE CLOSET AND I'M FEELIN' SO SAD
by Arthur Kopit; directed by Byron Ringland

1452   ONCE UPON A MATTRESS
book by Jay Thompson, Marshall Barer, and Dean Fuller, music by Mary Rodgers, lyrics by Marshall Barer; directed by Tullio Garzone

1453   PANTAGLEIZE
by Michel de Ghelderode, English version by Samuel Draper; directed by Philip Minor

1454   THE PLAYBOY OF THE WESTERN WORLD
by J.M. Synge; directed by Philip Minor

1455   THE TEMPEST
by William Shakespeare; directed by Stephen Porter

1456   UNCLE VANYA
by Anton Chekhov, translated by Robert W. Corrigan; directed by Adrian Hall

1457   UNDER MILK WOOD
by Dylan Thomas; directed by Byron Ringland

1965-1966

1458   ANATOL
by Arthur Schnitzler, adapted by Tom Jones; directed by Rocco
Bufano

1459   THE DIARY OF A SCOUNDREL
by Alexander Ostrovsky; directed by Stephen Porter

1460   THE GLASS MENAGERIE
by Tennessee Williams; directed by John A. McQuiggan

1461   HENRY IV (PART 1)
by William Shakespeare; directed by Stephen Porter

1462   MOTHER COURAGE
by Bertolt Brecht, English translation by Eric Bentley; directed
by Adrian Hall

1463   SAINT JOAN
by George Bernard Shaw; directed by Philip Minor

1464   THE SERVANT OF TWO MASTERS
by Carlo Goldoni, adapted by John A. McQuiggan; directed by
John A. McQuiggan

1465   THE TIME OF YOUR LIFE
by William Saroyan; directed by Tom Brennan

1966-1967

1466   DESIGN FOR LIVING
by Noel Coward; directed by Tunc Yalman

1467   ELECTRA
by Sophocles; directed by Tunc Yalman

1468   HEDDA GABLER
by Henrik Ibsen, translated by Eva Le Gallienne; directed by
Tunc Yalman

1469   HOT BUTTERED ROLL
by Rosalyn Drexler; directed by Thomas Bissinger. Theatre For
Tomorrow; performed the same evening as *The Investigation*

1470   THE INVESTIGATION
by Rosalyn Drexler; directed by Thomas Bissinger. Theatre For
Tomorrow; performed the same evening as *Hot Buttered Roll*

1471   THE MERCHANT OF VENICE
by William Shakespeare; directed by Gene Lesser

1472   THE MISER
by Moliere, translated and adapted by Kirk Denmark; directed by
Louis Criss

1473   THE PHYSICISTS
        by Friedrich Duerrenmatt, translated by James Kirkup; directed
        by Hy Kalus

1474   PUNTILA AND HIS HIRED MAN
        by Bertolt Brecht, translated by Gerhard Nelhaus; directed by
        Robert Kalfin

1475   THE SUDDEN AND ACCIDENTAL RE-EDUCATION OF HORSE JOHNSON
        by Douglas Taylor; directed by Robert Benedetti. Theatre For
        Tomorrow

                            1967-1968

1476   AMPHITRYON 38
        by Jean Giraudoux, adapted by S.N. Behrman; directed by Tunc
        Yalman

1477   THE BIG KNIFE
        by Clifford Odets; directed by Hy Kalus

1478   THE HEAD OF HAIR
        by Allen Davis III; directed by Robert Benedetti. Theatre For
        Tomorrow

1479   THE IMPORTANCE OF BEING EARNEST
        by Oscar Wilde; directed by Tunc Yalman

1480   MARY STUART
        by Friedrich von Schiller, translated by Sophie Wilkins;
        directed by Gene Lesser

1481   OH, PIONEERS
        by Douglas Taylor; directed by Tunc Yalman. Theatre For
        Tomorrow

1482   OTHELLO
        by William Shakespeare; directed by Robert Benedetti

1483   A STREETCAR NAMED DESIRE
        by Tennessee Williams; directed by Gene Lesser

1484   WAITING FOR GODOT
        by Samuel Beckett; directed by Gene Lesser

                            1968-1969

1485   DANGEROUS CORNER
        by J.B. Priestley; directed by Tunc Yalman

1486   DULCY
        by George S. Kaufman and Marc Connelly; directed by Tunc Yalman

1487   THE IMAGINARY INVALID
        by Moliere, adapted by Miles Malleson; directed by Anthony
        Perkins

1488   MARAT/SADE
        by Peter Weiss, English translation by Geoffrey Skelton, verse
        adaptation by Adrian Mitchell, music by Richard Peaslee;
        directed by Gene Lesser

1489   THE SKIN OF OUR TEETH
        by Thornton Wilder; directed by Tunc Yalman

1490   THAT'S THE GAME, JACK
        by Douglas Taylor; directed by Wayne Grice. Theatre For
        Tomorrow

1491   THE THREE SISTERS
        by Anton Chekhov, translated by Tyrone Guthrie and Leonid
        Kipnis; directed by Boris Tumarin

                        1969-1970

1492   THE BURGOMASTER
        by Gert Hofman, translated by Donald Watson; directed by
        Anthony Perkins

1493   THE CHAIRS
        by Eugene Ionesco; directed by Tunc Yalman. Performed the same
        evening as *The Lesson*

1494   THE KITCHEN
        by Arnold Wesker; directed by John Olon

1495   THE LESSON
        by Eugene Ionesco; directed by Tunc Yalman. Performed the same
        evening as *The Chairs*

1496   A MIDSUMMER NIGHT'S DREAM
        by William Shakespeare; directed by Boris Tumarin

1497   MISALLIANCE
        by George Bernard Shaw; directed by Ronald L. Hufham

1498   THE PRINCE OF PEASANTMANIA
        by Frank Gagliano, music by James Reichert, lyrics by Frank
        Gagliano; directed by Gene Lesser

1499   SHE STOOPS TO CONQUER
        by Oliver Goldsmith; directed by Ronald Hufham

                        1970-1971

1500   AS YOU LIKE IT
        by William Shakespeare; directed by Timothy S. Mayer

1501   A DOLL'S HOUSE
        by Henrik Ibsen, translated by Eva Le Gallienne; directed by
        Tunc Yalman

1502   THE LIAR
        by Carlo Goldoni, new version by Tunc Yalman; directed by Paul
        Weidner

1503   MEDEA
        by Euripides, translated by Philip Vellacott, music by James
        Reichert; directed by Tunc Yalman

1504   YOU CAN'T TAKE IT WITH YOU
        by Moss Hart and George S. Kaufman; directed by Ronald L. Hufham

                            1971-1972

1505   A DELICATE BALANCE
        by Edward Albee; directed by Charles Kimbrough

                            1972-1973

1506   THE CHERRY ORCHARD
        by Anton Chekhov, English version by Sir John Gielgud; directed
        by Nagle Jackson

1507   THE PLAY'S THE THING
        by Ferenc Molnar, adapted by P.G. Wodehouse; directed by Rod
        Alexander

1508   SCENES FROM AMERICAN LIFE
        by A.R. Gurney, Jr.; directed by Charles Kimbrough

1509   STICKS AND BONES
        by David Rabe; directed by Richard Risso

1510   THE TWO GENTLEMEN OF VERONA
        by William Shakespeare; directed by Nagle Jackson

                            1973-1974

1511   DOCTOR FAUSTUS
        by Christopher Marlowe; directed by Nagle Jackson

1512   KNOCK
        by Jules Romains, translated by James Gidney; directed by Tom
        Gruenewald

1513   LA TURISTA
        by Sam Shepard; directed by John Lion

1514   THE LITTLE FOXES
        by Lillian Hellman; directed by Richard Risso

1515   OUR TOWN
        by Thornton Wilder; directed by Nagle Jackson

1516   PRISONER OF THE CROWN
        (based on the story by Richard T. Herd) by Richard F. Stockton;
        directed by Nagle Jackson

1974-1975

1517 ANDROCLES AND THE LION
   by George Bernard Shaw; directed by Robert Lanchester

1518 BIG FISH, LITTLE FISH
   by Hugh Wheeler; directed by Jeffrey Tambor

1519 DOWN BY THE GRAVOIS (UNDER THE ANHEUSER-BUSCH)
   by James Nicholson; directed by Nagle Jackson

1520 JOE EGG
   by Peter Nichols; directed by Nagle Jackson

1521 THE REHEARSAL
   by Jean Anouilh, English version by Pamela Hansford Johnson
   and Kitty Black; directed by William McKereghan

1522a RICHARD II
   by William Shakespeare; directed by Nagle Jackson

Minneapolis, MN

CHILDREN'S THEATRE OF MINNEAPOLIS

1974-1975

1522b A CELEBRATION
   by Anton Chekhov, translated by Elisavita Fen; directed by
   John Clark Donahue. Performed the same evening as *On the*
   Harmfulness of Tobacco and *Swan Song*, under the title of
   Three by Chekhov

1523 THE CHATTERBOX
   adapted by Timothy Mason; directed by Myron Johnson. Performed
   the same evening as *The Fat Cat*, under the title of *Ukrainian*
   Tales

1524 CINDERELLA
   by Charles Perrault, adapted by John Davidson; directed by
   Bainbridge Boehlke

1525 THE FAT CAT
   adapted by Timothy Mason; directed by Myron Johnson. Performed
   the same evening as *The Chatterbox*, under the title of *Ukrainian*
   Tales

1526 HE WHO GETS SLAPPED
   by Leonid Andreyev, translated by Gregory Zilborg; directed by
   John Clark Donahue

1527 THE IMAGINARY INVALID
   by Moliere, translated by George Muschamp; directed by John
   Clark Donahue

1528   ON THE HARMFULNESS OF TOBACCO
           by Anton Chekhov, translated by S.S. Koteliansky; directed by
           John Clark Donahue. Performed the same evening as *A Celebration*
           and *Swan Song*, under the title of *Three by Chekhov*

1529   PETER AND THE WOLF
           music by Sergei Prokofiev; directed by Myron Johnson. Performed
           the same evening as *The Ugly Duckling*

1530   PINOCCHIO
           (based on the book by Carlo Collodi) adapted by Timothy Mason;
           directed by John Clark Donahue

1531   SWAN SONG
           by Anton Chekhov, translated by Marian Fell; directed by John
           Clark Donahue. Performed the same evening as *A Celebration* and
           On the Harmfulness of Tobacco, under the title of *Three by
           Chekhov*

1532   THE UGLY DUCKLING
           by Hans Christian Anderson, music by Sergei Prokofiev; directed
           by Wendy Lehr. Performed the same evening as *Peter and the Wolf*

THE GUTHRIE THEATRE

1963

1533   DEATH OF A SALESMAN
           by Arthur Miller; directed by Douglas Campbell

1534   HAMLET
           by William Shakespeare; directed by Tyrone Guthrie

1535   THE MISER
           by Moliere, translated by George Gravely; directed by Douglas
           Campbell

1536   THE THREE SISTERS
           by Anton Chekhov, translated by Tyrone Guthrie and Leonid
           Kipnis; directed by Tyrone Guthrie

1964*

1537   THE GLASS MENAGERIE
           by Tennessee Williams; directed by Alan Schneider

1538   HENRY V
           by William Shakespeare; directed by Tyrone Guthrie

1539   SAINT JOAN
           by George Bernard Shaw; directed by Douglas Campbell

---

* This season includes a program magazine containing interesting photographs and background information.

1540   VOLPONE
            by Ben Jonson; directed by Tyrone Guthrie

1965*

1541   THE CAUCASIAN CHALK CIRCLE
            by Bertolt Brecht, English version by Eric Bentley; directed
            by Edward Payson Call

1542   THE CHERRY ORCHARD
            by Anton Chekhov, translated by Tyrone Guthrie and Leonid
            Kipnis; directed by Tyrone Guthrie

1543   THE MISER˙
            by Moliere; directed by Douglas Campbell

1544   RICHARD III
            by William Shakespeare; directed by Tyrone Guthrie

1545   THE WAY OF THE WORLD
            by William Congreve; directed by Douglas Campbell

1966**

1546   AS YOU LIKE IT
            by William Shakespeare; directed by Edward Payson Call. Per-
            formed in Summer and Fall

1547   THE DANCE OF DEATH
            by August Strindberg, English translation by Norman Ginsbury;
            directed by Douglas Campbell. Performed in Summer and Fall

1548   THE DOCTOR'S DILEMMA
            by George Bernard Shaw; directed by Douglas Campbell

1549   S.S. GLENCAIRN
            by Eugene O'Neill; directed by Douglas Campbell and Edward
            Payson Call

1550   THE SKIN OF OUR TEETH
            by Thornton Wilder; directed by Douglas Campbell. Performed in
            Summer and Fall

1967

1551   HARPER'S FERRY
            by Bonnie Stavis; directed by Tyrone Guthrie

1552   THE HOUSE OF ATREUS
            (adapted from *Oresteia* by Aeschylus) by John Lewin; directed
            by Tyrone Guthrie

---

*   This season includes a program containing interesting photographs
     and background information.
** This season includes a program containing interesting background
     information on authors.

1553   SHOEMAKERS' HOLIDAY
        by Thomas Dekker; directed by John Olon

1554   THIEVES' CARNIVAL
        by Jean Anouilh, English version by Lucienne Hill; directed by
        Stephen Porter

1555   THE VISIT
        by Friedrich Duerrenmatt, adapted by Maurice Valency; directed
        by Mel Shapiro

                                1967-1968

1556   ENRICO IV
        by Luigi Pirandello, English version by Eric Bentley; directed
        by Mel Shapiro

1557   SHE STOOPS TO CONQUER
        by Oliver Goldsmith; directed by Douglas Campbell

1558   TANGO
        by Slawomir Mrozek, adapted by John Lewin; directed by Edward
        Payson Call

                                1968-1969

1559   THE MASTER BUILDER
        by Henrik Ibsen, adapted by Emlyn Williams; directed by Stephen
        Porter. Program contains interesting sketches, photographs, and
        biographical information

1560   MERTON OF THE MOVIES
        (based on the story by Harry Leon) by George S. Kaufman and
        Marc Connelly; directed by Mel Shapiro

1561   THE RESISTABLE RISE OF ARTURO UI
        by Bertolt Brecht, translated by George Tabori; directed by
        Edward Payson Call

1562   SERJEANT MUSGRAVE'S DANCE
        by John Arden; directed by Mel Shapiro. Program contains
        interesting sketches, photographs, and biographical information

1563   TWELFTH NIGHT
        by William Shakespeare; directed by Robert Lanchester. Program
        contains interesting sketches, photographs, and biographical
        information

                                 1969*

1564   THE BEAUTY PART
        by S.J. Perelman; directed by Philip Minor

----

* Programs for this season contain interesting sketches, photographs,
  and background information.

1565   JULIUS CAESAR
        by William Shakespeare; directed by Edward Payson Call

1566   MOURNING BECOMES ELECTRA
        by Eugene O'Neill; directed by Mel Shapiro. Performance in-
        cludes *Homecoming*, *The Hunted*, and *The Haunted*

1567   UNCLE VANYA
        by Anton Chekhov, translated by Tyrone Guthrie and Leonid
        Kipnis; directed by Tyrone Guthrie

                            1970

1568   A MAN'S A MAN
        by Bertolt Brecht, translated by Gerhard Nelhaus; directed by
        John Hirsch

1569   A PLAY
        by Aleksandr Solzhenitsyn, adapted by Paul Avila Mayer, trans-
        lated by Nicholas Bethell and David Burg; directed by Michael
        Langham

1570   THE TEMPEST
        by William Shakespeare; directed by Philip Minor

                            1971

1571   CYRANO DE BERGERAC
        by Edmond Rostand, translated and adapted by Anthony Burgess;
        directed by Michael Langham

1572   THE DIARY OF A SCOUNDREL
        by Alexander Ostrovsky, English version by Rodney Ackland;
        directed by Michael Langham

1573   FABLES HERE AND THEN
        by David Feldshuh; directed by David Feldshuh

1574   MISALLIANCE
        by George Bernard Shaw; directed by Edward Gilbert

1575   THE TAMING OF THE SHREW
        by William Shakespeare; by Michael Langham

1576   A TOUCH OF THE POET
        by Eugene O'Neill; directed by David Wheeler

                            1972

1577   AN ITALIAN STRAW HAT
        by Eugene Labiche and Marc-Michael, English version by David
        Ball and David Feldshuh; directed by David Feldshuh

1578   A MIDSUMMER NIGHT'S DREAM
        by William Shakespeare; directed by John Hirsch

1579   OEDIPUS THE KING
        by Sophocles, adapted and translated by Anthony Burgess;
        directed by Michael Langham

1580   OF MICE AND MEN
        by John Steinbeck; directed by Len Cariou

1581   THE RELAPSE
        by Sir John Vanbrugh; directed by Michael Langham

                              1973-1974

1582   BECKET
        by Jean Anouilh, translated by Lucienne Hill; directed by
        David Feldshuh

1583   THE GOVERNMENT INSPECTOR
        by Nikolai Gogol, adapted by Peter Roby, based on translation
        by Leonid Ignatieff; directed by Michael Langham

1584   I, SAID THE FLY
        by June Havoc; directed by Eric Christmas

1585   JUNO AND THE PAYCOCK
        by Sean O'Casey; directed by Tomas MacAnna

1586   THE MERCHANT OF VENICE
        by William Shakespeare; directed by Michael Langham

1587   WAITING FOR GODOT
        by Samuel Beckett; directed by Eugene Lion

                              1974-1975

1588   THE CRUCIBLE
        by Arthur Miller; directed by Len Cariou

1589   EVERYMAN
        by Cornelius Agrippa; directed by Robert Benedetti

1590   KING LEAR
        by William Shakespeare; directed by Michael Langham

1591   LOVE'S LABOUR'S LOST
        by William Shakespeare; directed by Michael Langham

1592   THE SCHOOL FOR SCANDAL
        by Richard Brinsley Sheridan; directed by Michael Langham

1593   TARTUFFE
        by Moliere, English translation by Richard Wilbur; directed by
        Michael Bawtree

                                1975

1594   ARSENIC AND OLD LACE
        by Joseph Kesselring; directed by Tom Gruenewald

1595   THE CARETAKER
           by Harold Pinter; directed by Stephen Kanel

1596   LOOT
           by Joe Orton; directed by Tom Moore

1597   MOTHER COURAGE AND HER CHILDREN
           by Bertolt Brecht, English version by Robert Hellman; directed
           by Eugene Lion

1598   A STREETCAR NAMED DESIRE
           by Tennessee Williams; directed by Ken Ruta

Montreal, Canada

CENTAUR THEATRE*

1971-1972

1599   THE ENTERTAINER
           by John Osborne; directed by Elsa Bolan. Excellent biographical
           notes on John Osborne and background information on *The*
           Entertainer

1600   SUMMER DAYS
           by Romain Weingarten, translated by Suzanne Grossmann; directed
           by Maurice Podbrey

1601   W.B. YEATS
           by W.B. Yeats; directed by James Flannery

New Haven, CT

LONG WHARF THEATRE

1965-1966**

1602   THE GREEN LUTE
           by J. Gladden Shrock; directed by Jon Jory. American premiere

1603   I'M NOBODY
           by David Kranes; directed by Jon Jory. American premiere; per-
           formed the same evening as *The Loon Hunt*, under the title of
           One Right After the Other

---

*   These were the only programs available.
** Programs for this season contain notes about the dramatist and the
     play by the artistic director and the executive director.

1604   LONG DAY'S JOURNEY INTO NIGHT
          by Eugene O'Neill; directed by Arvin Brown

1605   THE LOON HUNT
          by David Kranes; directed by Jon Jory. American premiere; per-
          formed the same evening as *I'm Nobody*, under the title of *One
          Right After the Other*

1606   THE PIRATES OF PENZANCE
          by W.S. Gilbert and Arthur Sullivan; directed by Frank Wicks

1607   THE PLOUGH AND THE STARS
          by Sean O'Casey; directed by Jon Jory

1608   THE RIVALS
          by Richard Brinsley Sheridan; directed by Jon Jory

1609   THE TROJAN WOMEN
          by Euripides, translated by Edith Hamilton; directed by Jon
          Jory

1610   UNCLE VANYA
          by Anton Chekhov, adapted by Robert Snook; directed by Jon Jory

1611   VOLPONE
          by Ben Jonson, freely adapted by Stefan Zweig; directed by Jon
          Jory

                               1966-1967

1612   THE MAN WHO CAME TO DINNER
          by George S. Kaufman and Moss Hart; directed by Jon Jory

1613   MISALLIANCE
          by George Bernard Shaw; directed by Arvin Brown

1614   MOTHER COURAGE
          by Bertolt Brecht, English version by Eric Bentley; directed
          by Michael Youngfellow; musical direction and special arrange-
          ments by Gordon Emerson

1615   THE NIGHT OF THE IGUANA
          by Tennessee Williams; directed by Jon Jory

1616   OH! WHAT A LOVELY WAR
          by Joan Littlewood and Charles Chilton, Palm Court scene
          written by Robert Ingham; directed by Jon Jory

1617   THE TAVERN
          by George M. Cohan; directed by Jon Jory

1618   THE THREE SISTERS
          by Anton Chekhov, translated by Tyrone Guthrie and Leonid
          Kipnis; directed by Arvin Brown

1967-1968

1619   THE BALD SOPRANO
        by Eugene Ionesco; directed by Jon Jory. Performed the same
        evening as *The Doctor in Spite of Himself*

1620   THE DOCTOR IN SPITE OF HIMSELF
        by Moliere; directed by Jon Jory. Performed the same evening
        as *The Bald Soprano*

1621   DON JUAN IN HELL
        by George Bernard Shaw; directed by Arvin Brown

1622   THE GLASS MENAGERIE
        by Tennessee Williams; directed by Arvin Brown

1623   THE PLAYBOY OF THE WESTERN WORLD
        by J.M. Synge; directed by Siobhan McKenna

1624   THE REHEARSAL
        by Jean Anouilh; directed by Arvin Brown

1625   ROOM SERVICE
        by John Murray and Allen Boretz; directed by Jon Jory

1626   TINY ALICE
        by Edward Albee; directed by Michael Youngfellow

1627   A WHISTLE IN THE DARK
        by Thomas Murphy; directed by Arvin Brown

1968-1969

1628   AMERICA HURRAH
        by Jean-Claude van Itallie; directed by Michael Youngfellow

1629   GHOSTS
        by Henrik Ibsen, translated by Peter Watts; directed by Arvin
        Brown

1630   THE LION IN WINTER
        by James Goldman; directed by Arvin Brown

1969-1970

1631   BLACK COMEDY
        by Peter Shaffer; directed by Maurice Breslow. Performed the
        same evening as *The White Liars*

1632   COUNTRY PEOPLE
        by Maxim Gorky, translated by Alexander Bakshy in collaboration
        with Paul S. Nathan; directed by Arvin Brown

1633   JOE EGG
        by Peter Nichols; directed by Barry Davis

1634   THE PIRATE
        (based on the play by S.N. Behrman) book by Lawrence Kasha and
        Hayden Griffin, music and lyrics by Cole Porter; directed by
        Maurice Breslow; musical director, Stuart Hamilton

1635   SPOON RIVER ANTHOLOGY
        by Edgar Lee Masters, conceived, adapted, and arranged by
        Charles Aidman, original music by Naomi Caryl Hirshorn,
        additional music by Michael Posnick; directed by Arvin Brown

1636   TANGO
        by Slawomir Mrozek, translated by Ralph Manheim and Teresa
        Dzieduscycka; directed by Arvin Brown

1637   TARTUFFE
        by Moliere, translated by Richard Wilbur, original music by
        Lee Hoiby; directed by Mark Healy

1638   A THOUSAND CLOWNS
        by Herb Gardner; directed by Harold Baldridge

1639   THE WHITE LIARS
        by Peter Shaffer; directed by Maurice Breslow. Performed the
        same evening as *Black Comedy*

1970-1971

1640   THE BLOOD KNOT
        by Athol Fugard; directed by Ted Cornell

1641   A PLACE WITHOUT DOORS
        by Marguerite Duras, translated by Barbara Bray; directed by
        Brian Murray. U.S. premiere

1642   THE PRICE
        by Arthur Miller; directed by Gilbert Cates

1643   SHE STOOPS TO CONQUER
        by Oliver Goldsmith; directed by Isaac Schambelan

1644   THE SKIN OF OUR TEETH
        by Thornton Wilder; directed by Jeff Bleckner

1645   SOLITAIRE/DOUBLE SOLITAIRE
        by Robert Anderson; directed by Arvin Brown. Premiere

1646   YEGOR BULICHOV
        by Maxim Gorky, translated and adapted by Joan Isserman;
        directed by Arvin Brown. U.S. premiere

1971-1972

1647   THE CONTRACTOR
        by David Storey; directed by Barry Davis. American premiere

1648   THE COUNTRY WOMAN
        by Ivan Turgenev; directed by Morris Carnovsky. American
        premiere; performed the same evening as *Swan Song* and *The
        Wedding*, under the title of *Troika*

1649   HAMLET
        by William Shakespeare; directed by Arvin Brown

1650   THE ICEMAN COMETH
        by Eugene O'Neill; directed by Arvin Brown

1651   PATRICK'S DAY
        by Bill Morrison; directed by Edward Gilbert

1652   SWAN SONG
        by Anton Chekhov; directed by Arvin Brown. Performed the same
        evening as *The Country Woman* and *The Wedding*, under the title
        of *Troika*

1653   THE WAY OF THE WORLD
        by William Congreve; directed by Malcolm Black

1654   THE WEDDING
        by Anton Chekhov; directed by Morris Carnovsky. Performed the
        same evening as *The Country Woman* and *Swan Song*, under the
        title of *Troika*

1655   YOU CAN'T TAKE IT WITH YOU
        by Moss Hart and George S. Kaufman; directed by Arvin Brown

                            1972-1973

1656   THE CHANGING ROOM
        by David Storey; directed by Michael Rudman. American premiere

1657   THE DANCE OF DEATH (PART 1)
        by August Strindberg, adapted by Austin Pendleton; directed by
        Austin Pendleton. Performed the same evening as *Miss Julie*

1658   FORGET-ME-NOT LANE
        by Peter Nichols; directed by Arvin Brown. American premiere

1659   JUNO AND THE PAYCOCK
        by Sean O'Casey; directed by Arvin Brown

1660   THE LADY'S NOT FOR BURNING
        by Christopher Fry; directed by Kent Paul

1661   MISS JULIE
        by August Strindberg, adapted by Austin Pendleton; directed by
        Austin Pendleton. Performed the same evening as *The Dance of
        Death (Part 1)*

1662   TRELAWNY OF THE "WELLS"
        by Sir Arthur Wing Pinero; directed by Max Stafford-Clark

1663   WHAT PRICE GLORY?
          by Maxwell Anderson and Lawrence Stallings; directed by Arvin
          Brown

                              1973-1974

1664   THE MASTER BUILDER
          by Henrik Ibsen, adapted by Austin Pendleton; directed by
          Austin Pendleton

1665   MORNING'S AT SEVEN
          by Paul Osborn; directed by William Francisco

1666   THE NATIONAL HEALTH
          by Peter Nichols; directed by Arvin Brown

1667   A PAGAN PLACE
          by Edna O'Brien; directed by John Lithgow

1668   THE RESISTABLE RISE OF ARTURO UI
          by Bertolt Brecht, translated by Ralph Manheim; directed by
          Brooks Jones

1669   THE SEA GULL
          by Anton Chekhov, translated by Stark Young; directed by Arvin
          Brown

1670   THE WIDOWING OF MRS. HOLROYD
          by D.H. Lawrence; directed by Arvin Brown

                              1974-1975

1671   AFORE NIGHT COME
          by David Rudkin; directed by Ron Daniels

1672   AH, WILDERNESS!
          by Eugene O'Neill; directed by Arvin Brown

1673   THE ISLAND
          devised by Athol Fugard, John Kani, and Winston Ntshona;
          directed by Athol Fugard. Performed the same evening as *Sizwe
          Banzi Is Dead*

1674   THE NIGHT OF THE BURNING PESTLE
          (based on the play by Francis Beaumont and John Fletcher)
          adapted by Brooks Jones, additional lyrics by Brooks Jones and
          Peter Schickele, music by Peter Schickele; directed by Brooks
          Jones. Performed the same evening as *A Soldier's Tale*

1675   PYGMALION
          by George Bernard Shaw; directed by Robin Gammell

1676   RICHARD III
          by William Shakespeare; directed by Barry Davis

1677   SIZWE BANZI IS DEAD
devised by Athol Fugard, John Kani, and Winston Ntshona;
directed by Athol Fugard. Performed the same evening as *The
Island*

1678   THE SOLDIER'S TALE
by C.F. Ramuz, translated by Michael Flanders and Kitty Black,
music by Igor Stravinsky; directed by Brooks Jones. Performed
the same evening as *The Knight of the Burning Pestle*

1679   YOU'RE TOO TALL, BUT COME BACK IN TWO WEEKS
by Richard Venture; directed by Arvin Brown. World premiere

YALE REPERTORY THEATRE

1967-1968

1680   CORIOLANUS
by William Shakespeare; directed by Jeff Bleckner and Larry
Arrick

1681   HENRY IV
by Luigi Pirandello, English version by Eric Bentley; directed
by Carl Weber

1682   'TIS PITY SHE'S A WHORE
by John Ford; directed by Kenneth Haigh

1683   WE BOMBED IN NEW HAVEN
by Joseph Heller; directed by Larry Arrick

1968-1969

1684   THE ANTIGONE OF SOPHOKLES
adapted for stage by Bertolt Brecht, based on German translation
by Friederich Holderlin, English translation by Judith Malina;
directed by Julian Beck and Judith Malina

1685   FRANKENSTEIN
by The Living Theatre Company; directed by Julian Beck and
Judith Malina

1686   GREATSHOT
book and lyrics by Arnold Weinstein; directed by Paul Sills

1687   MYSTERIES AND SMALLER PIECES
by The Living Theatre Company; directed by Julian Beck and
Judith Malina

1688   PARADISE NOW
by The Living Theatre Company

1969-1970

1689   MACBETH
by William Shakespeare; directed by Robert Brustein

1690   THE RIVALS
         by Richard Brinsley Sheridan; directed by Alvin Epstein

                            1970-1971

1691   THE LITTLE MAHAGONNY
         book and lyrics by Bertolt Brecht, music by Kurt Weill, trans-
         lated by Michael Feingold; directed by Michael Posnick.
         American premiere

1692   THE REVENGER'S TRAGEDY
         by Cyril Tourneur; directed by Robert Brustein

1693   THE SEVEN DEADLY SINS
         book and lyrics by Bertolt Brecht, music by Kurt Weill, trans-
         lated by W.H. Auden and Chester Kallman; directed by Alvin
         Epstein

                            1971-1972

1694   THE BIG HOUSE
         by Lonnie Carter; directed by Robert Brustein

1695   CALIGULA
         by Albert Camus, adapted from the French by Justin O'Brien;
         directed by Alvin Epstein

1696   HAPPY END
         by Dorothy Lane, lyrics by Bertolt Brecht, music by Kurt Weill,
         American adaptation and lyrics by Michael Feingold; directed by
         Michael Posnick

1697   I MARRIED YOU FOR THE FUN OF IT
         by Natalia Ginzburg, translated by John Hersey; directed by
         Roger Hendricks Simon

1698   LIFE IS A DREAM
         by Pedro Calderon De La Barca, English version by Roy Campbell;
         directed by Jacques Burdick

1699   WHEN WE DEAD AWAKEN
         by Henrik Ibsen, translated by Michael Feingold; directed by
         Tom Haas

                            1972-1973

1700   IN THE CLAP SHACK
         by William Styron; directed by Alvin Epstein

1701   LEAR
         by Edward Bond; directed by David Giles

                            1973-1974

1702   THE TEMPEST
         by William Shakespeare; directed by Moni Yakim and Alvin Epstein

1974-1975

1703   A MIDSUMMER NIGHT'S DREAM
        by William Shakespeare; directed by Alvin Epstein

1704   THE POSSESSED
        by Fyodor Dostoyevsky, a new dramatization by Andrzej Wajda
        based on the adaptation by Albert Camus, translated by Justin
        O'Brien; directed by Andrzej Wajda

New Orleans, LA

REPERTORY THEATRE OF NEW ORLEANS

1966-1967

1705   CHARLEY'S AUNT
        by Brandon Thomas; directed by Stuart Vaughan

1706   OUR TOWN
        by Thornton Wilder; directed by Stuart Vaughan

1707   THE RIVALS
        by Richard Brinsley Sheridan; directed by Stuart Vaughan

1708   ROMEO AND JULIET
        by William Shakespeare; directed by Stuart Vaughan

1967-1968

1709   SAINT JOAN
        by George Bernard Shaw; directed by Stuart Vaughan

1968-1969

1710   ARMS AND THE MAN
        by George Bernard Shaw; directed by Stuart Vaughan

1971-1972

1711   THE ROSE TATTOO
        by Tennessee Williams; directed by Paul Barry

1712   THE TAVERN
        by George M. Cohan; directed by Paul Barry

New York, NY

A.P.A.*

1968-1969**

1713   COCK-A-DOODLE DANDY
        by Sean O'Casey; directed by Jack O'Brien and Donald Moffat

1714   HAMLET
        by William Shakespeare; directed by Ellis Rabb

1715   THE MISANTHROPE
        by Moliere, English translation by Richard Wilbur; directed by
        Stephen Porter

1969-1970

1716   PRIVATE LIVES
        by Noel Coward; directed by Stephen Porter

THE ACTING COMPANY

1971-1972

1717   THE INDIAN WANTS THE BRONX
        by Israel Horovitz; directed by Gene Lesser. Performed the
        same evening as *Interview*

1718   INTERVIEW
        by Jean-Claude Van Itallie; directed by Gene Lesser. Performed
        the same evening as *The Indian Wants the Bronx*

1719   THE LOWER DEPTHS
        by Maxim Gorky, adapted by Alex Szogyi; directed by Boris
        Tumarin

1720   THE SCHOOL FOR SCANDAL
        by Richard Brinsley Sheridan; directed by Gerald Freedman

1721   WOMEN BEWARE WOMEN
        by Thomas Middleton; directed by Michael Kahn

1972-1973

1722   U.S.A.
        (based on the novel by John Dos Passos) by Paul Shyre and John
        Dos Passos; directed by Anne McNaughton

---

* These were the only programs available.
** The three plays this season are listed together in one program.

1973-1974

1723   THE BEGGAR'S OPERA
      by John Gay; directed by Gene Lesser; musical director, Roland
      Gagnon. Spa Summer Theatre, Saratoga Festival; also performed
      in N.Y.C.

1724   THE HOSTAGE
      by Brendan Behan; directed by Gene Lesser; musical director,
      Roland Gagnon. Spa Summer Theatre, Saratoga Festival

1725   THE KNACK
      by Ann Jellicoe; directed by Garland Wright. Spa Summer Theatre,
      Saratoga Festival

1726   MEASURE FOR MEASURE
      by William Shakespeare; directed by John Houseman. Spa Summer
      Theatre, Saratoga Festival; also performed in N.Y.C.

1727   NEXT TIME I'LL SING TO YOU
      by James Saunders; directed by Marian Seldes

1728   THE THREE SISTERS
      by Anton Chekhov, translated by Tyrone Guthrie and Leonid
      Kipnis; directed by Boris Tumarin; musical director, Gerald
      Shaw. Spa Summer Theatre, Saratoga Festival; also performed
      in N.Y.C.

1974-1975

1729   ARMS AND THE MAN
      by George Bernard Shaw; directed by Edward Payson Call. Spa
      Summer Theatre, Saratoga Festival

1730   EDWARD II
      by Christopher Marlowe, music by Bob James; directed by Ellis
      Rabb. Spa Summer Theatre, Saratoga Festival; also performed
      in N.Y.C.

1731   LOVE'S LABOUR'S LOST
      by William Shakespeare, music by John Morris; directed by
      Gerald Freedman

1732   ORCHESTRA
      by Jean Anouilh, translated by Miriam John, adapted by Jack
      O'Brien, musical arrangements by Fritz Rikko; directed by
      Jack O'Brien. Spa Summer Theatre, Saratoga Festival; performed
      the same evening as *Play*

1733   PLAY
      by Samuel Beckett, adapted by Jack O'Brien, musical arrange-
      ments by Fritz Rikko; directed by Jack O'Brien. Spa Summer
      Theatre, Saratoga Festival; performed the same evening as
      Orchestra

1734   THE ROBBER BRIDEGROOM
(based on the novella by Eudora Welty) book and lyrics by
Alfred Uhry, composed and arranged by Robert Waldman; directed
by Gerald Waldman. Spa Summer Theatre, Saratoga Festival; also
performed in N.Y.C.

1735   SHE STOOPS TO CONQUER
by Oliver Goldsmith, musical arrangements by Gerald Gutierrez;
directed by Stephen Porter. Spa Summer Theatre, Saratoga
Festival

1736   THE THREE SISTERS
by Anton Chekhov, translated by Tyrone Guthrie and Leonid
Kipnis; directed by Boris Tumarin; musical director, Gerald
Gutierrez

1737   THE TIME OF YOUR LIFE
by William Saroyan; directed by Jack O'Brien. Spa Summer
Theatre, Saratoga Festival; also performed in N.Y.C.

AMERICAN PLACE THEATRE

1965-1966

1738   THE FLOOR
by May Swenson; directed by Harvey Grossman. Performed the
same evening as *Miss Pete* and *23 Pat O'Brien Movies*, under
the title of *Doubles and Opposites*

1739   HOGAN'S GOAT
by William Alfred; directed by Frederick Rolf

1740   MISS PETE
by Andrew Glaze; directed by Richard B. McPhee. Performed the
same evening as *The Floor* and *23 Pat O'Brien Movies*, under
the title of *Doubles and Opposites*

1741   23 PAT O'BRIEN MOVIES
by Bruce Jay Friedman; directed by Gaby Rodgers. Performed
the same evening as *The Floor* and *Miss Pete*, under the title
of *Doubles and Opposites*

1966-1967

1742   THE DISPLACED PERSON
(adapted from the short stories by Flannery O'Connor) by Cecil
Dawkins; directed by Edward Parone

1968-1969

1743   THE ACQUISITION
by David Trainer; directed by Tom Bissinger. Performed the
same evening as *This Bird of Dawning Singeth All Night Long*
and *The Young Master Dante*, under the title of *Trainer, Dean,
Liepolt and Company*

1744   BOY ON THE STRAIGHT-BACK CHAIR
        by Ronald Tavel; directed by Wynn Handman

1745   PAPP
        by Kenneth Cameron; directed by Martin Fried

1746   THIS BIRD OF DAWNING SINGETH ALL NIGHT LONG
        by Phillip Dean; directed by Martin Fried. Performed the same
        evening as *The Acquisition* and *The Young Master Dante*, under
        the title of *Trainer, Dean, Liepolt and Company*

1747   THE YOUNG MASTER DANTE
        by Werner Liepolt; directed by Tom Bissinger. Performed the
        same evening as *The Acquisition* and *This Bird of Dawning
        Singeth All Night Long*, under the title of *Trainer, Dean,
        Liepolt and Company*

                        1969-1970

1748   MERCY STREET
        by Anne Sexton; directed by Charles Maryan

                        1970-1971

1749   BACK BOG BEAST BAIT
        by Sam Shepard; directed by Tony Barsha

1750   PINKVILLE
        by George Tabori; directed by Martin Fried

1751   SUNDAY DINNER
        by Joyce Carol Oates; directed by Curt Dempster

                        1972-1973

1752   BABA GOYA
        by Steve Tesich; directed by Edwin Sherin

1753   FREEMAN
        by Phillip Dean; directed by Lloyd Richards

1754   THE KARL MARX PLAY
        by Rochelle Owens; directed by Mel Shapiro

1755   THE KID
        by Robert Coover; directed by Jack Gelber

                        1973-1974

1756   BREAD
        by David Scott Milton; directed by Martin Fried

1757   CREAM CHEESE
        by Lonnie Carter; directed by Isaiah Sheffer. Performed the
        same evening as *Dr. Kheal* and *Love Scene*, under the title of
        A Festival of Short Plays

1758   DR. KHEAL
         by Maria Irene Fornes; directed by Maria Irene Fornes. Performed
         the same evening as *Cream Cheese* and *Love Scene*, under the title
         of *A Festival of Short Plays*

1759   HOUSE PARTY
         by Ed Bullins; directed by Roscoe Orman

1760   LOVE SCENE
         by Robert Coover; directed by Caymichael Patten. Performed the
         same evening as *Cream Cheese* and *Dr. Kheal*, under the title of
         A Festival of Short Plays

1761   SHEARWATER
         by William Hauptman

1762   THE YEAR OF THE DRAGON
         by Frank Chin; directed by Russell Treyz

                                1974-1975

1763   ACTION
         by Sam Shepard; directed by Nancy Meckler. Performed the same
         evening as *Killer's Head*

1764   THE BEAUTY PART
         by S.J. Perelman; directed by James Hammerstein

1765   KILLER'S HEAD
         by Sam Shepard; directed by Nancy Meckler. Performed the same
         evening as *Action*

1766   RUBBERS
         by Jonathan Reynolds; directed by Alan Arkin. Performed the
         same evening as *Yanks 3 Detroit 0 Top of the Seventh*

1767   STRAWS IN THE WIND: A THEATRICAL LOOK AHEAD
         by Donald Barthelme, Marshall Brickman, Cy Coleman, and others;
         directed by Phyllis Newman. A musical revue

1768   YANKS 3 DETROIT 0 TOP OF THE SEVENTH
         by Jonathan Reynolds; directed by Alan Arkin. Performed the
         same evening as *Rubbers*

                                1975-1976

1769   DOMINO COURTS
         by William Hauptman; directed by Barnet Kellman

CHELSEA THEATER CENTER (*see Brooklyn, NY*)

CIRCLE IN THE SQUARE

1969-1970

1770   CHICAGO 70
by Theodore Mann and Paul Libin; directed by George Luscombe

1771   THE WHITE HOUSE MURDER CASE
by Jules Feiffer; directed by Alan Arkin

1971-1972

1772   THE LAST ANALYSIS
by Saul Bellow; directed by Theodore Mann

1972-1973

1773   EURIPIDES' MEDEA
by Irene Papas, adapted by Minos Volanakis; directed by Minos
Volanakis

1774   HERE ARE LADIES
designed by Sean Kenny, music by Sean O'Riada; directed by
Sean Kelly

1775   MOURNING BECOMES ELECTRA
by Eugene O'Neill; directed by Theodore Mann

1973-1974

1776   AN AMERICAN MILLIONAIRE
by Murray Schisgal; directed by Theodore Mann. Program contains an article on Noel Coward

1777   THE ICEMAN COMETH
by Eugene O'Neill; directed by Theodore Mann. Program contains
biographical notes on Eugene O'Neill

1778   SCAPINO
by Moliere, adapted by Frank Dunlop and Jim Dale; directed by
Frank Dunlop

1779   THE WALTZ OF THE TOREADORS
by Jean Anouilh, translated by Lucienne Hill; directed by Brian
Murray

1974-1975

1780   AH, WILDERNESS!
by Eugene O'Neill; directed by Arvin Brown

1781   DEATH OF A SALESMAN
by Arthur Miller; directed by George C. Scott

1782   THE NATIONAL HEALTH
by Peter Nichols; directed by Arvin Brown

CIRCLE REPERTORY THEATRE COMPANY

1969-1970

1783   A PRACTICAL RITUAL TO EXORCISE FRUSTRATION AFTER FIVE DAYS
OF RAIN
by David Starkweather; directed by Rob Thirkield and David
Starkweather

1971-1972

1784   TIME SHADOWS
by Helen Duberstein; directed by Marshall Oglesby

1972-1973

1785   THE HOT L BALTIMORE
by Lanford Wilson; directed by Marshall W. Mason

1786   MRS. TIDINGS' MASON-DIXON MEDICINE MAN
by John Heuer; directed by Peter Tripp

1787   A ROAD WHERE THE WOLVES RUN
by Claris Nelson; directed by Marshall W. Mason

1788   THE TRAGEDY OF THOMAS ANDROS
by Ronald Wilcox; directed by Marshall Oglesby

1789   WHEN WE DEAD AWAKEN
by Henrik Ibsen, translated by Michael Feingold; directed by
Marshall Oglesby

1973-1974

1790   THE AMAZING ACTIVITY OF CHARLEY CONTRARE AND THE NINETY-EIGHTH
STREET GANG
by Roy London; directed by Richard A. Steel

1791   HIM
by E.E. Cummings; directed by Marshall Oglesby

1792   HOTHOUSE
by Megan Terry; directed by Barbara Rosoff

1793   THE PERSIANS
by Aeschylus; directed by Rob Thirkield

1794   PRODIGAL
by Richard Lortz; directed by Marshall W. Mason

1795   THE SEA HORSE
by James Irwin; directed by Marshall W. Mason

1796   WHEN YOU COMIN' BACK, RED RYDER?
by Mark Medoff; directed by Kenneth Frankel

1974-1975

1797   BATTLE OF ANGELS
        by Tennessee Williams; directed by Marshall W. Mason

1798   HURRY OUTSIDE
        by Corinne Jacker; directed by Marshall W. Mason

1799   THE MOUND BUILDERS
        by Lanford Wilson; directed by Marshall W. Mason

CITY CENTER ACTING COMPANY (*see THE ACTING COMPANY*)

THE JUILLIARD ACTING COMPANY (*see THE ACTING COMPANY*)

NEW YORK SHAKESPEARE FESTIVAL

1963 (Summer)

1800   AS YOU LIKE IT
        by William Shakespeare; directed by Gerald Freedman

1801   THE WINTER'S TALE
        by William Shakespeare; directed by Gladys Vaughan

1964 (Summer)

1802   ELECTRA
        by Sophocles, translated by H.D.F. Kitto; directed by Gerald
        Freedman

1965 (Summer)

1803   CORIOLANUS
        by William Shakespeare; directed by Gladys Vaughan

1804   LOVE'S LABOUR'S LOST
        by William Shakespeare; directed by Gerald Freedman

1805   TROILUS AND CRESSIDA
        by William Shakespeare; directed by Joseph Papp

1966 (Summer)

1806   ALL'S WELL THAT ENDS WELL
        by William Shakespeare; directed by Joseph Papp

1807   KING RICHARD III
        by William Shakespeare; directed by Gerald Freedman

1808   MACBETH
        by William Shakespeare; directed by Gladys Vaughan

1809   MEASURE FOR MEASURE
          by William Shakespeare; directed by Michael Kahn

                              1967 (Summer)

1810   THE COMEDY OF ERRORS
          by William Shakespeare; directed by Gerald Freedman

1811   VOLPONE
          by Ben Jonson; directed by George L. Sherman

                              1968 (Summer)

1812   HAMLET
          by William Shakespeare; directed by Joseph Papp

1813   KING HENRY IV (PARTS 1 & 2)
          by William Shakespeare; directed by Gerald Freedman

1814   ROMEO AND JULIET
          by William Shakespeare; directed by Joseph Papp

1815   TAKE ONE STEP
          book and lyrics by Gerald Freedman and John Morris, music by
          John Morris; directed by Gerald Freedman. Children's show at
          the Mobile Theatre

                              1969 (Summer)

1816   ELECTRA
          by Sophocles, translated by H.D.F. Kitto; directed by Gerald
          Freedman

1817   PEER GYNT
          by Henrik Ibsen, translated by Michael Meyer, adapted by Gerald
          Freedman; directed by Gerald Freedman

1818   TAKE ONE STEP
          book and lyrics by Gerald Freedman and John Morris, music by
          John Morris; directed by George and Ethel Martin. Children's
          show at the Mobile Theatre

1819   TWELFTH NIGHT
          by William Shakespeare; directed by Joseph Papp

                              1970 (Summer)

1820   THE CHRONICLES OF KING HENRY IV (PART 1)
          by William Shakespeare; directed by Stuart Vaughan. Listed
          under the heading of *The Wars of Roses*

1821   RICHARD III
          by William Shakespeare; directed by Stuart Vaughan. Listed
          under the heading of *The Wars of Roses*

1971 (Summer)

1822   THE TALE OF CYMBELINE
        by William Shakespeare; directed by A.J. Antoon

1972 (Summer)

1823   HAMLET
        by William Shakespeare; directed by Gerald Freedman

1824   MUCH ADO ABOUT NOTHING
        by William Shakespeare; directed by A.J. Antoon

1973 (Summer)

1825   AS YOU LIKE IT
        by William Shakespeare; directed by Joseph Papp

1826   KING LEAR
        by William Shakespeare; directed by Edwin Sherin

1827   THE TWO GENTLEMEN OF VERONA
        (based on the play by William Shakespeare) adapted by John
        Guare and Mel Shapiro, lyrics by John Guare, music by Galt
        MacDermot; directed by Kim Friedman

1975 (Summer)

1828   HAMLET
        by William Shakespeare; directed by Michael Rudman

1967-1968 (Winter)*

1829   ERGO
        by Jakov Lind; directed by Gerald Freedman

1830   HAIR
        book and lyrics by Gerome Ragni and James Rado, music by Galt
        MacDermot; directed by Gerald Freedman

1831   HAMLET
        by William Shakespeare; directed by Joseph Papp

1832   THE MEMORANDUM
        by Vaclav Havel, translated by Vera Blackwell; directed by
        Joseph Papp

1968-1969 (Winter)

1833   CITIES IN BEZIQUE
        by Adrienne Kennedy; directed by Gerald Freedman

1834   HUUI, HUUI
        by Anne Burr; directed by Joseph Papp

---

* First season of performances at the Florence Sutro Anspacher Theatre.

1835   INVITATION TO A BEHEADING
        by Vladimir Nabokov, adapted by Russell McGrath; directed by
        Gerald Freedman

1836   NO PLACE TO BE SOMEBODY
        by Charles Gordone; directed by Ted Cornell

                        1969-1970 (Winter)

1837   MOD DONNA
        book and lyrics by Myrna Lamb, music by Susan Hulsman Bingham;
        directed by Joseph Papp

1838   SAMBO
        words by Ron Steward, music by Ron Steward and Neal Tate;
        directed by Gerald Freedman

                        1970-1971 (Winter)

1839   THE BASIC TRAINING OF PAVLO HUMMEL
        by David Rabe; directed by Jeff Bleckner

1840   SUBJECT TO FITS
        by Robert Montgomery; directed by A.J. Antoon

1841   TRELAWNY OF THE "WELLS"
        by Sir Arthur Wing Pinero; directed by Robert Roman

                        1971-1972 (Winter)

1842   COP AND BLOW
        by Neil Harris; directed by Kris Keiser. Performed the same
        evening as *Gettin' It Together*, *Players Inn*, and *Sister Son/JI*,
        under the title of *Black Visions*

1843   GETTIN' IT TOGETHER
        by Richard Wesley; directed by Kris Keiser. Performed the same
        evening as *Cop and Blow*, *Players Inn*, and *Sister Son/JI*, under
        the title of *Black Visions*

1844   OLDER PEOPLE
        by John Ford Noonan; directed by Mel Shapiro

1845   PLAYERS INN
        by Neil Harris; directed by Kris Keiser. Performed the same
        evening as *Cop and Blow*, *Gettin' It Together*, and *Sister
        Son/JI*, under the title of *Black Visions*

1846   SISTER SON/JI
        by Sonia Sanchez; directed by Novella Nelson. Performed the
        same evening as *Cop and Blow*, *Gettin' It Together*, and *Players
        Inn*, under the title of *Black Visions*

1847   STICKS AND BONES
        by David Rabe; directed by Jeff Bleckner

1848 THAT CHAMPIONSHIP SEASON
   by Jason Miller; directed by A.J. Antoon

1849 THE TWO GENTLEMEN OF VERONA
   (based on the play by William Shakespeare) adapted by John
   Guare and Mel Shapiro, lyrics by John Guare, music by Galt
   MacDermot; directed by Mel Shapiro

1972-1973 (Winter)

1850 THE CHERRY ORCHARD
   by Anton Chekhov; directed by Michael Schultz

1851 THE CHILDREN
   by Michael McGuire; directed by Paul Schneider

1852 MORE THAN YOU DESERVE
   book by Michael Weller, lyrics by Michael Weller and Jim
   Steinman, music by Jim Steinman; directed by Kim Friedman

1853 THE ORPHAN
   by David Rabe; directed by Jeff Bleckner

1854 SIAMESE CONNECTIONS
   by Dennis J. Reardon; directed by David Schweizer

1855 WEDDING BAND
   by Alice Childress; directed by Alice Childress and Joseph Papp

1856 WINNING HEARTS AND MINDS
   (adapted from *Winning Hearts and Minds: War Poems by Vietnam
   Veterans*) adapted by Paula Kay Pierce, edited by Larry Rottman,
   Jan Barry, and Basil T. Paquet; directed by Paula Kay Pierce

1973-1974 (Winter)

1857 THE AU PAIR MAN
   by Hugh Leonard; directed by Gerald Freedman

1858 THE DANCE OF DEATH
   by August Strindberg, adapted by A.J. Antoon from the Elizabeth
   Sprigge translation; directed by A.J. Antoon

1859 IN THE BOOM BOOM ROOM
   by David Rabe; directed by Joseph Papp

1860 SHORT EYES
   by Miguel Pinero; directed by Marvin Felix Camillo

1861 THE TEMPEST
   by William Shakespeare; directed by Edward Berkeley

1862 WHAT THE WINE-SELLERS BUY
   by Ron Milner; directed by Michael Schultz

1974-1975 (Winter)

1863   APPLE PIE (AN OPEN REHEARSAL)
        by Myrna Lamb, music by Nicholas Meyers; directed by Rae Allen

1864   A CHORUS LINE
        book by James Kirkwood and Nicholas Dante, music by Marvin
        Hamlisch, lyrics by Edward Kleban; directed by Michael Bennett

1865   THE LEAF PEOPLE
        by Dennis Reardon; directed by Tom O'Horgan

1866   TRELAWNY OF THE "WELLS"
        by Sir Arthur Wing Pinero; directed by A.J. Antoon

PHOENIX THEATRE

1960-1961

1867   SHE STOOPS TO CONQUER
        by Oliver Goldsmith, music by Lee Hoiby; directed by Stuart
        Vaughan

1964-1965

1868   WAR AND PEACE
        (based on the novel by Leo Tolstoy) adapted by Alfred Neumann,
        Erwin Piscator, and Guntram Prufer, English version of novel
        by Robert David MacDonald; directed by Ellis Rabb

1969-1970

1869   THE CRIMINALS
        by Jose Triana, adapted by Adrian Mitchell; directed by David
        Wheeler

1970-1971

1870   THE TRIAL OF THE CATONSVILLE NINE
        by Daniel Berrigan, S.J.; directed by Gordon Davidson

1971-1972

1871   MURDEROUS ANGELS
        by Conor Cruise O'Brien; directed by Gordon Davidson

1972-1973

1872   DON JUAN
        by Moliere, adapted by Stephen Porter; directed by Stephen
        Porter. Performed the same evening as *The Great God Brown*

1873   THE GREAT GOD BROWN
        by Eugene O'Neill; directed by Harold Prince. Performed the
        same evening as *Don Juan*

1973-1974*

1874   CHEMIN DE FER
        by Georges Feydeau, adapted by Suzanne Grossmann and Paxton
        Whitehead; directed by Stephen Porter

1875   HOLIDAY
        by Philip Barry; directed by Michael Montel

1876   THE VISIT
        by Friedrich Duerrenmatt, adapted by Maurice Valency; directed
        by Harold Prince

1974-1975*

1877   LOVE FOR LOVE
        by William Congreve; directed by Harold Prince

1878   THE MEMBER OF THE WEDDING
        by Carson McCullers; directed by Michael Montel

1879   THE RULES OF THE GAME
        by Luigi Pirandello, translated by William Murray; directed by
        Stephen Porter

REPERTORY THEATRE OF LINCOLN CENTER

1964-1965

1880   AFTER THE FALL
        by Arthur Miller; directed by Elia Kazan

1881   THE CHANGELING
        by Thomas Middleton and William Rowley; directed by Elia Kazan

1882   INCIDENT AT VICHY
        by Arthur Miller; directed by Harold Clurman

1883   TARTUFFE
        by Moliere, translated by Richard Wilbur; directed by William
        Ball

1965-1966

1884   THE CAUCASIAN CHALK CIRCLE
        by Bertolt Brecht, English version by Eric Bentley; directed
        by Jules Irving

1885   THE CONDEMNED OF ALTONA
        by Jean-Paul Sartre, adapted by Justin O'Brien; directed by
        Herbert Blau

---

* The three plays for this season are contained in one program.

1886   THE COUNTRY WIFE
         by William Wycherley; directed by Robert Symonds

1887   DANTON'S DEATH
         by Georg Buechner; directed by Herbert Blau

                              1966-1967

1888   THE ALCHEMIST
         by Ben Jonson; directed by Jules Irving

1889   THE EAST WIND
         by Leo Lehman; directed by Robert Symonds

1890   GALILEO
         by Bertolt Brecht, English version by Charles Laughton;
         directed by John Hirsch

1891   YERMA
         by Federico Garcia Lorca, translated by W.S. Merwin; directed
         by John Hirsch

                              1967-1968

1892   CYRANO DE BERGERAC
         by Edmond Rostand, English version by James Forsyth; directed
         by Carl Weber

1893   HAPPINESS
         by Mayo Simon; directed by George L. Sherman. Performed at the
         Forum, the same evening as *Walking to Waldheim*

1894   THE LITTLE FOXES
         by Lillian Hellman; directed by Mike Nichols

1895   MAVROMICHAELIS
         by Patricia Broderick; directed by Patricia Broderick. Per-
         formed at the Forum

1896   SAINT JOAN
         by George Bernard Shaw; directed by John Hirsch

1897   SUMMERTREE
         by Ron Cowan; directed by David Pressman. Performed at the Forum

1898   TIGER AT THE GATES
         by Jean Giraudoux, adapted by Christopher Fry; directed by
         Anthony Quayle

1899   WALKING TO WALDHEIM
         by Mayo Simon; directed by George L. Sherman. Performed at the
         Forum, the same evening as *Happiness*

                              1968-1969

1900   A CRY OF PLAYERS
         by William Gibson; directed by Gene Frankel

1901   AN EVENING FOR MERLIN FINCH
          by Charles Dizenzo; directed by George L. Sherman. Performed
          at the Forum

1902   GEORGE DANDIN
          by Moliere; directed by Roger Planchon

1903   IN THE MATTER OF J. ROBERT OPPENHEIMER
          (a play freely adapted on the basis of documents by Heinar
          Kipphardt) by Heinar Kipphardt, translated by Ruth Speirs;
          directed by Gordon Davidson

1904   THE INNER JOURNEY
          by James Hanley; directed by Jules Irving

1905   KING LEAR
          by William Shakespeare; directed by Gerald Freedman

1906   LOVERS
          by Brian Friel; directed by Hilton Edwards

1907   THE MISER
          by Moliere, translated by H. Baker and J. Miller; directed by
          Carl Weber

1908   THE PROGRESS OF BORA, THE TAILOR*
          by Alexander Popovic; directed by Branko Plesa

1909   TARTUFFE
          by Moliere; directed by Roger Planchon

1910   THE THREE MUSKETEERS
          by Alexandre Dumas, adapted by Roger Planchon; directed by
          Roger Planchon

1911   UBU-ROI (KING UBU)*
          by Alfred Jarry, translated by Ivanka Markovic and Svetlana
          Termacic, songs adapted by Ivan Lalic, music by Vojislav Kostic
          and adapted by Ljubomir Draskic; directed by Ljubomir Draskic

1912   VICTOR, OR THE CHILDREN TAKE OVER*
          by Roger Vitrac; directed by Mica Popovic

1913   WHO'S AFRAID OF VIRGINIA WOOLF?*
          by Edward Albee, translated by Ileana Cosic; directed by Mica
          Trailovic

1914   THE YEAR BOSTON WON THE PENNANT
          by John Ford Noonan; directed by Tim Ward

                            1969-1970

1915   CAMINO REAL
          by Tennessee Williams; directed by Milton Katselas

---

* Performed by Atelje 212, an avant-guard theatre group from Yugoslavia.

1916   OPERATION SIDEWINDER
        by Sam Shepard; directed by Michael Schultz

                            1970-1971

1917   ANTIGONE
        by Sophocles, English version by Dudley Fitts and Robert
        Fitzgerald; directed by John Hirsch

1918   AN ENEMY OF THE PEOPLE
        by Henrik Ibsen, adapted by Arthur Miller; directed by Jules
        Irving

1919   THE GOOD WOMAN OF SETZUAN
        by Bertolt Brecht, translated by Ralph Manheim; directed by
        Robert Symonds

1920   LANDSCAPE
        by Harold Pinter; directed by Peter Gill. Performed at the
        Forum, the same evening as *Silence*

1921   PICTURES IN THE HALLWAY
        by Sean O'Casey, adapted by Paul Shyre; directed by Paul Shyre.
        Performed at the Forum

1922   PLAY STRINDBERG
        by Friedrich Duerrenmatt, translated by James Kirkup; directed
        by Daniel Sullivan. Performed at the Forum; American premiere

1923   THE PLAYBOY OF THE WESTERN WORLD
        by J.M. Synge; directed by John Hirsch

1924   SCENES FROM AMERICAN LIFE
        by A.R. Gurney, Jr.; directed by Daniel Sullivan. Performed at
        the Forum

1925   SILENCE
        by Harold Pinter; directed by Peter Gill. Performed at the
        Forum, the same evening as *Landscape*

                            1971-1972

1926   MARY STUART
        by Friedrich Schiller, translated and adapted by Stephen
        Spender; directed by Jules Irving. Performed at the Forum

1927   PEOPLE ARE LIVING THERE
        by Athol Fugard; directed by John Berry. Performed at the Forum

                            1972-1973

1928   ACT WITHOUT WORDS
        by Samuel Beckett; directed by Alan Schneider. Performed at
        the Forum, the same evening as *Happy Days*, *Krapp's Last Tape*,
        and *Not I*, under the title of *Samuel Beckett Festival*

1929 ENEMIES
   by Maxim Gorky, English version by Jeremy Brooks and Kitty
   Hunter-Blair; directed by Ellis Rabb

1930 HAPPY DAYS
   by Samuel Beckett; directed by Alan Schneider. Performed at
   the Forum, the same evening as *Act Without Words*, *Krapp's Last*
   Tape, and *Not I*, under the title of *Samuel Beckett Festival*

1931 KRAPP'S LAST TAPE
   by Samuel Beckett; directed by Alan Schneider. Performed at
   the Forum, the same evening as *Act Without Words*, *Happy Days*,
   and *Not I*, under the title of *Samuel Beckett Festival*

1932 THE MERCHANT OF VENICE
   by William Shakespeare; directed by Ellis Rabb

1933 NOT I
   by Samuel Beckett; directed by Alan Schneider. Performed at
   the Forum, the same evening as *Act Without Words*, *Happy Days*,
   and *Krapp's Last Tape*, under the title of *Samuel Beckett*
   Festival

1934 THE PLOUGH AND THE STARS
   by Sean O'Casey; directed by Daniel Sullivan

ROUNDABOUT THEATRE COMPANY

1966-1967

1935 THE FATHER
   by August Strindberg; directed by Gene Feist

1936 PELLEAS AND MELISANDE
   by Maurice Maeterlinck; directed by Gene Feist

1970-1971

1937 HAMLET
   by William Shakespeare; directed by Gene Feist

1938 UNCLE VANYA
   by Anton Chekhov; directed by Gene Feist

1971-1972

1939 CONDITIONS OF AGREEMENT
   by John Whiting; directed by Gene Feist

1940 THE CREDITORS
   by August Strindberg; directed by Nancy Rhodes and Sterling B.
   Jensen. Summer season; performed the same evening as *The Lover*

1941   THE LOVER
        by Harold Pinter; directed by Nancy Rhodes and Sterling B.
        Jensen. Summer season; performed the same evening as *The
        Creditors*

1942   THE MASTER BUILDER
        by Henrik Ibsen, translated by Michael Meyer; directed by
        Gene Feist

1943   THE TAMING OF THE SHREW
        by William Shakespeare; directed by Gene Feist and Gui Andrisano

1972-1973

1944   ANTON CHEKHOV'S GARDEN PARTY
        (adapted from the works of Anton Chekhov) by Elihu Winer;
        directed by Gene Feist

1945   FILLING THE HOLE
        by Donald Kvares; directed by Nancy Rubin. Performed the same
        evening as *Modern Statuary*, *A Piece of Fog*, and *Strangulation*,
        under the title of *American Gothic*

1946   GHOSTS
        by Henrik Ibsen; directed by Gene Feist

1947   MODERN STATUARY
        by Donald Kvares; directed by Nancy Rhodes. Performed the same
        evening as *Filling the Hole*, *A Piece of Fog*, and *Strangulation*,
        under the title of *American Gothic*

1948   A PIECE OF FOG
        by Donald Kvares; directed by Frank Errante. Performed the
        same evening as *Filling the Hole*, *Modern Statuary*, and
        Strangulation, under the title of *American Gothic*

1949   THE PLAY'S THE THING
        by Ferenc Molnar, adapted by P.G. Wodehouse; directed by Gene
        Feist

1950   RIGHT YOU ARE (IF YOU THINK YOU ARE)
        by Luigi Pirandello, English version by Eric Bentley; directed
        by Gene Feist

1951   STRANGULATION
        by Donald Kvares; directed by Frank Errante. Performed the
        same evening as *Filling the Hole*, *Modern Statuary*, and *A Piece
        of Fog*, under the title of *American Gothic*

1973-1974

1952   THE BURNT FLOWER BED
        by Ugo Betti; directed by Paul Aaron

1953   THE CARETAKER
        by Harold Pinter; directed by Gene Feist

1954   THE CIRCLE
        by W. Somerset Maugham; directed by Gene Feist

1955   THE DEATH OF LORD CHATTERLY
        by Christopher Frank; directed by Henry Pillsbury. Performed
        the same evening as *Miss Julie*

1956   THE FATHER
        by August Strindberg, adapted by Gene Feist; directed by Gene
        Feist

1957   MISS JULIE
        by August Strindberg; directed by Henry Pillsbury. Performed
        the same evening as *The Death of Lord Chatterly*

1958   THE SEA GULL
        by Anton Chekhov, adapted by Gene Feist; directed by Gene Feist

                        1974-1975

1959   ALL MY SONS
        by Arthur Miller; directed by Gene Feist. Inaugural performance

1960   JAMES JOYCE'S DUBLINERS
        by J.W. Riordan, music and lyrics by Philip Campenella;
        directed by Gene Feist

1961   A MUSICAL MERCHANT OF VENICE
        by William Shakespeare, music by Jim Smith, lyrics by Tony
        Tanner; directed by Tony Tanner. A Stage Two production

1962   THE RIVALS
        by Richard Brinsley Sheridan; directed by Michael Bawtree

1963   ROSMERSHOLM
        by Henrik Ibsen; directed by Raphael Kelly. A Stage Two
        production

                        1975-1976

1964   SUMMER AND SMOKE
        by Tennessee Williams; directed by Gene Feist

Oklahoma City, OK

MUMMERS THEATRE

                        1964-1965

1965   BUS STOP
        by William Inge; directed by Jack Jones

1966   HARVEY
        by Mary Chase; directed by Jack Jones

1967   LONG DAY'S JOURNEY INTO NIGHT
            by Eugene O'Neill; directed by Mack Scism

1968   THE NIGHT OF THE IGUANA
            by Tennessee Williams; directed by Mack Scism

1969   ONLY IN AMERICA
            (based on the book by Harry Golden) by Jerome Lawrence and
            Robert E. Lee; directed by Jack Jones

1970   THE REMARKABLE MR. PENNYPACKER
            by Liam O'Brien; directed by Mack Scism

1971   WHO'LL SAVE THE PLOWBOY?
            by Frank Gilroy; directed by Mack Scism

                                1965-1966

1972   ARSENIC AND OLD LACE
            by Joseph Kesselring; directed by Joseph B. Sax

1973   THE DEVIL'S DISCIPLE
            by George Bernard Shaw; directed by Jack Jones

1974   THE DISENCHANTED
            (based on the novel by Budd Schulberg) by Budd Schulberg and
            Harvey Breit; directed by Mack Scism

1975   THE GLASS MENAGERIE
            by Tennessee Williams; directed by Mack Scism

1976   THE LITTLE FOXES
            by Lillian Hellman; directed by Jack Jones

1977   LOOK HOMEWARD, ANGEL
            (based on the novel by Thomas Wolfe) by Ketti Frings; directed
            by Jack Jones

1978   VOLPONE
            by Ben Jonson; directed by Mack Scism

                                1966-1967

1979   AH, WILDERNESS!
            by Eugene O'Neill; directed by Dallet Norris

1980   MADEMOISELLE COLOMBE
            by Jean Anouilh; directed by Joseph B. Sax

1981   MAJOR BARBARA
            by George Bernard Shaw; directed by Mack Scism

1982   RASHOMON
            (based on stories by Ryunosuke Akutagawa) by Fay and Michael
            Kanin; directed by Jack Jones

1983   THE TAVERN
            by George M. Cohan; directed by Joanne Combs

1984   TWO FOR THE SEESAW
            by William Gibson; directed by Jack Jones

                            1967-1968

1985   ARMS AND THE MAN
            by George Bernard Shaw; directed by Jean E. McFaddin

1986   LIFE WITH MOTHER
            (based on the book by Clarence Day, Jr.) by Howard Lindsay and
            Russel Crouse; directed by Jack Jones

1987   THE MEMBER OF THE WEDDING
            by Carson McCullers; directed by Mack Scism

1988   NIGHT OF THE DUNCE
            by Frank Gagliano; directed by Mack Scism

1989   RIGHT YOU ARE (IF YOU THINK YOU ARE)
            by Luigi Pirandello; directed by Mack Scism

1990   STRANGE BEDFELLOWS
            by Florence Ryerson and Colin Clements; directed by Jean E.
            McFaddin

1991   THE THREE SISTERS
            by Anton Chekhov, translated by Anya Lachman and Mack Scism;
            directed by Mack Scism

                            1968-1969

1992   BIG FISH, LITTLE FISH
            by Hugh Wheeler; directed by Jean E. McFaddin

1993   HEDDA GABLER
            by Henrik Ibsen; directed by Andrew Way

1994   MISALLIANCE
            by George Bernard Shaw; directed by Jean E. McFaddin

1995   STATE OF THE UNION
            by Howard Lindsay and Russel Crouse, newly adapted by Jeanette
            Edmondson; directed by Mack Scism

                            1969-1970

1996   BLACK COMEDY
            by Peter Shaffer; directed by Jean E. McFaddin

1997   BLITHE SPIRIT
            by Noel Coward; directed by Mack Scism

1998   THE PURSUIT OF HAPPINESS
          by Lawrence Langner and Armina Marshall Langner; directed by
          Jean E. McFaddin

1999   SPOON RIVER ANTHOLOGY
          by Edgar Lee Masters, conceived, adapted, and arranged by
          Charles Aidman; directed by John Wylie

                            1970-1971*

2000   ARSENIC AND OLD LACE
          by Joseph Kesselring; directed by John Wylie

2001   DEAR LIAR
          (based on correspondence of George Bernard Shaw and Mrs.
          Patricia Campbell) by Jerome Kilty; directed by Mack Scism

2002   A MAN FOR ALL SEASONS
          by Robert Bolt; directed by Porter Van Zandt

2003   THE MISANTHROPE
          by Moliere, translated by Richard Wilbur; directed by John
          Wylie

2004   THE RIVALRY
          by Norman Corwin; directed by John Wylie

2005   THE WORLD OF CARL SANDBERG
          by Norman Corwin; directed by Saylor Creswell

                            1971-1972

2006   DAMES AT SEA
          book and lyrics by George Haimsohn and Robin Miller, music by
          Jim Wise; directed by David Christmas

2007   THE MAN WHO CAME TO DINNER
          by Moss Hart and George S. Kaufman; directed by John (Jack)
          Going

2008   THE ODD COUPLE
          by Neil Simon; directed by Mack Scism

2009   THE TAMING OF THE SHREW
          by William Shakespeare, adapted by John Wylie; directed by
          John Wylie

---

* Inaugural season in new theatre.

Pasadena, CA

PASADENA PLAYHOUSE

1965-1966

2010   DARK OF THE MOON
by Howard Richardson and William Berney; directed by Charles Rome Smith

2011   THE DEVIL'S DISCIPLE
by George Bernard Shaw; directed by Stuart Margolin

2012   THE FIREBUGS
by Max Frisch, translated by Mordecai Gorelik; directed by C. Lowell Lees. Performed the same evening as *The Shoemaker's Prodigious Wife*

2013   LOVE FOR LOVE
by William Congreve; directed by Claude Woolman

2014   PEER GYNT
by Henrik Ibsen, adapted by C. Lowell Lees; directed by C. Lowell Lees

2015   RICHARD III
by William Shakespeare; directed by C. Lowell Lees

2016   THE SHOEMAKER'S PRODIGIOUS WIFE
by Federico Garcia Lorca, translated by James Graham-Lujan and Richard L. O'Connell; directed by C. Lowell Lees. Performed the same evening as *The Firebugs*

Philadelphia, PA

PHILADELPHIA DRAMA GUILD

1973-1974

2017   DEATH OF A SALESMAN
by Arthur Miller; directed by George C. Scott

2018   THE LITTLE FOXES
by Lillian Hellman; directed by Philip Minor

2019   THE ROSE TATTOO
by Tennessee Williams; directed by Jeff Bleckner

2020   THE TAMING OF THE SHREW
by William Shakespeare; directed by Malcolm Black

1974-1975

2021   ARDELE
by Jean Anouilh, translated by Lucienne Hill; directed by
Douglas Seale

2022   THE IMPORTANCE OF BEING EARNEST
by Oscar Wilde; directed by Douglas Seale

2023   LONG DAY'S JOURNEY INTO NIGHT
by Eugene O'Neill; directed by Richard Maltby, Jr.

2024   MISALLIANCE
by George Bernard Shaw; directed by Paxton Whitehead

THEATRE OF THE LIVING ARTS

1964-1965*

2025   DESIRE UNDER THE ELMS
by Eugene O'Neill; directed by Charles Olsen

2026   ENDGAME
by Samuel Beckett; directed by Andre Gregory

2027   GALILEO
by Bertolt Brecht; directed by Andre Gregory

2028   THE MISANTHROPE
by Moliere, translated by Richard Wilbur; directed by George L.
Sherman

2029   TIGER AT THE GATES
by Jean Giraudoux; directed by John O'Shaughnessy

1965-1966

2030   THE CRITIC
by Richard Brinsley Sheridan; directed by George L. Sherman

2031   THE LAST ANALYSIS
by Saul Bellow; directed by George L. Sherman

2032   MISS JULIE
by August Strindberg, translated by Arvid Paulson; directed by
George L. Sherman

2033   POOR BITOS
by Jean Anouilh; directed by Andre Gregory

2034   THE STRONGER
by August Strindberg, translated by Alex Szogyi; directed by
George L. Sherman

* Inaugural season.

2058   IT SHOULD HAPPEN TO A DOG
        by Wolf Mankowitz; directed by Pamela Hawthorn. Performed the
        same evening as *The Second Shepherds Pageant* and *The Words
        Upon the Window Pane*, under the title of *Three One Act Plays*

2059   THE SECOND SHEPHERDS PAGEANT
        directed by Bryan Hull. Performed the same evening as *It Should
        Happen To a Dog* and *The Words Upon the Window Pane*, under the
        title of *Three One Act Plays*

2060   TWELFTH NIGHT
        by William Shakespeare; directed by Jon Jory

2061   THE WORDS UPON THE WINDOW PANE
        by W.B. Yeats; directed by Arthur W. Lithgow. Performed the
        same evening as *It Should Happen To a Dog* and *The Second
        Shepherds Pageant*, under the title of *Three One Act Plays*

                            1968-1969

2062   AS YOU LIKE IT
        by William Shakespeare; directed by John Lithgow

2063   CHARLEY'S AUNT
        by Brandon Thomas; directed by Robert Blackburn

2064   THE GLASS MENAGERIE
        by Tennessee Williams; directed by Gordon Phillips

2065   KRAPP'S LAST TAPE
        by Samuel Beckett; directed by Arthur W. Lithgow and Gordon
        Phillips. Performed the same evening as *Oedipus the King*

2066   OEDIPUS THE KING
        by Sophocles; directed by Arthur W. Lithgow and Gordon
        Phillips. Performed the same evening as *Krapp's Last Tape*

2067   THE SCARECROW
        by Percy MacKaye; directed by Robert Blackburn

2068   THE THREE SISTERS
        by Anton Chekhov; directed by Tom Brennan

2069   THE VILLAGE: A PARTY
        by Charles H. Fuller, Jr.; directed by Arthur W. Lithgow

                            1969-1970

2070   AH, WILDERNESS!
        by Eugene O'Neill; directed by Robert Blackburn

2071   THE BIRTHDAY PARTY
        by Harold Pinter; directed by Arthur W. Lithgow

2072   THE FIREBUGS
        by Max Frisch, translated by Mordecai Gorelik; directed by
        Tom Brennan

2073   MUCH ADO ABOUT NOTHING
        by William Shakespeare; directed by John Lithgow

2074   OF MICE AND MEN
        by John Steinbeck; directed by Robert Blackburn

2075   PYGMALION
        by George Bernard Shaw; directed by Brendan Burke

2076   THE WAY OF THE WORLD
        by William Congreve; directed by John Lithgow

                        1970-1971

2077   ALL MY SONS
        by Arthur Miller; directed by Arthur W. Lithgow

2078   CAESAR AT THE RUBICON
        by Theodore H. White; directed by Arthur W. Lithgow. World
        premiere

2079   THE HOMECOMING
        by Harold Pinter; directed by Louis Criss

2080   THE IMPORTANCE OF BEING EARNEST
        by Oscar Wilde; directed by Russell L. Treyz

2081   LITTLE MURDERS
        by Jules Feiffer; directed by Russell L. Treyz

2082   MACBETH
        by William Shakespeare; directed by Russell L. Treyz

2083   A RAISIN IN THE SUN
        by Lorraine Hansberry; directed by Eric Krebs

                        1972-1973

2084   AGAMEMNON
        by William Alfred; directed by Hovhanness I. Pilikian

2085   LOOT
        by Joe Orton; directed by Edward Payson Call

2086   ROSMERSHOLM
        by Henrik Ibsen; directed by Louis Criss

2087   THE TEMPEST
        by William Shakespeare; directed by Louis Criss

2088   THE TOOTH OF THE CRIME
        by Sam Shepard; directed by Louis Criss

                        1973-1974

2089   THE DAUGHTER IN LAW
        by D.H. Lawrence; directed by John Pasquin

2090   THE ENTERTAINER
        by John Osborne; directed by Carl Weber

2091   THE SEA GULL
        by Anton Chekhov; directed by Louis Criss

                        1974-1975

2092   BEYOND THE HORIZON
        by Eugene O'Neill; directed by Michael Kahn

2093   KINGDOM OF EARTH
        by Tennessee Williams; directed by Garland Wright

2094   MOTHER COURAGE AND HER CHILDREN
        by Bertolt Brecht, English version by Eric Bentley; directed
        by Michael Kahn

2095   ROMEO AND JULIET
        by William Shakespeare; directed by Michael Kahn

2096   'TIS PITY SHE'S A WHORE
        by John Ford; directed by Michael Kahn

Providence, RI

TRINITY SQUARE REPERTORY COMPANY

                        1964-1965

2097   ALL TO HELL LAUGHING
        by Trevanian; directed by Adrian Hall

2098   THE AMERICAN DREAM
        by Edward Albee; directed by Adrian Hall

2099   ADAPTATION
        by Elaine May; directed by Joel J. Friedman. Performed the
        same evening as *Next*
2100   DARK OF THE MOON
        by Howard Richardson and William Berney; directed by Adrian
        Hall

2101   DESIRE UNDER THE ELMS
        by Eugene O'Neill; directed by Adrian Hall

2102   DON JUAN IN HELL
        by George Bernard Shaw; directed by Adrian Hall

2103   THE HOUSE OF BERNARDA ALBA
        by Federico Garcia Lorca; directed by Ira Zuckerman

2104   THE REHEARSAL
          by Jean Anouilh, English version by Pamela Hansford Johnson
          and Kitty Black; directed by Adrian Hall

2105   UNCLE VANYA
          by Anton Chekhov, translated by Robert W. Corrigan; directed
          by George Keathley

2106   THE ZOO STORY
          by Edward Albee; directed by Adrian Hall

                              1965-1966

2107   THE BALCONY
          by Jean Genet; directed by Adrian Hall

2108   THE CRUCIBLE
          by Arthur Miller; directed by Adrian Hall

2109   THE ETERNAL HUSBAND
          (based on the novelette by Fyodor Dostoevsky) by Gabriel
          Gladstone; directed by Adrian Hall

2110   LONG DAY'S JOURNEY INTO NIGHT
          by Eugene O'Neill; directed by Adrian Hall

2111   THE PLAYBOY OF THE WESTERN WORLD
          by J.M. Synge; directed by Philip Minor

2112   TARTUFFE
          by Moliere, English translation by Richard Wilbur; directed by
          Adrian Hall

2113   TWELFTH NIGHT
          by William Shakespeare; directed by Stephen Porter

                              1966-1967

2114   AH, WILDERNESS!
          by Eugene O'Neill; directed by Rocco Bufano

2115   THE BIRTHDAY PARTY
          by Harold Pinter; directed by Adrian Hall

2116   THE GRASS HARP
          (based on the novel by Truman Capote) book and lyrics by
          Kenward Elmslie; directed by Adrian Hall. World premiere

2117   A MIDSUMMER NIGHT'S DREAM
          by William Shakespeare; directed by Louis Beachner

2118   SAINT JOAN
          by George Bernard Shaw; directed by Adrian Hall

2119   A STREETCAR NAMED DESIRE
          by Tennessee Williams; directed by Adrian Hall

2120 THE THREE SISTERS
   by Anton Chekhov, translated by Robert W. Corrigan; directed
   by Adrian Hall

1967-1968

2121 THE IMPORTANCE OF BEING EARNEST
   by Oscar Wilde; directed by Henry Butler

2122 JULIUS CAESAR
   by William Shakespeare; directed by Adrian Hall

2123 PHAEDRA
   by Jean-Baptiste Racine, English version by Robert Lowell;
   directed by Adrian Hall

2124 THE THREEPENNY OPERA
   text and lyrics by Bertolt Brecht, music by Kurt Weill, English
   adaptation by Marc Blitzstein; directed by Adrian Hall

2125 YEARS OF THE LOCUST
   by Norman Holland; directed by Adrian Hall

1968-1969

2126 BILLY BUDD
   by Herman Melville; directed by Adrian Hall

2127 BROTHER TO DRAGONS
   by Robert Penn Warren; directed by Adrian Hall

2128 EXILES
   by James Joyce; directed by Adrian Hall

2129 MACBETH
   by William Shakespeare; directed by Adrian Hall

2130 RED ROSES FOR ME
   by Sean O'Casey; directed by Adrian Hall

1969-1970

2131 HOUSE OF BREATH
   by William Goyen; directed by Adrian Hall

2132 THE OLD GLORY
   by Robert Lowell; directed by Adrian Hall

2133 WILSON IN THE PROMISED LAND
   by Roland Van Zandt; directed by Adrian Hall

1970-1971

2134 ADAPTATION
   by Elaine May; directed by Wayne Carson. Bridgham Street
   Series; performed the same evening as *Next*

2135 THE GOOD AND BAD TIMES OF CADY FRANCIS McCULLUM AND FRIENDS
by Portia Bohn; directed by Adrian Hall. Bridgham Street Series

2136 HARVEY
by Mary Chase; directed by Philip Minor. Bridgham Street Series

2137 LITTLE MURDERS
by Jules Feiffer; directed by William Cain. Bridgham Street
Series

2138 LOVE FOR LOVE
by William Congreve; directed by Philip Minor. Market Square
Series

2139 NEXT
by Terrence McNally; directed by Wayne Carson. Bridgham Street
Series; performed the same evening as *Adaptation*

2140 SON OF MAN AND THE FAMILY
by Timothy Taylor and Adrian Hall; directed by Adrian Hall.
Market Square Series

2141 THE TAMING OF THE SHREW
by William Shakespeare; directed by Adrian Hall. Market Square
Series

2142 THE THREEPENNY OPERA
text and lyrics by Bertolt Brecht, music by Kurt Weill, English
adaptation by Marc Blitzstein; directed by Adrian Hall

2143 YOU CAN'T TAKE IT WITH YOU
by Moss Hart and George S. Kaufman; directed by Adrian Hall.
Bridgham Street Series

1971-1972

2144 CHILD'S PLAY
by Robert Marasco; directed by Adrian Hall

2145 DOWN BY THE RIVER WHERE WATERLILIES ARE DISFIGURED EVERY DAY
by Julie Bovasso; directed by Adrian Hall

2146 THE PRICE
by Arthur Miller; directed by Larry Arrick

2147 THE SCHOOL FOR WIVES
by Moliere, English translation by Richard Wilbur; directed by
Adrian Hall

2148 TROILUS AND CRESSIDA
by William Shakespeare; directed by Adrian Hall

1972-1973

2149   LADY AUDLEY'S SECRET
        (adapted from the novel by Mary Elizabeth Bradden) by Douglas
        Seale, music by George Goehring, lyrics by John Kuntz; directed
        by Word Baker

2150   OLD TIMES
        by Harold Pinter; directed by Jacques Cartier

2151   THE ROYAL HUNT OF THE SUN
        by Peter Shaffer; directed by Adrian Hall

2152   THE SCHOOL FOR WIVES
        by Moliere, English translation by Richard Wilbur; directed by
        Adrian Hall

1973-1974*

2153   AIMEE
        book and lyrics by William Goyen; directed by Adrian Hall

2154   ALFRED THE GREAT
        by Israel Horovitz; directed by James Hammerstein

2155   BROTHER TO DRAGONS
        by Robert Penn Warren; directed by Adrian Hall

2156   FOR THE USE OF THE HALL
        by Oliver Hailey; directed by Word Baker. World premiere

2157   GHOST DANCE
        by Stuart Vaughan; directed by Stuart Vaughan

2158   A MAN FOR ALL SEASONS
        by Robert Bolt; directed by Adrian Hall

2159   SHERLOCK HOLMES
        by William Gillette, adapted by Dennis Rosa; directed by
        Dennis Rosa

2160   THE TOOTH OF THE CRIME
        by Sam Shepard; directed by Larry Arrick

1974-1975*

2161   THE EMPEROR HENRY
        by Luigi Pirandello; directed by Brooks Jones

2162   JUMPERS
        by Tom Stoppard; directed by Word Baker

---

* Programs for these seasons contain interesting biographical notes and
  background information.

2163   PEER GYNT
       by Henrik Ibsen, adapted by Adrian Hall and Richard Cumming;
       directed by Adrian Hall

2164   SEVEN KEYS TO BALDPATE
       by George M. Cohan; directed by Adrian Hall

2165   TOM JONES
       by Henry Fielding, adapted by Larry Arrick and Barbara
       Damashek; directed by Larry Arrick

2166   WELL HUNG
       by Robert Lord; directed by Adrian Hall. American premiere

Richmond, VA

VIRGINIA MUSEUM THEATRE

1961-1962

2167   LIFE WITH MOTHER
       (based on the book by Clarence Day, Jr.) by Howard Lindsay and
       Russel Crouse; directed by Robert S. Telford

1963-1964

2168   ALL THE WAY HOME
       (based on *A Death in the Family* by James Agee) by Tad Mosel;
       directed by Zeke Berlin

2169   AUNTIE MAME
       (based on the novel by Patrick Dennis) by Jerome Lawrence and
       Robert E. Lee; directed by Robert S. Telford

2170   HAMLET
       by William Shakespeare; directed by Robert S. Telford

2171   THE KING AND I
       (based on *Anna and the King of Siam* by Margaret Landon) book
       and lyrics by Oscar Hammerstein II, music by Richard Rodgers;
       directed by Robert S. Telford

2172   A THOUSAND CLOWNS
       by Herb Gardner; directed by Robert S. Telford

1964-1965

2173   THE ADMIRABLE CRICHTON
       by Sir James Barrie; directed by Robert S. Telford

2174   HEDDA GABLER
       by Henrik Ibsen, translated by Kai Jurgensen and Robert
       Shenkkan; directed by Kai Jurgensen

2175   NO TIME FOR SERGEANTS
          by Ira Levin; directed by Robert S. Telford

1966-1967

2176   THE MIRACLE WORKER
          by William Gibson; directed by James Dyas

2177   OKLAHOMA!
          (based on *Green Grow the Lilacs* by Lynn Riggs) book and lyrics
          by Oscar Hammerstein II, music by Richard Rodgers; directed by
          James Dyas

2178   THE SUBJECT WAS ROSES
          by Frank D. Gilroy; directed by James Dyas

1967-1968

2179   THE SCHOOL FOR WIVES
          by Moliere, free version by Miles Malleson; directed by James
          Dyas

2180   THE WOMEN
          by Clare Booth Luce; directed by James Dyas

1972-1973*

2181   A CHRISTMAS CAROL
          by Charles Dickens; directed by Keith Fowler and James Kirkland

2182   CYRANO DE BERGERAC
          by Edmond Rostand; directed by Keith Fowler

2183   JACQUES BREL IS ALIVE AND WELL AND LIVING IN PARIS
          (based on Brel's lyrics and commentary) production conception,
          English lyrics, and additional material by Eric Blau and Mort
          Shuman; directed by Ken Letner and Don Pasco

2184   LOOT
          by Joe Orton; directed by William Prosser

2185   MACBETH
          by William Shakespeare; directed by Keith Fowler

2186   THE NIGHT THOREAU SPENT IN JAIL
          by Jerome Lawrence and Robert E. Lee; directed by Ken Letner

2187   THE ROYAL RAPE OF RUARI MACASMUNDE
          (based on the story by Richard T. Herd) by Richard F. Stockton;
          directed by Alfred Drake

---

* Inaugural professional season.

1973-1974

2188   THE BLOOD KNOT
        by Athol Fugard; directed by Robert Colston

2189   DEMOCRACY
        (based on the novels by Esther and Henry Adams) by Romulus
        Linney; directed by Keith Fowler

2190   INDIANS
        by Arthur Kopit; directed by Keith Fowler

2191   MAN WITH A LOAD OF MISCHIEF
        by Ben Tarver; directed by James Kirkland

2192   SAINT JOAN
        by George Bernard Shaw; directed by James Kirkland

2193   THE TAMING OF THE SHREW
        by William Shakespeare; directed by Keith Fowler

2194   VICTORIAN CHRISTMAS SHOW
        directed by Keith Fowler and Robert Gainer; musical director,
        William M. Smith

1974-1975

2195   KASPAR
        by Peter Handke; English version by Michael Roloff; directed
        by Gene Snow

2196   THE MISER
        by Moliere; directed by Keith Fowler

2197   OUR FATHER
        by Maxim Gorky, English adaptation by William Marion Smith;
        directed by Keith Fowler. American premiere

2198   OUR TOWN
        by Thornton Wilder; directed by R.S. Cohen

2199   PURLIE
        (a musical based on the play *Purlie Victorious* by Ossie Davis)
        by Ossie Davis, Gary Geld, Philip Rose, and Peter Udell;
        directed by Albert Reyes

2200   TOBACCO ROAD
        (based on the novel by Erskine Caldwell) by Jack Kirkland;
        directed by James Kirkland

Rochester, MI

MEADOW BROOK THEATRE

1966-1967

2201   THE CAUCASIAN CHALK CIRCLE
by Bertolt Brecht; English version by Eric Bentley; directed
by John Fernald

2202   THE IMPERIAL NIGHTINGALE
by Nicholas Stuart Gray; directed by Robin Ray

2203   LOVE'S LABOUR'S LOST
by William Shakespeare; directed by John Fernald

2204   THE THREE SISTERS
by Anton Chekhov, translated by J.P. Davis; directed by John
Fernald

2205   THE WALTZ OF THE TOREADORS
by Jean Anouilh; directed by Robin Ray

2206   YOU NEVER CAN TELL
by George Bernard Shaw; directed by Robin Ray

1967-1968

2207   AND PEOPLE ALL AROUND
by George Sklar, music, lyrics, and arrangements by Booker T.
Bradshaw, Jr.; directed by John Broome and George Guidall

2208   CHARLEY'S AUNT
by Brandon Thomas; directed by John Fernald

2209   THE FIREBUGS
by Max Frisch, translated by Mordecai Gorelik; directed by
Milo Sperber. Performed the same evening as *No Exit*

2210   THE IMPORTANCE OF BEING EARNEST
by Oscar Wilde; directed by Eric Berry

2211   KING LEAR
by William Shakespeare; directed by John Fernald

2212   NO EXIT
by Jean-Paul Sartre, adapted by Paul Bowles; directed by Milo
Sperber. Performed the same evening as *The Firebugs*

1968-1969

2213   AH, WILDERNESS!
by Eugene O'Neill; directed by Terence Kilburn

2214   THE APPLE CART
            by George Bernard Shaw; directed by Richard Curnock

2215   THE SECOND COMING OF BERT
            by Ronald Chudley; directed by John Fernald

1969-1970

2216   THE AMERICAN DREAM
            by Edward Albee; directed by Anthony J. Stimac. Performed the
            same evening as *Black Comedy*

2217   BLACK COMEDY
            by Peter Shaffer; directed by John Fernald. Performed the same
            evening as *The American Dream*

2218   THE COCKTAIL PARTY
            by T.S. Eliot; directed by Malcolm Morrison

1970-1971

2219   THE CRUCIBLE
            by Arthur Miller; directed by Terence Kilburn

2220   THE FANTASTICKS
            words by Tom Jones, music by Harvey Schmidt; directed by
            Christopher Hewett

2221   LIFE WITH FATHER
            (based on the book by Clarence Day, Jr.) by Howard Lindsay and
            Russel Crouse; directed by Joseph Shaw

2222   THE RAINMAKER
            by N. Richard Nash; directed by Terence Kilburn

2223   THE SKIN OF OUR TEETH
            by Thornton Wilder; directed by Terence Kilburn

2224   TARTUFFE
            by Moliere, English translation by Richard Wilbur; directed by
            Terence Kilburn

2225   A THOUSAND CLOWNS
            by Herb Gardner; directed by Terence Kilburn

2226   WHO'S AFRAID OF VIRGINIA WOOLF?
            by Edward Albee; directed by John Ulmer

1971-1972

2227   THE ANDERSONVILLE TRIAL
            by Saul Levitt; directed by Charles Nolte

2228   THE BOY FRIEND
            by Sandy Wilson; directed by Joseph Shaw

2229   THE GLASS MENAGERIE
by Tennessee Williams; directed by Terence Kilburn

2230   HEARTBREAK HOUSE
by George Bernard Shaw; directed by Terence Kilburn

2231   THE MATCHMAKER
by Thornton Wilder; directed by Terence Kilburn

2232   THE PRICE
by Arthur Miller; directed by John Ulmer

1972-1973

2233   BEDTIME STORY
by Sean O'Casey; directed by Terence Kilburn. Performed the same evening as *The Doctor in Spite of Himself*

2234   COUNT DRACULA
(adapted from the novel by Bram Stoker) by Ted Tiller; directed by John Ulmer

2235   THE COUNTRY GIRL
by Clifford Odets; directed by Michael Sinclair

2236   THE DOCTOR IN SPITE OF HIMSELF
by Moliere; directed by Terence Kilburn. Performed the same evening as *Bedtime Story*

2237   THE FRONT PAGE
by Ben Hecht and Charles MacArthur; directed by Charles Nolte

2238   INHERIT THE WIND
by Jerome Lawrence and Robert E. Lee; directed by Charles Nolte

2239   THE MIRACLE WORKER
by William Gibson; directed by Warren Enters

2240   RIGHT YOU ARE (IF YOU THINK YOU ARE)
by Luigi Pirandello; directed by Terence Kilburn

2241   THE TORCH BEARERS
by George Kelly; directed by Terence Kilburn

1973-1974

2242   HOW THE OTHER HALF LOVES
by Alan Ayckbourn; directed by Terence Kilburn

2243   I DO! I DO!
(based on *The Fourposter* by Jan De Hartog) by Tom Jones and Harvey Schmidt; directed by Judith Haskell; musical director, Marsha Whitaker

2244   THE MEMBER OF THE WEDDING
by Carson McCullers; directed by Terence Kilburn

2245   OEDIPUS REX
        by Sophocles, new adaptation by Charles Nolte; directed by
        Charles Nolte

2246   SPOON RIVER ANTHOLOGY
        by Edgar Lee Masters, conceived, adapted, and arranged by
        Charles Aidman; directed by John Ulmer

2247   A STREETCAR NAMED DESIRE
        by Tennessee Williams; directed by Charles Nolte

                              1974-1975

2248   DEATH OF A SALESMAN
        by Arthur Miller; directed by Charles Nolte

2249   THE DRUNKARD
        by W.H.S. Smith, adapted by Bro Herrod, music and lyrics by
        Barry Manilow; directed by John Ulmer

2250   HARVEY
        by Mary Chase; directed by Donald Ewer

2251   THE MISANTHROPE
        by Moliere, translated by Richard Wilbur; directed by Terence
        Kilburn

2252   TONIGHT AT 8:30
        by Noel Coward; directed by Terence Kilburn

2253   TWELFTH NIGHT
        by William Shakespeare; directed by Terence Kilburn

Rochester, NY

ROCHESTER SHAKESPEARE THEATRE

                              1972-1973*

2254   FABLES HERE AND THEN
        by David Feldshuh; directed by Robert E. Bilheimer

2255   RICHARD II
        by William Shakespeare; directed by Robert E. Bilheimer

2256   TWELFTH NIGHT
        by William Shakespeare; directed by Robert E. Bilheimer

---

* Inaugural season.

1973-1974

2257 THE BRUTE
by Anton Chekhov; directed by Robert E. Bilheimer. Performed the same evening as *A Marriage Proposal* and *Swan Song*, under the title of *Three By Chekhov*

2258 A MARRIAGE PROPOSAL
by Anton Chekhov; directed by Robert E. Bilheimer. Performed the same evening as *The Brute* and *Swan Song*, under the title of *Three By Chekhov*

2259 ONE FLEW OVER THE CUCKOO'S NEST
(based on the book by Ken Kesey) by Dale Wasserman; directed by Robert E. Bilheimer

2260 SWAN SONG
by Anton Chekhov; directed by Robert E. Bilheimer. Performed the same evening as *The Brute* and *A Marriage Proposal*, under the title of *Three By Chekhov*

St. Louis, MO

LORETTO-HILTON REPERTORY THEATRE

1967-1968

2261 THE CAUCASIAN CHALK CIRCLE
by Bertolt Brecht, English version by Eric Bentley; directed by Philip Minor

2262 THE MISER
by Moliere; directed by Michael Flanagan

2263 THE TIME OF YOUR LIFE
by William Saroyan; directed by James Bernardi

1969-1970

2264 ARMS AND THE MAN
by George Bernard Shaw; directed by J. Robert Dietz

2265 THE IDES OF MARCH
(adapted from the novel by Thornton Wilder) by Jerome Kilty; directed by Nagle Jackson. American premiere

2266 ONCE UPON A MATTRESS
book by Jay Thompson, Marshall Barer, and Dean Fuller, music by Mary Rodgers, lyrics by Marshall Barer; directed by Milton Lyon

2267 OTHELLO
by William Shakespeare; directed by William Woodman

2268   WILL ROGERS' U.S.A.
         adapted by Paul Shyre; directed by Paul Shyre

2269   YOU CAN'T TAKE IT WITH YOU
         by Moss Hart and George S. Kaufman; directed by Robert H.
         Livingston

1973-1974

2270   DETECTIVE STORY
         by Sidney Kingsley; directed by Davey Marlin-Jones

2271   HENRY V
         by William Shakespeare; directed by David Frank

2272   THE HOT L BALTIMORE
         by Lanford Wilson; directed by Davey Marlin-Jones

2273   THE IMAGINARY INVALID
         by Moliere; adapted by Miles Malleson; directed by John Going

2274   IRMA LA DOUCE
         original book and lyrics by Alexandre Breffort, music by
         Marguerite Monnot, English book and lyrics by Julian More,
         David Heneker, and Monty Norman; directed by Davey Marlin-Jones

1974-1975

2275   CAESAR AND CLEOPATRA
         by George Bernard Shaw; directed by Davey Marlin-Jones

2276   THE CRUCIBLE
         by Arthur Miller; directed by Gene Lesser

2277   HAVE I STAYED TOO LONG AT THE FAIR?
         by the Loretto-Hilton Company; directed by Davey Marlin-Jones

2278   INDIANS
         by Arthur Kopit; directed by Davey Marlin-Jones

2279   THE REAL INSPECTOR HOUND
         by Tom Stoppard; directed by John Dillon. Performed the same
         evening as *Trevor*

2280   TREVOR
         by John Bowen; directed by John Dillon. Performed the same
         evening as *The Real Inspector Hound*

San Diego, CA

OLD GLOBE THEATRE

1964

2281　MACBETH
　　　by William Shakespeare; directed by W. Duncan Ross

2282　MEASURE FOR MEASURE
　　　by William Shakespeare; directed by Allen Fletcher

2283　MUCH ADO ABOUT NOTHING
　　　by William Shakespeare; directed by B. Iden Payne

1965

2284　CORIOLANUS
　　　by William Shakespeare; directed by Milton Katselas

2285　KING HENRY VIII
　　　by William Shakespeare; directed by Philip Minor

2286　THE MERRY WIVES OF WINDSOR
　　　by William Shakespeare; directed by Mel Shapiro

1967

2287　ALL'S WELL THAT ENDS WELL
　　　by William Shakespeare; directed by Malcolm Black

2288　OTHELLO
　　　by William Shakespeare; directed by Milton Katselas

2289　TWELFTH NIGHT
　　　by William Shakespeare; directed by Edward Payson Call

1968

2290　AS YOU LIKE IT
　　　by William Shakespeare; directed by Robert Moss

2291　HAMLET
　　　by William Shakespeare; directed by Ellis Rabb

2292　KING JOHN
　　　by William Shakespeare; directed by Craig Noel

1972

2293　KING RICHARD III
　　　by William Shakespeare; directed by Edward Payson Call

2294   LOVE'S LABOUR'S LOST
        by William Shakespeare; directed by Eric Christmas

2295   THE MERRY WIVES OF WINDSOR
        by William Shakespeare; directed by Jack O'Brien

1973

2296   I DO! I DO!
        (based on *The Fourposter* by Jan De Hartog) by Tom Jones and
        Harvey Schmidt; directed by Craig Noel

2297   KING LEAR
        by William Shakespeare; directed by Edward Payson Call

2298   THE MERCHANT OF VENICE
        by William Shakespeare; directed by Eric Christmas

2299   PRIVATE LIVES
        by Noel Coward; directed by Craig Noel

2300   THE TWO GENTLEMEN OF VERONA
        by William Shakespeare; directed by Allen Fletcher

1974

2301   KING HENRY IV (PART 2)
        by William Shakespeare; directed by Edward Payson Call

2302   ROMEO AND JULIET
        by William Shakespeare; directed by Diana Maddox

2303   TWELFTH NIGHT
        by William Shakespeare; directed by Eric Christmas and Craig
        Noel

1974-1975

2304   ABELARD AND HELOISE
        by Ronald Miller; directed by Robert Bonaventura

2305   AFTER MAGRITTE
        by Tom Stoppard; directed by Ken Ruta. Performed the same
        evening as *The Real Inspector Hound*

2306   BUTLEY
        by Simon Gray; directed by Asaad Kelada

2307   GODSPELL
        (a musical based upon the Gospel according to *St. Matthew*)
        conceived by John-Michael Tebelak, music and lyrics by Stephen
        Schwartz; directed by Jack Tygett

2308   AN INSPECTOR CALLS
        by J.B. Priestley; directed by Craig Noel

2309   MACBETT
           by Eugene Ionesco, English translation by Charles Marowitz;
           directed by Floyd Gaffrey

2310   THE REAL INSPECTOR HOUND
           by Tom Stoppard; directed by Ken Ruta. Performed the same
           evening as *After Magritte*

2311   THE SCHOOL FOR WIVES
           by Moliere, translated by Richard Wilbur; directed by Bertram
           Tanswell

2312   THE TENTH MAN
           by Paddy Chayefsky; directed by Mark Feder

2313   YOU NEVER CAN TELL
           by George Bernard Shaw; directed by Craig Noel

2314   6 RMS RIV VU
           by Bob Randall; directed by Craig Noel

1975

2315   MEASURE FOR MEASURE
           by William Shakespeare; directed by Diana Maddox

2316   MUCH ADO ABOUT NOTHING
           by William Shakespeare; directed by Jack O'Brien

2317   THE TEMPEST
           by William Shakespeare; directed by Ellis Rabb

San Francisco, CA

ACADEMY THEATRE

1962 (Summer)

2318a   HENRY IV (PART 1)
           by William Shakespeare; directed by Mel Shapiro

2318b   MANDRAGOLA
           by Machiavelli; directed by Sydney Walter

2319a   OTHELLO
           by William Shakespeare; directed by Sydney Walter

2319b   TWELFTH NIGHT
           by William Shakespeare; directed by Mel Shapiro

1963-1964

2320a   THE HOSTAGE
           by Brendan Behan; directed by Frank Whittow

2320b   SHE STOOPS TO CONQUER
          by Oliver Goldsmith; directed by Frank Whittow

ACTOR'S WORKSHOP

1959-1960

2321   THE BIRTHDAY PARTY
          by Harold Pinter; directed by Glynne Wickham

2322   THE BUSY MARTYR
          by George Hitchcock; directed by Robert W. Goldsby

2323   THE CHAIRS
          by Eugene Ionesco, translated by Donald M. Allen; directed by
          Morgan Upton. Performed the same evening as *Jack or the
          Submission*

2324   JACK OR THE SUBMISSION
          by Eugene Ionesco, translated by Donald M. Allen; directed by
          Robert Symonds. Performed the same evening as *The Chairs*

2325   THE MARRIAGE OF MR. MISSISSIPPI
          by Friedrich Duerrenmatt; directed by Herbert Blau

2326   SAINT'S DAY
          by John Whiting; directed by David Sarvis

1960-1961

2327   KING LEAR
          by William Shakespeare; directed by Herbert Blau

2328   KRAPP'S LAST TAPE
          by Samuel Beckett; directed by Jules Irving. Performed the
          same evening as *The Zoo Story*

2329   THE MAIDS
          by Jean Genet; directed by Robert Symonds. Performed the same
          evening as *The Widow*

2330   MISALLIANCE
          by George Bernard Shaw; directed by Jules Irving

2331   THE ROCKS CRIED OUT
          by Miriam Stovall; directed by Jules Irving

2332   A TOUCH OF THE POET
          by Eugene O'Neill; directed by Herbert Blau

2333   TWINKLING OF AN EYE
          by H.W. Wright and Guy Andros; directed by Alan Schneider

2334   THE WIDOW
          by Edwin Honig; directed by Robert Symonds. Performed the same
          evening as *The Maids*

2335   THE ZOO STORY
        by Edward Albee; directed by Jules Irving. Performed the same
        evening as *Krapp's Last Tape*

1961-1962

2336   BECKET
        by Jean Anouilh, translated by Lucienne Hill; directed by
        Robert W. Goldsby. Program contains an introduction by the
        author

2337   THE DANCE OF DEATH
        by August Strindberg, adapted by Elizabeth Sprigge; directed
        by Robert Symonds

2338   HENRY IV (PART 1)
        by William Shakespeare; directed by Jules Irving

2339   KRAPP'S LAST TAPE
        by Samuel Beckett; directed by Jules Irving

2340   SERJEANT MUSGRAVE'S DANCE
        by John Arden; directed by Herbert Blau

2341   THE THREE SISTERS
        by Anton Chekhov; directed by Robert Symonds

2342   WAITING FOR GODOT
        by Samuel Beckett; directed by Herbert Blau

2343   THE ZOO STORY
        by Edward Albee; directed by Jules Irving

1962-1963

2344   THE BALCONY
        by Jean Genet; directed by Herbert Blau

2345   THE DUMB WAITER
        by Harold Pinter; directed by Timothy Ward

2346   GALILEO
        by Bertolt Brecht; directed by Herbert Blau

2347   THE GLASS MENAGERIE
        by Tennessee Williams; directed by Jules Irving

2348   MAJOR BARBARA
        by George Bernard Shaw; directed by Herbert Blau

2349   A SLIGHT ACHE
        by Harold Pinter; directed by Lee Breuer

2350   TELEGRAPH HILL
        by Herbert Blau; directed by Jules Irving

2351   TWELFTH NIGHT
         by William Shakespeare; directed by Robert Symonds

2352   THE UNDERPANTS
         by Carl Sternheim, translated by Eric Bentley; directed by
         Lee Breuer

2353   VOLPONE
         by Ben Jonson; directed by Robert Symonds

2354   WAITING FOR GODOT
         by Samuel Beckett; directed by Herbert Blau

                              1963-1964

2355   THE BIRDS
         by Aristophanes; directed by Herbert Blau

2356   THE CARETAKER
         by Harold Pinter; directed by Jules Irving

2357   THE CHALK GARDEN
         by Enid Bagnold; directed by Timothy Ward

2358   THE DEFENSE OF TAIPEI
         by Conrad Bromberg; directed by Robert Symonds

2359   THE FIREBUGS
         by Max Frisch, adapted by Mordecai Gorelik; directed by Jules
         Irving and Herbert Blau

2360   THE NIGHT OF THE IGUANA
         by Tennessee Williams; directed by Robert Symonds

2361   THE TAMING OF THE SHREW
         by William Shakespeare; directed by Robert Symonds

                              1964-1965

2362   THE COUNTRY WIFE
         by William Wycherley; directed by Robert Symonds

2363   THE ROOMING HOUSE
         by Conrad Bromberg; directed by Jules Irving and Herbert Blau

2364   UNCLE VANYA
         by Anton Chekhov; directed by Herbert Blau

2365   THE WALL
         (based on the novel by John Hersey) by Millard Lampell;
         directed by Jules Irving

                              1965-1966

2366   DON JUAN
         by Moliere, translated by Robert W. Goldsby; directed by Tom
         Gruenewald

2367   THE FATHER
        by August Strindberg, translated by Michael Meyer; directed by
        John Hancock

2368   THE HISTORY OF EDWARD II
        by Eric Bentley; directed by John Hancock

2369   THE LAST ANALYSIS
        by Saul Bellow; directed by John Hancock

2370   A MIDSUMMER NIGHT'S DREAM
        by William Shakespeare; directed by John Hancock

AMERICAN CONSERVATORY THEATRE*

1965-1966

2371   ANTIGONE
        by Jean Anouilh, adapted by Lewis Galantiere; directed by Jay
        Harnick

2372   BEYOND THE FRINGE
        by Alan Bennett, Peter Cook, Jonathan Miller, and Dudley Moore;
        directed by Hugh Alexander

2373   DEATH OF A SALESMAN
        by Arthur Miller; directed by Allen Fletcher

2374   THE DEVIL'S DISCIPLE
        by George Bernard Shaw; directed by Harold Stone

2375   IN WHITE AMERICA
        by Martin Duberman; directed by Harold Stone

2376   KING LEAR
        by William Shakespeare; directed by William Ball

2377   NOAH
        by Andre Obey, translated by Arthur Wilmurt; directed by
        William Young

2378   THE ROSE TATTOO
        by Tennessee Williams; directed by William Francisco

2379   THE SERVANT OF TWO MASTERS
        by Carlo Goldoni, English version by Edward J. Dent; directed
        by William Francisco

---

* ACT was established in 1965 in Pittsburgh, PA with the help of the
  Rockefeller Foundation, Carnegie-Mellon University, and the Pittsburgh
  Playhouse. All ACT programs contain interesting photographs; Performing
  Arts magazines contain articles about the contemporary theatre, per-
  sonalities, history of theatre, and informative notes about plays in
  repertory.

2380   SIX CHARACTERS IN SEARCH OF AN AUTHOR
           by Luigi Pirandello, adapted by Paul Avila Mayer; directed by
           William Ball

2381   TARTUFFE
           by Moliere, translated by Richard Wilbur; directed by William
           Ball

2382   TINY ALICE
           by Edward Albee; directed by William Ball

                              1966-1967

2383   THE AMERICAN DREAM
           by Edward Albee; directed by William Ball. Performed at the
           Marines' Memorial Theatre, the same evening as *The Zoo Story*,
           under the title of *Albee Acts*

2384   ARSENIC AND OLD LACE
           by Joseph Kesselring; directed by Allen Fletcher

2385   BEYOND THE FRINGE
           by Alan Bennett, Peter Cook, Jonathan Miller, and Dudley Moore;
           directed by Rene Auberjonois

2386   CHARLEY'S AUNT
           by Brandon Thomas; directed by Edward Hastings

2387   DEAR LIAR
           (based on correspondence of George Bernard Shaw and Mrs.
           Patricia Campbell) by Jerome Kilty; directed by Jerome Kilty.
           Performed at the Geary Theatre

2388   DEATH OF A SALESMAN
           by Arthur Miller; directed by Allen Fletcher

2389   ENDGAME
           by Samuel Beckett; directed by Patrick Tovatt

2390   KRAPP'S LAST TAPE
           by Samuel Beckett; directed by Scott Hylands

2391   LONG DAY'S JOURNEY INTO NIGHT
           by Eugene O'Neill; directed by Byron Ringland. Performed at
           the Marines' Memorial Theatre

2392   MAN AND SUPERMAN
           by George Bernard Shaw; directed by Jerome Kilty

2393   OUR TOWN
           by Thornton Wilder; directed by Edward Hastings

2394   THE SEA GULL
           by Anton Chekhov; directed by Edward Payson Call

2395   SIX CHARACTERS IN SEARCH OF AN AUTHOR
by Luigi Pirandello, adapted by Paul Avila Mayer; directed by
William Ball and Byron Ringland. Performed at the Marines'
Memorial Theatre

2396   TARTUFFE
by Moliere, translated by Richard Wilbur; directed by William
Ball. Performed at the Geary Theatre

2397   TINY ALICE
by Edward Albee; directed by William Ball

2398   THE TORCH BEARERS
by George Kelly; directed by Edward Payson Call

2399   TWO FOR THE SEESAW
by William Gibson; directed by Byron Ringland. Performed at
the Marines' Memorial Theatre

2400   UNDER MILK WOOD
by Dylan Thomas; directed by Byron Ringland

2401   THE ZOO STORY
by Edward Albee; directed by Richard Dysart. Performed at the
Marines' Memorial Theatre, the same evening as *The American
Dream*, under the title of *Albee Acts*

1967-1968

2402   DEAR LIAR
(based on correspondence of George Bernard Shaw and Mrs.
Patricia Campbell) by Jerome Kilty; directed by Jerome Kilty

2403   TARTUFFE
by Moliere, translated by Richard Wilbur; directed by William
Ball

2404   THIEVES' CARNIVAL
by Jean Anouilh, translated by Lucienne Hill; directed by
Jerome Kilty

2405   TWELFTH NIGHT
by William Shakespeare; directed by William Ball

2406   UNDER MILK WOOD
by Dylan Thomas; directed by William Ball

1968-1969

2407   THE ARCHITECT AND THE EMPEROR OF ASSYRIA
by Fernando Arrabal, translated by Everard D'Harnoncourt and
Adele Shank; directed by Robert W. Goldsby

2408   THE DEVIL'S DISCIPLE
by George Bernard Shaw; directed by Edward Hastings

2409   A FLEA IN HER EAR
            by Georges Feydeau, translated by Barnett Shaw; directed by
            Gower Champion

2410   LITTLE MURDERS
            by Jules Feiffer; directed by Nagle Jackson

2411   THE PROMISE
            by Aleksei Arbuzov, translated by Edward Hastings and Dwight
            Stevens; directed by Edward Hastings

2412   STAIRCASE
            by Charles Dyer; directed by Robert W. Goldsby

2413   THE THREE SISTERS
            by Anton Chekhov; directed by William Ball

1969-1970

2414   THE BLOOD KNOT
            by Athol Fugard; directed by Gilbert Moses

2415   A FLEA IN HER EAR
            by Georges Feydeau, translated by Barnett Shaw; directed by
            Gower Champion

2416   HADRIAN VII
            by Peter Luke; directed by Allen Fletcher

2417   THE IMPORTANCE OF BEING EARNEST
            by Oscar Wilde; directed by Jack O'Brien

2418   LITTLE MALCOLM AND HIS STRUGGLE AGAINST THE EUNUCHS
            by David Halliwell; directed by Nagle Jackson

2419   OEDIPUS REX
            by Sophocles; directed by William Ball

2420   THE ROSE TATTOO
            by Tennessee Williams; directed by Louis Criss

2421   ROSENCRANTZ AND GUILDENSTERN ARE DEAD
            by Tom Stoppard; directed by William Ball

2422   SAINT JOAN
            by George Bernard Shaw; directed by Edward Gilbert

2423   SIX CHARACTERS IN SEARCH OF AN AUTHOR
            by Luigi Pirandello, English adaptation by Paul Avila Mayer;
            directed by Mark Healy

2424   THE TAVERN
            by George M. Cohan; directed by Ellis Rabb

2425   THE TEMPEST
            by William Shakespeare; directed by William Ball

2426   THE THREE SISTERS
        by Anton Chekhov; directed by William Ball

2427   TINY ALICE
        by Edward Albee; directed by William Ball

                        1970-1971

2428   AN ENEMY OF THE PEOPLE
        by Henrik Ibsen, translated by Allen Fletcher; directed by
        Allen Fletcher

2429   HADRIAN VII
        by Peter Luke; directed by Allen Fletcher

2430   THE LAST SWEET DAYS OF ISAAC
        by Gretchen Cryer; directed by Arthur Sherman

2431   THE LATENT HETEROSEXUAL
        by Paddy Chayefsky; directed by Allen Fletcher

2432   MAX MORATH AT THE TURN OF THE CENTURY
        by Max Morath; directed by Dennis Dougherty

2433   THE MERCHANT OF VENICE
        by William Shakespeare; directed by Ellis Rabb

2434   THE RELAPSE
        by Sir John Vanbrugh; directed by Edward Hastings

2435   THE SELLING OF THE PRESIDENT
        by John Flaxman; directed by Ellis Rabb

2436   THE TEMPEST
        by William Shakespeare; directed by William Ball

2437   THE TIME OF YOUR LIFE
        by William Saroyan; directed by Edward Hastings

2438   WILL ROGERS' U.S.A.
        adapted by Paul Shyre; directed by Paul Shyre. Program con-
        tains biographical notes about Will Rogers

                        1971-1972

2439   ANTONY AND CLEOPATRA
        by William Shakespeare; directed by Allen Fletcher

2440   CAESAR AND CLEOPATRA
        by George Bernard Shaw; directed by William Ball

2441   THE CONTRACTOR
        by David Storey; directed by William Ball

2442   DANDY DICK
        by Sir Arthur Wing Pinero; directed by Edward Hastings

2443   PARADISE LOST
        by Clifford Odets; directed by Allen Fletcher

2444   PRIVATE LIVES
        by Noel Coward; directed by Francis Ford Coppola

2445   ROSENCRANTZ AND GUILDENSTERN ARE DEAD
        by Tom Stoppard; directed by William Ball

2446   SLEUTH
        by Anthony Shaffer; directed by Ellis Rabb

2447   THE TAVERN
        by George M. Cohan; directed by Ellis Rabb

1972-1973

2448   THE CRUCIBLE
        by Arthur Miller; directed by William Ball

2449   CYRANO DE BERGERAC
        by Edmond Rostand, translated by Brian Hooker, adapted by
        Dennis Powers; directed by William Ball

2450   A DOLL'S HOUSE
        by Henrik Ibsen, translated by Allen Fletcher; directed by
        Allen Fletcher

2451   DON'T BOTHER ME I CAN'T COPE
        by Micki Grant, conceived by Vinette Carroll; directed by
        Vinette Carroll

2452   THE HOUSE OF BLUE LEAVES
        by John Guare; directed by Edward Hastings

2453   THE MERCHANT OF VENICE
        by William Shakespeare; directed by Robert Bonaventura

2454   A MIDSUMMER NIGHT'S DREAM
        by William Shakespeare; directed by Peter Brook

2455   THE MYSTERY CYCLE
        by Nagle Jackson; directed by Nagle Jackson

2456   THAT CHAMPIONSHIP SEASON
        by Jason Miller; directed by Allen Fletcher

2457   YOU CAN'T TAKE IT WITH YOU
        by Moss Hart and George S. Kaufman; directed by Jack O'Brien

1973-1974

2458   BROADWAY
        by Philip Dunning and George Abbott; directed by Edward
        Hastings

2459   THE CHERRY ORCHARD
        by Anton Chekhov, English translation by William Ball and
        Dennis Powers; directed by William Ball

2460   CYRANO DE BERGERAC
        by Edmond Rostand, translated by Brian Hooker, adapted by
        Dennis Powers; directed by William Ball

2461   FAMILY ALBUM
        by Noel Coward; directed by Edward Hastings. Performed the
        same evening as *Red Peppers* and *Shadow Play*, under the title
        of *Tonight at 8:30*

2462   GODSPELL
        (a musical based upon the Gospel according to *St. Matthew*)
        conceived by John-Michael Tebelak, music and lyrics by Stephen
        Schwartz; directed by Larry Whiteley

2463   THE HOT L BALTIMORE
        by Lanford Wilson; directed by Allen Fletcher

2464   THE HOUSE OF BERNARDA ALBA
        by Federico Garcia Lorca, English translation by Tom Stoppard;
        directed by Joy Carlin

2465   THE MISER
        by Moliere; translated by Donald M. Frame; directed by Allen
        Fletcher

2466   OH COWARD!
        by Noel Coward, devised by Roderick Cook; directed by Roderick
        Cook

2467   RED PEPPERS
        by Noel Coward, music by Paul Blake; directed by Paul Blake.
        Performed the same evening as *Family Album* and *Shadow Play*,
        under the title of *Tonight at 8:30*

2468   SHADOW PLAY
        by Noel Coward, music by Paul Blake; directed by Paul Blake.
        Performed the same evening as *Family Album* and *Red Peppers*,
        under the title of *Tonight at 8:30*

2469   THE SUNSHINE BOYS
        by Neil Simon; directed by Jeremiah Morris

2470   THE TAMING OF THE SHREW
        by William Shakespeare; directed by William Ball

2471   WILL ROGERS' U.S.A.
        adapted by Paul Shyre; directed by Paul Shyre. Performed at
        the Marines' Memorial Theatre

2472   YOU CAN'T TAKE IT WITH YOU
        by Moss Hart and George S. Kaufman; directed by Jack O'Brien

1974-1975

2473   CYRANO DE BERGERAC
        by Edmond Rostand, translated by Brian Hooker, adapted by
        Dennis Powers; directed by William Ball

2474   JUMPERS
        by Tom Stoppard; directed by William Ball

2475   THE RULING CLASS
        by Peter Barnes; directed by Allen Fletcher

2476   STREET SCENE
        by Elmer Rice; directed by Edward Hastings

2477   THE TAMING OF THE SHREW
        by William Shakespeare; directed by William Ball

2478   THE THREEPENNY OPERA
        text and lyrics by Bertolt Brecht, music by Kurt Weill, English
        adaptation by Marc Blitzstein; directed by Andrei Serban

Santa Clara, CA

CALIFORNIA SHAKESPEARE FESTIVAL

1966 (Summer)

2479   HAMLET
        by William Shakespeare; directed by Roger D. Gross. Program
        contains photographs of past *Hamlet* performers

2480   THE TAMING OF THE SHREW
        by William Shakespeare; directed by James Dunn. Program con-
        tains photographs of past *Shrew* performers

1968*

2481   THE COMEDY OF ERRORS
        by William Shakespeare; directed by Roger D. Gross

2482   A MIDSUMMER NIGHT'S DREAM
        by William Shakespeare; directed by James Dunn

2483   OTHELLO
        by William Shakespeare; directed by James Dunn

2484   RICHARD III
        by William Shakespeare; directed by Roger D. Gross

2485   THE TAMING OF THE SHREW
        by William Shakespeare; directed by James Dunn

* Program contains interesting notes and photographs.

Sarasota, FL

ASOLO THEATRE*

1963

2486   CYRANO DE BERGERAC
by Edmond Rostand, English adaptation by James Forsyth;
directed by Richard G. Fallon; dueling scenes directed by
Paul Brumer

2487   THE MISTRESS OF THE INN
by Carlo Goldoni, translated by Robert Strane; directed by
Robert Strane

2488   THE RIVALS
by Richard Brinsley Sheridan; directed by Robert Strane

2489   THE SCHOOL FOR WIVES
by Moliere, translated by Eberle Thomas; directed by Eberle
Thomas

2490   THE TAMING OF THE SHREW
by William Shakespeare; directed by Eberle Thomas

1967

2491   AS YOU LIKE IT
by William Shakespeare; directed by Eberle Thomas

2492   THE CHERRY ORCHARD
by Anton Chekhov; directed by Robert Strane

2493   ELEONORA DUSE
by Mario Fratti; directed by Richard G. Fallon

2494   THE FAN
by Carlo Goldoni, translated by Eberle Thomas; directed by
Eberle Thomas

2495   THE MADWOMAN OF CHAILLOT
by Jean Giraudoux, adapted by Maurice Valency; directed by
Eberle Thomas

2496   MAJOR BARBARA
by George Bernard Shaw; directed by Robert Strane

2497   ROMEO AND JULIET
by William Shakespeare; directed by Robert Strane

* Award winning souvenir books and playbills are of exceptional quality,
  containing photographs of cast and prints of contributing artists.

2498   SCAPIN
         by Moliere, translated by Paul Weidner; directed by Paul
         Weidner

                                1969

2499   THE HOSTAGE
         by Brendan Behan; directed by Eberle Thomas

2500   THE LARK
         by Jean Anouilh, English adaptation by Lillian Hellman; directed
         by Richard G. Fallon

2501   UNCLE VANYA
         by Anton Chekhov; directed by Richard D. Meyer

2502   YOU CAN'T TAKE IT WITH YOU
         by Moss Hart and George S. Kaufman; directed by Robert Strane

                                1971

2503   BORN YESTERDAY
         by Garson Kanin; directed by Howard J. Millman

2504   CANDIDA
         by George Bernard Shaw; directed by Eberle Thomas

2505   CHARLEY'S AUNT
         by Brandon Thomas; directed by Robert Lanchester

2506   THE COMEDY OF ERRORS
         by William Shakespeare; directed by Bradford Wallace

2507   INDIANS
         by Arthur Kopit; directed by Eberle Thomas

2508   JOE EGG
         by Peter Nichols; directed by Jon Spelman

2509   LOVE FOR LOVE
         by William Congreve; directed by Robert Strane

2510   OUR TOWN
         by Thornton Wilder; directed by Robert Strane

2511   THE PUPPET PRINCE
         by Alan Cullen; directed by Jon Spelman

2512   THE SNOW QUEEN
         (based on the story by Hans Christian Anderson) by Suria Magito
         and Rudolph Weil; directed by Moses Goldberg

2513   THE SUBJECT WAS ROSES
         by Frank D. Gilroy; directed by Richard G. Fallon

1972

2514   THE BEST MAN
by Gore Vidal; directed by Bradford Wallace

2515   THE DEVIL'S DISCIPLE
by George Bernard Shaw; directed by Richard D. Meyer

2516   DRACULA
(adapted from the novel by Bram Stoker) by Frederick Gaines;
directed by Jon Spelman

2517   THE FRONT PAGE
by Ben Hecht and Charles MacArthur; directed by Howard J.
Millman

2518   HAY FEVER
by Noel Coward; directed by Eberle Thomas

2519   THE HOUSE OF BLUE LEAVES
by John Guare; directed by Robert Strane

2520   THE KING STAG
(based on a play by Carlo Gozzi) by Eberle Thomas; directed by
Moses Goldberg

2521   THE LEGEND OF SLEEPY HOLLOW
by Frederick Gaines; directed by Jon Spelman

2522   THE MATCHMAKER
by Thornton Wilder; directed by Robert Lanchester

2523   THE THREE MUSKETEERS
(adapted from the novel by Alexander Dumas) adapted by Roger
Planchon, music by Claude Lochy, English version by Eberle
Thomas and Robert Strane; directed by M. Jean-Louis Martin-
Barbaz

2524   THE TIME OF YOUR LIFE
by William Saroyan; directed by Richard G. Fallon

2525   TWELFTH NIGHT
by William Shakespeare; directed by Robert Strane

2526   THE YELLOW LAUGH
by Arthur Fauquez, translated and adapted by Eberle Thomas;
directed by Moses Goldberg

1973

2527   ANGEL STREET
by Patrick Hamilton; directed by Howard J. Millman

2528   BIG KLAUS AND LITTLE KLAUS
(based on the tale by Hans Christian Anderson) by Dean Wenstrom;
directed by Richard Hopkins

2529   THE CANTERVILLE GHOST
         (based on the story by Oscar Wilde) by Barbara Reid McIntyre
         and Richard Strane; directed by Richard Hopkins

2530   THE CRUCIBLE
         by Arthur Miller; directed by Bradford Wallace

2531   THE EFFECT OF GAMMA RAYS ON MAN-IN-THE-MOON MARIGOLDS
         by Paul Zindel; directed by Richard D. Meyer

2532   HOTEL PARADISO
         by Georges Feydeau and Maurice Desvallieres, English version
         by Peter Glenville; directed by Robert Strane

2533   THE MERCHANT OF VENICE
         by William Shakespeare; directed by Eberle Thomas

2534   THE PHILADELPHIA STORY
         by Philip Barry; directed by Eberle Thomas

2535   PYGMALION
         by George Bernard Shaw; directed by Richard G. Fallon

2536   THE WIND IN THE WILLOWS
         by Kenneth Grahame; directed by Eberle Thomas

                                 1974

2537   ARSENIC AND OLD LACE
         by Joseph Kesselring; directed by Amnon Kabatchnik

2538   BROADWAY
         Philip Dunning and George Abbott; directed by Howard J. Millman

2539   A DELICATE BALANCE
         by Edward Albee; directed by Bradford Wallace

2540   THE DEVIL'S GENERAL
         by Carl Zuckmayer, adapted by Tunc Yalman from a translation
         by Ingrid G. Gilbert and William F. Gilbert; directed by Tunc
         Yalman

2541   INHERIT THE WIND
         by Jerome Lawrence and Robert E. Lee; directed by Howard J.
         Millman

2542   MACBETH
         by William Shakespeare; directed by Robert Strane

2543   PRIVATE LIVES
         by Noel Coward; directed by Howard J. Millman

2544   RING AROUND THE MOON
         by Jean Anouilh, adapted by Christopher Fry; directed by Jim
         Hoskins

2545   TRELAWNY OF THE "WELLS"
        by Sir Arthur Wing Pinero; directed by Robert Strane

                              1975

2546   GUYS AND DOLLS
        (based on stories by Damon Runyon) book by Jo Swerling and
        Abe Burrows, music and lyrics by Frank Loesser; directed by
        Howard J. Millman

2547   HEARTBREAK HOUSE
        by George Bernard Shaw; directed by Paxton Whitehead

2548   KING LEAR
        by William Shakespeare; directed by William Woodman

2549   MISTRESS OF THE INN
        by Carlo Goldoni, translated and adapted by Robert Strane;
        directed by Bradford Wallace

2550   THE SEA
        by Edward Bond; directed by John Dillon

2551   TARTUFFE
        by Moliere, translated and adapted by Eberle Thomas and Robert
        Strane; directed by Robert Strane

2552   THERE'S ONE IN EVERY MARRIAGE
        by Georges Feydeau, adapted by Suzanne Grossmann and Paxton
        Whitehead; directed by Howard J. Millman

2553   TOBACCO ROAD
        (based on the novel by Erskine Caldwell) by Jack Kirkland;
        directed by S.C. Hastie

Seattle, WA

A CONTEMPORARY THEATRE

                              1972

2554   BUTTERFLIES ARE FREE
        by Leonard Gershe; directed by Clayton Corzatte

2555   ECHOES
        by N. Richard Nash; directed by Gregory A. Falls

2556   THE EFFECT OF GAMMA RAYS ON MAN-IN-THE-MOON MARIGOLDS
        by Paul Zindel; directed by William F. West

2557   THE ME NOBODY KNOWS
        (based on the book edited by Stephen M. Joseph) adapted by
        Robert H. Livingston and Herb Shapiro, music by Gary William
        Friedman, lyrics by Will Holt; directed by Allie Woods

2558   MOONCHILDREN
         by Michael Weller; directed by Pirie MacDonald

2559   THE TRIAL OF THE CATONSVILLE NINE
         by Daniel Berrigan, S.J.; directed by Tunc Yalman

2560   WHAT THE BUTLER SAW
         by Joe Orton; directed by Gregory A. Falls

                              1972-1973

2561   GILGAMESH
         adapted by Larry Arrick; directed by Larry Arrick. National
         Theatre for the Deaf

2562   UNDER MILK WOOD
         by Dylan Thomas; directed by Robert Loper

                                1973

2563   A CONFLICT OF INTEREST
         by Jay Broad; directed by Allie Woods

2564   THE CONTRACTOR
         by David Storey; directed by Gregory A. Falls

2565   A DAY IN THE DEATH OF JOE EGG
         by Peter Nichols; directed by Tunc Yalman

2566   THE DECLINE AND FALL OF THE ENTIRE WORLD AS SEEN THROUGH THE
         EYES OF COLE PORTER
         by Ben Bagley, words and music by Cole Porter; directed by
         Robert Loper

2567   NO PLACE TO BE SOMEBODY
         by Charles Gordone; directed by Allie Woods

2568   OLD TIMES
         by Harold Pinter; directed by Robert Loper

2569   ONE FLEW OVER THE CUCKOO'S NEST
         (based on the book by Ken Kesey) by Dale Wasserman; directed
         by M. Burke Walker

                                1974

2570   ABSURD MUSICAL REVUE FOR CHILDREN: THE LOCOMOTION SHOW
         directed by Arne Zaslove; musical director, Stan Keen.
         Children's Theatre; toured state of Washington, performing
         at schools

2571   THE ANNIVERSARY
         by Anton Chekhov, English version by Theodore Hoffman; directed
         by Jack Sydow. Performed the same evening as *The Brute* and *The
         Marriage Proposal*, under the title of *Three Early Farces by
         Anton Chekhov*

2572 THE BALD SOPRANO
by Eugene Ionesco; directed by M. Burke Walker. Performed the
same evening as *The Chairs*

2573 THE BRUTE
by Anton Chekhov, English version by Eric Bentley; directed by
Jack Sydow. Performed the same evening as *The Anniversary* and
The Marriage Proposal, under the title of *Three Early Farces
by Anton Chekhov*

2574 THE CHAIRS
by Eugene Ionesco; directed by M. Burke Walker. Performed the
same evening as *The Bald Soprano*

2575 THE CHRISTMAS SHOW
by the Contemporary Theatre Company; directed by Gregory A.
Falls; musical director, Stan Keen. Children's Theatre

2576 COUNT DRACULA
(adapted from the novel by Bram Stoker) by Ted Tiller; directed
by Gregory A. Falls

2577 THE DYBBUK
by S. Ansky; directed by John Broome. National Theatre for the
Deaf; performed the same evening as *Priscilla, Princess of
Power*

2578 GODSPELL
(a musical based upon the Gospel according to *St. Matthew*)
conceived by John-Michael Tebelak, music and lyrics by Stephen
Schwartz; directed by Gregory A. Falls; musical director, Stan
Keen

2579 THE HEIRESS
(based on *Washington Square* by Henry James) by Ruth and Augustus
Goetz; directed by Gregory A. Falls

2580 THE HOT L BALTIMORE
by Lanford Wilson; directed by Gregory A. Falls

2581 IN CELEBRATION
by David Storey; directed by Robert Loper

2582 THE MARRIAGE PROPOSAL
by Anton Chekhov, English version by Theodore Hoffman; directed
by Jack Sydow. Performed the same evening as *The Anniversary*
and *The Brute*, under the title of *Three Early Farces by Anton
Chekhov*

2583 PRISCILLA, PRINCESS OF POWER
by James Stevenson, adapted by the Contemporary Theatre Company;
directed by Ed Waterstreet, Jr. National Theatre for the Deaf;
performed the same evening as *The Dybbuk*

2584 A STREETCAR NAMED DESIRE
by Tennessee Williams; directed by Pirie MacDonald

2585   TWIGS
         by George Furth; directed by William F. West

                              1975

2586   THE HOLLOW CROWN
         by John Barton; directed by Margaret Booker; musical director,
         Stan Keen

2587   OF MICE AND MEN
         by John Steinbeck; directed by Robert Loper

2588   OH COWARD!
         by Noel Coward, devised by Roderick Cook; directed by Jack
         Sydow

2589   QUIET CARAVANS
         by Barry Dinerman; directed by Gregory A. Falls

2590   THE RESISTIBLE RISE OF ARTURO UI
         by Bertolt Brecht, adapted by George Tabori; directed by
         Gregory A. Falls

2591   SLEUTH
         by Anthony Shaffer; directed by James Higgins

2592   WHEN YOU COMIN' BACK, RED RYDER?
         by Mark Medoff; directed by M. Burke Walker

SEATTLE REPERTORY THEATRE

                         1963-1964*

2593   DEATH OF A SALESMAN
         by Arthur Miller; directed by Thomas Hill

2594   THE FIREBUGS
         by Max Frisch; directed by Andre Gregory

2595   KING LEAR
         by William Shakespeare; directed by Stuart Vaughan

2596   THE LADY'S NOT FOR BURNING
         by Christopher Fry; directed by Stuart Vaughan

2597   SHADOW OF HEROES
         by Robert Ardrey; directed by Stuart Vaughan

                         1964-1965

2598   AH, WILDERNESS!
         by Eugene O'Neill; directed by Thomas Hill

---

* Inaugural season.

2599 THE CHERRY ORCHARD
   by Anton Chekhov; directed by Thomas Hill

2600 DEATH OF A SALESMAN
   by Arthur Miller; directed by Thomas Hill

2601 HAMLET
   by William Shakespeare; directed by Stuart Vaughan

2602 KING LEAR
   by William Shakespeare; directed by Stuart Vaughan

2603 THE LADY'S NOT FOR BURNING
   by Christopher Fry; directed by Stuart Vaughan

2604 MAN AND SUPERMAN
   by George Bernard Shaw; directed by Stuart Vaughan and Archie
   Smith. A special program with photographs is included in the
   fiche collection

2605 TWELFTH NIGHT
   by William Shakespeare; directed by Stuart Vaughan

1965-1966

2606 AH, WILDERNESS!
   by Eugene O'Neill; directed by Thomas Hill

2607 THE CHERRY ORCHARD
   by Anton Chekhov; directed by Thomas Hill

2608 GALILEO
   by Bertolt Brecht, English version by Charles Laughton;
   directed by Pirie MacDonald

2609 HAMLET
   by William Shakespeare; directed by Pirie MacDonald

2610 HEARTBREAK HOUSE
   by George Bernard Shaw; directed by Stuart Vaughan

2611 THE IMPORTANCE OF BEING EARNEST
   by Oscar Wilde; directed by Stuart Vaughan

2612 JULIUS CAESAR
   by William Shakespeare; directed by Stuart Vaughan

2613 LONG DAY'S JOURNEY INTO NIGHT
   by Eugene O'Neill; directed by Pirie MacDonald

2614 THE TINDER BOX
   (based on the story by Hans Christian Anderson) by Nicholas
   Stuart Gray; directed by Pirie MacDonald

2615 TWELFTH NIGHT
   by William Shakespeare; directed by Pirie MacDonald

1966-1967

2616   BLITHE SPIRIT
        by Noel Coward; directed by Allen Fletcher

2617   THE CRUCIBLE
        by Arthur Miller; directed by Allen Fletcher

2618   THE HOSTAGE
        by Brendan Behan; directed by Pirie MacDonald

2619   THE NIGHT OF THE IGUANA
        by Tennessee Williams; directed by Allen Fletcher

2620   TARTUFFE
        by Moliere, translated by Richard Wilbur; directed by Allen
        Fletcher

2621   THE VISIT
        by Friedrich Duerrenmatt, adapted by Maurice Valency; directed
        by Pirie MacDonald. Programme lists plays performed from
        1963-1966

1967-1968

2622   THE AMERICAN DREAM
        by Edward Albee; directed by Allen Fletcher. Off-Center Theatre;
        performed the same evening as *The Death of Bessie Smith*

2623   BRECHT ON BRECHT
        arranged and translated by George Tabori; directed by Archie
        Smith. Off-Center Theatre

2624   CHILDHOOD
        by Thornton Wilder; directed by Patrick Hines. Off-Center
        Theatre; performed the same evening as *Infancy* and *Krapp's
        Last Tape*, under the title of *Two Against One*

2625   CHRISTOPHER
        by Clarence Morley; directed by James Bertholf. Off-Center
        Theatre

2626   THE DEATH OF BESSIE SMITH
        by Edward Albee; directed by Allen Fletcher. Off-Center Theatre;
        performed the same evening as *The American Dream*

2627   THE FATHER
        by August Strindberg; directed by Pirie MacDonald

2628   HENRY IV (PART 1)
        by William Shakespeare; directed by Allen Fletcher

2629   INFANCY
        by Thornton Wilder; directed by Patrick Hines. Off-Center
        Theatre; performed the same evening as *Childhood* and *Krapp's
        Last Tape*, under the title of *Two Against One*

2630   KRAPP'S LAST TAPE
        by Samuel Beckett; directed by Patrick Hines. Off-Center
        Theatre; performed the same evening as *Childhood* and *Infancy*,
        under the title of *Two Against One*

2631   LITTLE MURDERS
        by Jules Feiffer; directed by Hal Todd. Off-Center Theatre

2632   THE REHEARSAL
        by Jean Anouilh, English version by Pamela Hansford Johnson
        and Kitty Black; directed by Byron Ringland

2633   THE RIVALS
        by Richard Brinsley Sheridan; directed by Allen Fletcher

2634   THE THREEPENNY OPERA
        text and lyrics by Bertolt Brecht, music by Kurt Weill, English
        adaptation by Marc Blitzstein; directed by Allen Fletcher;
        musical director, Stan Keen

2635   U.S.A.
        (based on the novel by John Dos Passos) by Paul Shyre and John
        Dos Passos; directed by George Vogel. Off-Center Theatre

2636   YOU CAN'T TAKE IT WITH YOU
        by Moss Hart and George S. Kaufman; directed by Allen Fletcher

                            1968-1969

2637   BIG NOSE MARY IS DEAD
        arranged by Archie Smith; directed by Archie Smith. Off-Center
        Theatre; performed the same evening as *The Quickies*

2638   THE BLACKS
        by Jean Genet; directed by Jason Bernard. Off-Center Theatre

2639   JUNO AND THE PAYCOCK
        by Sean O'Casey; directed by Byron Ringland

2640   LOOK BACK IN ANGER
        by John Osborne; directed by Archie Smith. Off-Center Theatre

2641   A MIDSUMMER NIGHT'S DREAM
        by William Shakespeare; directed by Allen Fletcher

2642   MOURNING BECOMES ELECTRA
        by Eugene O'Neill; directed by Allen Fletcher. Off-Center
        Theatre

2643   OUR TOWN
        by Thornton Wilder; directed by Allen Fletcher

2644   THE QUICKIES
        arranged by Archie Smith; directed by Archie Smith. Off-Center
        Theatre; performed the same evening as *Big Nose Mary Is Dead*

2645   SERJEANT MUSGRAVE'S DANCE
         by John Arden; directed by Allen Fletcher

2646   THREE CHEERS FOR WHAT'S-ITS-NAME!
         by Jon Swan; directed by Josef Sommer. Off-Center Theatre

2647   A VIEW FROM THE BRIDGE
         by Arthur Miller; directed by Allen Fletcher

                              1969-1970

2648   IN THE MATTER OF J. ROBERT OPPENHEIMER
         (a play freely adapted on the basis of documents by Heinar
         Kipphardt) by Heinar Kipphardt, translated by Ruth Speirs;
         directed by Allen Fletcher

2649   JOE EGG
         by Peter Nichols; directed by Robert Loper. Off-Center Theatre

2650   SUMMERTREE
         by Ron Cowen; directed by Clayton Corzatte

2651   THE THREE SISTERS
         by Anton Chekhov, translated by Allen Fletcher; directed by
         Allen Fletcher

2652   VOLPONE
         by Ben Jonson; directed by Pirie MacDonald

                              1970-1971

2653   DAY OF ABSENCE
         by Douglas Ward Turner; directed by Israel Hicks. Performed
         the same evening as *Happy Ending*

2654   EMLYN WILLIAMS AS CHARLES DICKENS
         (scenes from Dickens' novels and stories) production supervisor,
         Robert Crawley. Solo performance

2655   A FLEA IN HER EAR
         by Georges Feydeau, new English version by Carol Johnston;
         directed by W. Duncan Ross

2656   HAPPY ENDING
         by Douglas Ward Turner; directed by Israel Hicks. Performed
         the same evening as *Day of Absence*

2657   HAY FEVER
         by Noel Coward; directed by Arthur Storch

2658   INDIANS (A THEATRICAL EXTRAVAGANZA)
         by Arthur Kopit; directed by Arne Zaslove

2659   THE MISER
         by Moliere, original translation by Nagle Jackson; directed by
         Nagle Jackson

2660   THE PRICE
        by Arthur Miller; directed by Robert Loper

2661   RICHARD II
        by William Shakespeare; directed by W. Duncan Ross. World
        premiere performance by Richard Chamberlain

                        1971-1972

2662   ADAPTATION
        by Elaine May; directed by Wayne Carson. Performed the same
        evening as *Next*

2663   AND MISS REARDON DRINKS A LITTLE
        by Paul Zindel; directed by Robert Loper

2664   GETTING MARRIED
        by George Bernard Shaw; directed by Clayton Corzatte

2665   HOTEL PARADISO
        by Georges Feydeau and Maurice Desvallieres, translated by
        Peter Glenville; directed by W. Duncan Ross

2666   THE HOUSE OF BLUE LEAVES
        by John Guare; directed by W. Duncan Ross

2667   NEXT
        by Terrence McNally; directed by Wayne Carson. Performed the
        same evening as *Adaptation*

2668   RING AROUND THE MOON
        by Jean Anouilh, adapted by Christopher Fry; directed by
        W. Duncan Ross

                        1972-1973

2669   ALL OVER
        by Edward Albee; directed by W. Duncan Ross

2670   CHARLEY'S AUNT
        by Brandon Thomas; directed by Mario Siletti

2671   CHILD'S PLAY
        by Robert Marasco; directed by Edward Payson Call

2672   MACBETH
        by William Shakespeare; directed by W. Duncan Ross

                        1973-1974

2673   JACQUES BREL IS ALIVE AND WELL AND LIVING IN PARIS
        (based on Brel's lyrics and commentary) production conception,
        English lyrics, and additional material by Eric Blau and Mort
        Shuman; directed by Jay Broad

2674   THE SEA GULL
        by Anton Chekhov; directed by W. Duncan Ross

2675   THE SKIN OF OUR TEETH
        by Thornton Wilder; directed by Edward Payson Call

2676   THAT CHAMPIONSHIP SEASON
        by Jason Miller; directed by W. Duncan Ross

2677   THREE MEN ON A HORSE
        by George Abbott and John Cecil Holm; directed by Robert Loper

1974-1975

2678   AFTER MAGRITTE
        by Tom Stoppard; directed by William Glover. The 2nd Stage;
        performed the same evening as *The Real Inspector Hound*

2679   THE ARCHITECT AND THE EMPEROR OF ASSYRIA
        by Fernando Arrabal, translated by Everhard D'Harnoncourt and
        Adele Shank; directed by Arne Zaslove. The 2nd Stage

2680   A DOLL'S HOUSE
        by Henrik Ibsen, translated by Eva Le Gallienne; directed by
        Eva Le Gallienne

2681   A GRAVE UNDERTAKING
        by Lloyd Gold; directed by W. Duncan Ross

2682   HALLOWEEN
        by Leonard Melfi; directed by Asaad Kelada. The 2nd Stage;
        performed the same evening as *Lunchtime*

2683   HAMLET
        by William Shakespeare; directed by W. Duncan Ross

2684   LIFE WITH FATHER
        (based on the book by Clarence Day, Jr.) by Howard Lindsay and
        Russel Crouse; directed by George Abbott

2685   A LOOK AT THE FIFTIES
        book, music, and lyrics by Al Carmines; directed by Arne
        Zaslove. The 2nd Stage

2686   LUNCHTIME
        by Leonard Melfi; directed by W. Duncan Ross. The 2nd Stage;
        performed the same evening as *Halloween*

2687   THE REAL INSPECTOR HOUND
        by Tom Stoppard; directed by William Glover. The 2nd Stage;
        performed the same evening as *After Magritte*

2688   THE WALTZ OF THE TOREADORS
        by Jean Anouilh; directed by Harold Scott

Stanford, CA

STANFORD REPERTORY THEATRE

1966-1967

2689   ANTONY AND CLEOPATRA
        by William Shakespeare; directed by Erik Vos

2690   THE BEGGAR'S OPERA
        by John Gay; directed by John Wright

2691   THE CAVERN
        by Jean Anouilh, translated by Lucienne Hill; directed by
        Sirin Devrim

2692   THE CHERRY ORCHARD
        by Anton Chekhov; directed by Mel Shapiro

2693   INADMISSABLE EVIDENCE
        by John Osborne; directed by Robert Loper

2694   ONCE IN A LIFETIME
        by Moss Hart and George S. Kaufman; directed by Edward Parone

2695   OUT AT SEA
        by Slawomir Mrozek; directed by Erik Vos. Performed the same
        evening as *A Slight Ache*

2696   A SLIGHT ACHE
        by Harold Pinter; directed by Erik Vos. Performed the same
        evening as *Out at Sea*

Stratford, CT

AMERICAN SHAKESPEARE THEATRE

1964*

2697   HAMLET
        by William Shakespeare; directed by Douglas Seale

2698   MUCH ADO ABOUT NOTHING
        by William Shakespeare; directed by Allen Fletcher

2699   RICHARD III
        by William Shakespeare; directed by Allen Fletcher

---

* Charles Wilson was musical director for the season.

1965*

2700   CORIOLANUS
         by William Shakespeare; directed by Allen Fletcher

2701   KING LEAR
         by William Shakespeare; directed by Allen Fletcher

2702   ROMEO AND JULIET
         by William Shakespeare; directed by Allen Fletcher

2703   THE TAMING OF THE SHREW
         by William Shakespeare; directed by Joseph Anthony

1966

2704   FALSTAFF; HENRY IV (PART 2)
         by William Shakespeare; directed by Joseph Anthony

2705   JULIUS CAESAR
         by William Shakespeare; musical director, John Duffy

2706   MURDER IN THE CATHEDRAL
         by T.S. Eliot; directed by John Houseman

2707   TWELFTH NIGHT
         by William Shakespeare; directed by Frank Hauser

1967

2708   ANTIGONE
         by Jean Anouilh, translated by Lewis Galantiere; directed by
         Jerome Kilty

2709   MACBETH
         by William Shakespeare; directed by John Houseman

2710   THE MERCHANT OF VENICE
         by William Shakespeare; directed by Michael Kahn

2711   A MIDSUMMER NIGHT'S DREAM
         by William Shakespeare; directed by Cyril Ritchard

1968

2712   ANDROCLES AND THE LION
         by George Bernard Shaw; directed by Nikos Psacharopoulos

2713   AS YOU LIKE IT
         by William Shakespeare; directed by Stephen Porter

2714   LOVE'S LABOUR'S LOST
         by William Shakespeare; directed by Michael Kahn

---

* Jose Serebrier was musical director for the season.

2715   RICHARD II
        by William Shakespeare; directed by Michael Kahn

                        1969

2716   HAMLET
        by William Shakespeare; directed by John Dexter

2717   HENRY V
        by William Shakespeare; directed by Michael Kahn; associate
        director, Moni Yakim

2718   MUCH ADO ABOUT NOTHING
        by William Shakespeare; directed by Peter Gill

2719   THE THREE SISTERS
        by Anton Chekhov, translated by Moura Budberg; directed by
        Michael Kahn

                        1970

2720   ALL'S WELL THAT ENDS WELL
        by William Shakespeare; directed by Michael Kahn

2721   THE DEVIL'S DISCIPLE
        by George Bernard Shaw; directed by Cyril Ritchard

2722   OTHELLO
        by William Shakespeare; directed by Michael Kahn

                        1971

2723   THE MERRY WIVES OF WINDSOR
        by William Shakespeare; directed by Michael Kahn

2724   MOURNING BECOMES ELECTRA
        by Eugene O'Neill; directed by Michael Kahn

2725   THE TEMPEST
        by William Shakespeare; directed by Edward Payson Call

2726   TWELFTH NIGHT
        by William Shakespeare; directed by Garland Wright

                        1972

2727   ANTONY AND CLEOPATRA
        by William Shakespeare; directed by Michael Kahn

2728   JULIUS CAESAR
        by William Shakespeare; directed by Michael Kahn

2729   MAJOR BARBARA
        by George Bernard Shaw; directed by Edwin Sherin

1973

2730   THE COUNTRY WIFE
        by William Wycherley; directed by David Giles

2731   JULIUS CAESAR
        by William Shakespeare; directed by Garland Wright

2732   MACBETH
        by William Shakespeare; directed by Michael Kahn

2733   MEASURE FOR MEASURE
        by William Shakespeare; directed by Michael Kahn

1974

2734   CAT ON A HOT TIN ROOF
        by Tennessee Williams; directed by Michael Kahn

2735   ROMEO AND JULIET
        by William Shakespeare; directed by Michael Kahn

2736   TWELFTH NIGHT
        by William Shakespeare; directed by David William

1975

2737   KING LEAR
        by William Shakespeare; directed by Anthony Page

2738   OUR TOWN
        by Thornton Wilder; directed by Michael Kahn

2739   THE WINTER'S TALE
        by William Shakespeare; directed by Michael Kahn

Syracuse, NY

SYRACUSE REPERTORY THEATRE

1970-1971

2740   THE FANTASTICKS
        words by Tom Jones, music by Harvey Schmidt; directed by Gary
        Gage

2741   INDIANS
        by Arthur Kopit; directed by Rex Henriot

2742   ROOM SERVICE
        by John Murray and Allen Boretz; directed by Rex Henriot

2743   THE TAVERN
        by George M. Cohan; directed by Rex Henriot

2744   THE TIME OF YOUR LIFE
        by William Saroyan; directed by Rex Henriot

                    1972-1973

2745   BYE BYE BIRDIE
        by Michael Stewart; directed by David Gold

2746   CHILD'S PLAY
        by Robert Marasco; directed by Rex Henriot

2747   DEAR LIAR
        (based on correspondence of George Bernard Shaw and Mrs.
        Patricia Campbell) by Jerome Kilty; directed by Rex Henriot

2748   GALILEO
        by Bertolt Brecht; directed by Gerard E. Moses

2749   THE GINGERBREAD LADY
        by Neil Simon; directed by Rex Henriot

2750   MISS LONELYHEARTS
        (based on the novel by Nathanael West) by Howard Teichman;
        directed by Jack Collard and Rex Henriot

2751   THE SECRET LIFE OF WALTER MITTY
        (based on the story by James Thurber) by Rex Henriot; directed
        by Rex Henriot; musical director, Tony Riposo

SYRACUSE STAGE

                    1973-1974

2752   AN ENEMY OF THE PEOPLE
        by Henrik Ibsen, adapted by Arthur Miller; directed by George L.
        Sherman

2753   NOON
        by Terrence McNally; directed by Arthur Storch. Performed the
        same evening as *Waiting for Lefty*

2754   WAITING FOR LEFTY
        by Clifford Odets; directed by Arthur Storch. Performed the
        same evening as *Noon*

                    1974-1975

2755   ARMS AND THE MAN
        by George Bernard Shaw; directed by Tom Gruenewald

2756   THE BUTTERFINGERS ANGEL, MARY & JOSEPH, HEROD THE NUT, AND THE
        SLAUGHTER OF 12 HIT CAROLS IN A PEAR TREE
        by William Gibson; directed by Arthur Storch. World premiere

2757   HEDDA GABLER
        by Henrik Ibsen, adapted by John Dillon; directed by John Dillon

2758   THE IMPORTANCE OF BEING EARNEST
            by Oscar Wilde; directed by Pirie MacDonald

2759   LA RONDE
            by Arthur Schnitzler, adapted by Arthur Storch; directed by
            Arthur Storch

Washington, DC

ARENA STAGE*

1958-1959

2760   THE DEVIL'S DISCIPLE.
            by George Bernard Shaw; directed by Zelda Fichandler

2761   EPITAPH FOR GEORGE DILLON
            by John Osborne and Anthony Creighton; directed by Alan
            Schneider

2762   THE FRONT PAGE
            by Ben Hecht and Charles MacArthur; directed by John
            O'Shaughnessy

2763   THE HOLLOW
            by Agatha Christie; directed by Zelda Fichandler

2764   THE LADY'S NOT FOR BURNING
            by Christopher Fry; directed by Zelda Fichandler

2765   A MEMORY OF TWO MONDAYS
            by Arthur Miller; directed by Zelda Fichandler. Performed the
            same evening as *Once Around the Block* and *The Purification*

2766   A MONTH IN THE COUNTRY
            by Ivan Turgenev, adapted by Emlyn Williams; directed by
            William Ball

2767   ONCE AROUND THE BLOCK
            by William Saroyan; directed by Zelda Fichandler. Performed the
            same evening as *A Memory of Two Mondays* and *The Purification*

2768   THE PLOUGH AND THE STARS
            by Sean O'Casey; directed by John O'Shaughnessy

2769   THE PURIFICATION
            by Tennessee Williams; directed by Zelda Fichandler. Performed
            the same evening as *A Memory of Two Mondays* and *Once Around the
            Block*

---

* Programs are excellent sources of information on director, dramatist,
  and particularly historical detail for American period plays.

1959-1960

2770   THE CAINE MUTINY COURT-MARTIAL
        by Herman Wouk; directed by F. Cowles Strickland

2771   THE CHERRY ORCHARD
        by Anton Chekhov, adapted by Stark Young; directed by Alan
        Schneider

2772   CLANDESTINE ON THE MORNING LINE
        by Josh Greenfield; directed by Alan Schneider

2773   THE DISENCHANTED
        (based on the story by Budd Schulberg) by Budd Schulberg and
        Harvey Breit; directed by F. Cowles Strickland

2774   THE ICEMAN COMETH
        by Eugene O'Neill; directed by F. Cowles Strickland

2775   MAJOR BARBARA
        by George Bernard Shaw; directed by F. Cowles Strickland

2776   RING AROUND THE MOON
        by Jean Anouilh, adapted by Christopher Fry; directed by
        F. Cowles Strickland

2777   THREE MEN ON A HORSE
        by John Cecil Holm and George Abbott; directed by F. Cowles
        Strickland

1960-1961

2778   THE EGG
        by Felicien Marceau, translated by Robert Schlitt; directed by
        F. Cowles Strickland

2779   THE END OF THE BEGINNING
        by Sean O'Casey; directed by F. Cowles Strickland. Performed
        the same evening as *In the Zone* and *Krapp's Last Tape*

2780   THE GANG'S ALL HERE
        by Jerome Lawrence and Robert E. Lee; directed by F. Cowles
        Strickland

2781   IN THE ZONE
        by Eugene O'Neill; directed by F. Cowles Strickland. Performed
        the same evening as *The End of the Beginning* and *Krapp's Last
        Tape*

2782   KRAPP'S LAST TAPE
        by Samuel Beckett; directed by Alan Schneider. Performed the
        same evening as *The End of the Beginning* and *In the Zone*

2783   MAN AND SUPERMAN
        by George Bernard Shaw; directed by F. Cowles Strickland

2784 THE RIVALS
   by Richard Brinsley Sheridan; directed by F. Cowles Strickland

2785 SILENT NIGHT, LONELY NIGHT
   by Robert Anderson; directed by Zelda Fichandler

2786 SIX CHARACTERS IN SEARCH OF AN AUTHOR
   by Luigi Pirandello, new version by Paul Avila Mayer; directed
   by Zelda Fichandler

2787 TIGER AT THE GATES
   by Jean Giraudoux, translated by Christopher Fry; directed by
   F. Cowles Strickland

1961-1962

2788 THE AMERICAN DREAM
   by Edward Albee; directed by Alan Schneider. Performed the
   same evening as *What Shall We Tell Caroline?*

2789 THE BURNING OF THE LEPERS
   by Wallace Hamilton; directed by Alan Schneider

2790 THE MADWOMAN OF CHAILLOT
   by Jean Giraudoux, adapted by Maurice Valency; directed by
   F. Cowles Strickland

2791 MISALLIANCE
   by George Bernard Shaw; directed by Warren Enters

2792 THE MOON IN THE YELLOW RIVER
   by Denis Johnston; directed by F. Cowles Strickland

2793 THE TIME OF YOUR LIFE
   by William Saroyan; directed by Alan Schneider

2794 UNCLE VANYA
   by Anton Chekhov, translated by Stark Young; directed by Alan
   Schneider

2795 WHAT SHALL WE TELL CAROLINE?
   by John Mortimer; directed by Alan Schneider. Performed the
   same evening as *The American Dream*

1962-1963

2796 ALL THE WAY HOME
   (based on *A Death in the Family* by James Agee) by Tad Mosel;
   directed by Alan Schneider

2797 THE HOSTAGE
   by Brendan Behan; directed by John O'Shaughnessy

2798 ONCE IN A LIFETIME
   by Moss Hart and George S. Kaufman; directed by Zelda
   Fichandler

2799   OTHELLO
        by William Shakespeare; directed by Alan Schneider

2800   THE THREEPENNY OPERA
        text and lyrics by Bertolt Brecht, music by Kurt Weill, English
        adaptation by Marc Blitzstein; directed by Alan Schneider;
        musical director, Richard Dirksen

2801   TWELVE ANGRY MEN
        by Reginald Rose; directed by Zelda Fichandler

2802   UNDER MILK WOOD
        by Dylan Thomas; directed by John O'Shaughnessy

2803   VOLPONE
        by Ben Jonson, adapted by Stefan Zweig; directed by Nina Vance

                        1963-1964

2804   THE AFFAIR
        (adapted from the novel by C.P. Snow) by Ronald Millar;
        directed by Mel Shapiro

2805   BATTLE DREAM
        by Herbert Boland; directed by George L. Sherman

2806   DARK OF THE MOON
        by Howard Richardson and William Berney; directed by Edwin
        Sherin; musical director, Ronn Carroll

2807   THE DEVILS
        by John Whiting; directed by Zelda Fichandler

2808   ENRICO IV
        by Luigi Pirandello, adapted by John Reich; directed by Zelda
        Fichandler

2809   HOTEL PARADISO
        by Georges Feydeau and Maurice Desvallieres, adapted by Peter
        Glenville

2810   THE TAMING OF THE SHREW
        by William Shakespeare; directed by Mel Shapiro

2811   THE WALL
        (based on the novel by John Hersey) by Millard Lampell;
        directed by Edwin Sherin

                        1964-1965

2812   BILLY BUDD
        (based on the novel by Herman Melville) by Louis O. Coxe and
        Robert Chapman; directed by Edwin Sherin

2813   GALILEO
        by Bertolt Brecht, English version by Charles Laughton;
        directed by Edwin Sherin

2814   HARD TRAVELIN'
        by Millard Lampell; directed by Edwin Sherin; musical director,
        George Manos. World premiere; performed the same evening as
        The Lonesome Train

2815   HE WHO GETS SLAPPED
        by Leonid Andreyev, English version by F.D. Reeve; directed
        by Edwin Sherin

2816   HEARTBREAK HOUSE
        by George Bernard Shaw; directed by Mel Shapiro

2817   THE LONESOME TRAIN
        by Millard Lampell; directed by Edwin Sherin; musical director,
        George Manos. Performed the same evening as *Hard Travelin'*

2818   LONG DAY'S JOURNEY INTO NIGHT
        by Eugene O'Neill; directed by Mel Shapiro

2819   THE REHEARSAL
        by Jean Anouilh, translated by Pamela Hansford Johnson and
        Kitty Black; directed by Mel Shapiro

                           1965-1966

2820   THE COLLECTION
        by Harold Pinter; directed by Dana Elcar

2821   THE LESSON
        by Eugene Ionesco; directed by Edwin Sherin

2822   MR. WELK AND JERSEY JIM
        by Howard Sackler; directed by Edwin Sherin

2823   OH! WHAT A LOVELY WAR
        by J. Littlewood and C. Chilton; directed by Edward Parone

2824   PROJECT IMMORTALITY
        by Loring Mandel; directed by Edwin Sherin

2825   SAINT JOAN
        by George Bernard Shaw; directed by Edwin Sherin

2826   SERJEANT MUSGRAVE'S DANCE
        by John Arden; directed by Edwin Sherin

2827   THE SKIN OF OUR TEETH
        by Thornton Wilder; directed by Zelda Fichandler

                           1966-1967

2828   THE ANDERSONVILLE TRIAL
        by Saul Levitt; directed by Edwin Sherin

2829   THE CRUCIBLE
        by Arthur Miller; directed by Milton Katselas

2830   THE INSPECTOR GENERAL
       by Nicolai Gogol; directed by Edwin Sherin

2831   LOOK BACK IN ANGER
       by John Osborne; directed by Hy Kalus

2832   MACBETH
       by William Shakespeare; directed by Edwin Sherin

2833   THE MAGISTRATE
       by Sir Arthur Wing Pinero; directed by David William

1967-1968

2834   THE GREAT WHITE HOPE
       by Howard Sackler; directed by Edwin Sherin

2835   THE ICEMAN COMETH
       by Eugene O'Neill; directed by Edwin Sherin

2836   MAJOR BARBARA
       by George Bernard Shaw; directed by Edwin Sherin

2837   POOR BITOS
       by Jean Anouilh, translated by Lucienne Hill; directed by
       Harold Stone

2838   ROOM SERVICE
       by John Murray and Allen Boretz; directed by Donald Moreland

2839   THE TENTH MAN
       by Paddy Chayefsky; directed by Donald Moreland

1968-1969

2840   INDIANS
       by Arthur Kopit; directed by Gene Frankel

2841   MARAT/SADE
       by Peter Weiss, English version by Geoffrey Skelton, verse
       adaptation by Adrian Mitchell, music by Richard Peaslee;
       directed by Alfred Ryder

2842   SIX CHARACTERS IN SEARCH OF AN AUTHOR
       by Luigi Pirandello, translated by Paul Avila Mayer; directed
       by Zelda Fichandler

2843   THE THREEPENNY OPERA
       text and lyrics by Bertolt Brecht, music by Kurt Weill, English
       adaptation by Marc Blitzstein; directed by Donald Moreland and
       Zelda Fichandler; musical director, Richard Dirksen

1969-1970

2844   THE CHEMMY CIRCLE
       by Georges Feydeau, translated and adapted by Suzanne Grossmann
       and Paxton Whitehead; directed by Alfred Ryder

2845   THE CHERRY ORCHARD
           by Anton Chekhov, translated by Stark Young; directed by Alfred
           Ryder

2846   THE DANCE OF DEATH
           by August Strindberg, adapted by Paul Avila Mayer; directed by
           Alfred Ryder

2847   EDITH STEIN
           by Arthur Giroń; directed by Zelda Fichandler. World premiere

2848   ENCHANTED NIGHT
           by Slawomir Mrozek, translated by Nicholas Bethell; directed
           by Norman Gevanthor. Performed the same evening as *The Police*

2849   NO PLACE TO BE SOMEBODY
           by Charles Gordone; directed by Gilbert Moses

2850   THE POLICE
           by Slawomir Mrozek, translated by Nicholas Bethell; directed
           by Norman Gevanthor. Performed the same evening as *Enchanted
           Night*

2851   YOU CAN'T TAKE IT WITH YOU
           by Moss Hart and George S. Kaufman; directed by Alfred Ryder

                                1970-1971

2852   MOTHER COURAGE
           by Bertolt Brecht, American version by George Tabori; directed
           by Gilbert Moses

2853   THE NIGHT THOREAU SPENT IN JAIL
           by Jerome Lawrence and Robert E. Lee; directed by Norman
           Gevanthor

2854   PUEBLO
           by Stanley R. Greenberg; directed by Gene Frankel

2855   THE RULING CLASS
           by Peter Barnes; directed by David William

2856   THE SIGN IN SIDNEY BRUSTEIN'S WINDOW
           by Lorraine Hansberry; directed by Gene Lesser

2857   WHAT THE BUTLER SAW
           by Joe Orton; directed by David William

2858   WIPE-OUT GAMES
           by Eugene Ionesco, translated by Donald Watson; directed by
           Mel Shapiro

                                1971-1972

2859   A CONFLICT OF INTEREST
           by Jay Broad; directed by Jerry Adler

2860 THE HOUSE OF BLUE LEAVES
      by John Guare; directed by Norman Gevanthor

2861 MOONCHILDREN
      by Michael Weller; directed by Alan Schneider

2862 PANTAGLEIZE
      by Michel de Ghelderode, translated by George Hauger; directed
      by Gene Lesser

2863 STATUS QUO VADIS
      by Donald Driver; directed by Donald Driver

2864 TRICKS
      (a musical comedy based on *Scapin* by Moliere) book by Jon Jory,
      music by Jerry Blatt, lyrics by Lonnie Burstein; directed by
      Jon Jory

2865 TWELFTH NIGHT
      by William Shakespeare; directed by Jeff Bleckner

                    1972-1973

2866 ENEMIES
      by Maxim Gorky, English version by Kitty Hunter-Blair and
      Jeremy Brooks; directed by Alan Schneider

2867 THE FOURSOME
      by E.A. Whitehead; directed by Alan Schneider

2868 THE HOSTAGE
      by Brendan Behan; directed by Norman Gevanthor

2869 I AM A WOMAN
      by Viveca Lindfors, music by David Horowitz; directed by Paul
      Austin

2870 A LOOK AT THE FIFTIES
      book, music, and lyrics by Al Carmines; directed by Lawrence
      Kornfeld

2871 ONE FLEW OVER THE CUCKOO'S NEST
      (based on the book by Ken Kesey) by Dale Wasserman; directed
      by Norman Gevanthor

2872 OUR TOWN
      by Thornton Wilder; directed by Alan Schneider

2873 A PUBLIC PROSECUTOR IS SICK OF IT ALL
      by Max Frisch; directed by Zelda Fichandler

2874 RAISIN
      (a musical based on *A Raisin in the Sun* by Lorraine Hansberry)
      book by Robert Nemiroff and Charlotte Zaltzberg, music by Judd
      Woldin, lyrics by Robert Brittan; directed by Donald McKayle

1973-1974*

2875   HORATIO
        play and lyrics by Ron Whyte, music by Mel Marvin; directed by
        Charles Haid

2876   IN CELEBRATION
        by David Storey; directed by John Dillon. Performed the same
        evening as *Relatively Speaking*

2877   INHERIT THE WIND
        by Jerome Lawrence and Robert E. Lee; directed by Zelda
        Fichandler

2878   LEONCE AND LENA
        by Georg Buechner, English version by Eric Bentley; directed
        by Liviu Bentley

2879   THE MADNESS OF GOD
        by Elie Wiesel, stage adaptation by Marion Wiesel, based on
        a translation by Nathan Edelman; directed by Alan Schneider

2880   OUR TOWN
        by Thornton Wilder; directed by Alan Schneider

2881   RELATIVELY SPEAKING
        by Alan Ayckbourn; directed by John Dillon. Performed the same
        evening as *In Celebration*

2882   THE RESISTABLE RISE OF ARTURO UI
        by Bertolt Brecht, translated by Ralph Manheim; directed by
        Carl Weber

2883   THREE MEN ON A HORSE
        by John Cecil Holm and George Abbott; directed by Norman
        Gevanthor

2884   TOM
        by Alexander Buzo; directed by Alan Schneider

2885   TWO BY SAMUEL BECKETT
        by Samuel Beckett; directed by Alan Schneider

1974-1975

2886   THE ASCENT OF MOUNT FUJI
        by Chingiz Aitmatov and Kaltai Mukhamedzhanov, translated by
        Nicholas Bethell; directed by Zelda Fichandler

2887   BOCCACCIO
        (based on stories from *The Decameron*) by Kenneth Cavander,
        music by Richard Peaslee; directed by Gene Lesser

---

* Programs for this season contain supplemantary notes on the dramatist.

2888   DEATH OF A SALESMAN
        by Arthur Miller; directed by Zelda Fichandler

2889   THE DYBBUK
        by S. Ansky, adapted by John Hirsch; directed by Gene Lesser

2890   THE FRONT PAGE
        by Ben Hecht and Charles MacArthur; directed by Edward Payson
        Call

2891   JULIUS CAESAR
        by William Shakespeare; directed by Carl Weber

2892   THE LAST MEETING OF THE KNIGHTS OF THE WHITE MAGNOLIA
        by Preston Jones; directed by Alan Schneider

2893   WHO'S AFRAID OF VIRGINIA WOOLF?
        by Edward Albee; directed by John Dillon

WASHINGTON THEATER CLUB

1969-1970

2894   THE DECLINE AND FALL OF THE ENTIRE WORLD AS SEEN THROUGH THE
        EYES OF COLE PORTER
        by Ben Bagley, words and music by Cole Porter; directed by
        Darwin Knight

2895   THE MOTHS
        by Raffi Arzoomanian; directed by Davey Marlin-Jones

1970-1971

2896   THE CHINESE AND DR. FISH
        by Murray Schisgal; directed by Leland Ball

2897   THE EFFECT OF GAMMA RAYS ON MAN-IN-THE-MOON MARIGOLDS
        by Paul Zindel; directed by Davey Marlin-Jones

2898   THE LAST SWEET DAYS OF ISAAC
        book and lyrics by Gretchen Cryer; directed by Davey Marlin-Jones

2899   THE WEB AND THE ROCK
        (based on the novel by Thomas Wolfe) by Dolores Sutton; directed
        by Davey Marlin-Jones

1971-1972

2900   ADAPTATION
        by Elaine May; directed by Joel J. Friedman. Performed the
        same evening as *Next*

2901   ALL OVER
        by Edward Albee; directed by Davey Marlin-Jones

2902   LEMON SKY
           by Lanford Wilson; directed by Davey Marlin-Jones

2903   NEXT
           by Terrence McNally; directed by Joel J. Friedman. Performed
           the same evening as *Adaptation*

1972-1973

2904   THE ECSTASY OF RITA JOE
           by George Ryga; directed by Harold Stone

W. Springfield, MA

STAGE/WEST

1968-1969

2906   ARMS AND THE MAN
           by George Bernard Shaw; directed by Jon Jory

1969-1970

2907   THE FANTASTICKS
           words by Tom Jones, music by Harvey Schmidt; directed by John
           Ulmer

2908   THE TAMING OF THE SHREW
           by William Shakespeare; directed by John Ulmer

2909   WAITING FOR GODOT
           by Samuel Beckett; directed by John Ulmer

1970-1971

2910   HAMLET
           by William Shakespeare; directed by John Ulmer

2911   LOVERS
           by Brian Friel; directed by John Ulmer

2912   THE PRICE
           by Arthur Miller; directed by John Ulmer

2913   TARTUFFE
           by Moliere; translated by Richard Wilbur; directed by J. Ulmer

1971-1972

2914   THE MIRACLE WORKER
           by William Gibson; directed by John Ulmer

2915   SCAPIN
           by Moliere; directed by John Ulmer

2916   SLOW DANCE ON THE KILLING GROUND
        by William Hanley; directed by William Guild

2917   THIS AGONY, THIS TRIUMPH
        by Reginald Rose; directed by John Ulmer. World premiere

                        1972-1973*

2918   BUTTERFLIES ARE FREE
        by Leonard Gershe; directed by William Guild

2919   THE EFFECT OF GAMMA RAYS ON MAN-IN-THE-MOON MARIGOLDS
        by Paul Zindel; directed by John Ulmer

2920   THE GOOD NEWS
        by Paul G. Enger; directed by William Guild. World premiere

2921   HEDDA GABLER
        by Henrik Ibsen; directed by John Ulmer

2922   THE IMPORTANCE OF BEING EARNEST
        by Oscar Wilde; directed by John Ulmer

2923   OLD TIMES
        by Harold Pinter; directed by John Ulmer

2924   TEN LITTLE INDIANS
        by Agatha Christie; directed by William Guild

                        1973-1974

2925   CAT ON A HOT TIN ROOF
        by Tennessee Williams; directed by John Ulmer

2926   THE CHERRY ORCHARD
        by Anton Chekhov; directed by John Ulmer

2927   THE DRUNKARD
        by W.H.S. Smith, adapted by Bro Herrod, music and lyrics by
        Barry Manilow; directed by John Ulmer; musical director,
        Thomas Babbitt. A new musical

2928   PRIVATE LIVES
        by Noel Coward; directed by John Ulmer

2929   THE SHOW-OFF
        by George Kelly; directed by John Ulmer

2930   THE WHITE HOUSE MURDER CASE
        by Jules Feiffer; directed by William Guild

---

* Programs for this season contain photographs from past performances.

1974-1975

2931   ECHOES
            by N. Richard Nash with Bruce Bouchard; directed by Steve
            Rothman

2932   THE GUARDSMAN
            by Ferenc Molnar, English version by Grace I. Colbron and Hans
            Bartsch, acting version by Philip Moeller; directed by John
            Ulmer

2933   MARCUS BRUTUS
            by Paul Foster; directed by John Ulmer. World premiere

2934   MASQUERADE
            (based on *The Servant of Two Masters* by Carlo Goldoni) by John
            Ulmer; directed by John Ulmer; musical director, Thomas
            Babbitt. World premiere

2935   ONE FLEW OVER THE CUCKOO'S NEST
            (based on the book by Ken Kesey) by Dale Wasserman; directed
            by Peter J. Hajduk

2936   PROMENADE, ALL!
            by David V. Robison; directed by Harry Ellerbe

2937   THAT CHAMPIONSHIP SEASON
            by Jason Miller; directed by John Ulmer

Williamstown, MA

WILLIAMSTOWN THEATRE

1975

2938   ABE LINCOLN IN ILLINOIS
            by Robert Sherwood; directed by Kenneth Frankel

2939   RING AROUND THE MOON
            by Jean Anouilh, adapted by Christopher Fry; directed by Nikos
            Psacharopoulos

2940   SAVAGES
            by Christopher Hampton; directed by Peter Hunt

2941   SIX CHARACTERS IN SEARCH OF AN AUTHOR
            by Luigi Pirandello, new translation by David Calicchio;
            directed by Olympia Dukakis

2942   SUMMER AND SMOKE
            by Tennessee Williams; directed by Edward Berkeley

Winnipeg, Canada

MANITOBA THEATRE CENTRE

1963-1964

2943   THE HOSTAGE
           by Brendan Behan; directed by John Hirsch

2944   LITTLE MARY SUNSHINE
           by Rick Besoyan; directed by Brian MacDonald

2945   A MIDSUMMER NIGHT'S DREAM
           by William Shakespeare; directed by John Hirsch and Robert
           Sherrin

2946   PRIVATE LIVES
           by Noel Coward; directed John Holden

2947   PYGMALION
           by George Bernard Shaw; directed by John Hirsch

1964-1965

2948   ALL ABOUT US
           by Len Peterson; directed by John Hirsch

2949   HAY FEVER
           by Noel Coward; directed by Warren Enters

2950   HEARTBREAK HOUSE
           by George Bernard Shaw; directed by Edward Gilbert

2951   IRMA LA DOUCE
           original book and lyrics by Alexandre Breffort, music by
           Marguerite Monnot, English book and lyrics by Julian More,
           David Heneker, and Monty Norman; directed by Rocco Bufano

2952   MOTHER COURAGE
           by Bertolt Brecht, adapted by Eric Bentley; directed by John
           Hirsch

2953   THE TAMING OF THE SHREW
           by William Shakespeare; directed by John Hirsch

2954   THE TIGER
           by Murray Schisgal; directed by Warren Enters. Performed the
           same evening as *The Typists*

2955   THE TYPISTS
           by Murray Schisgal; directed by Warren Enters. Performed the
           same evening as *The Tiger*

2956   WHO'S AFRAID OF VIRGINIA WOOLF?
          by Edward Albee; directed by John Hirsch

                              1965-1966

2957   ANDORRA
          by Max Frisch; directed by John Hirsch

2958   THE DANCE OF DEATH
          by August Strindberg; directed by Jean Gascon

2959   THE FANTASTICKS
          words by Tom Jones, music by Harvey Schmidt; directed by
          Edward Gilbert

2960   THE IMPORTANCE OF BEING EARNEST
          by Oscar Wilde; directed by John Hirsch

2961   NICHOLAS ROMANOV
          by William Kinsolving; directed by Michael Langham

2962a   THE PRIVATE EAR
          by Peter Shaffer; directed by Edward Gilbert. Performed the
          same evening as *The Public Eye*

2962b   THE PUBLIC EYE
          by Peter Shaffer; directed by Edward Gilbert. Performed the
          same evening as *The Private Ear*

2963   THE TEMPEST
          by William Shakespeare; directed by Edward Gilbert

2964   THE THREEPENNY OPERA
          text and lyrics by Bertolt Brecht, music by Kurt Weill, English
          adaptation by Marc Blitzstein; directed by John Hirsch

                              1966-1967

2965   CHARLEY'S AUNT
          by Brandon Thomas; directed by Edward Gilbert

2966   A FUNNY THING HAPPENED ON THE WAY TO THE FORUM
          book by Burt Shevlove and Larry Gelbart, music and lyrics by
          Stephen Sondheim; directed by Marvin Gordon

2967   GALILEO
          by Bertolt Brecht; directed by Edward Gilbert

2968   LULU STREET
          by Ann Henry; directed by Edward Gilbert

2969   LUV
          by Murray Schisgal; directed by Harvey Medlinsky

2970   THE RAINMAKER
          by N. Richard Nash; directed by Robert Kalfin

2971   ROMEO AND JULIET
            by William Shakespeare; directed by Edward Gilbert

1967-1968

2972   ANTIGONE
            by Sophocles; directed by Edward Gilbert. Performed the same
            evening as *Sganarelle*

2973   A DELICATE BALANCE
            by Edward Albee; directed by Edward Gilbert

2974   THE FANTASTICKS
            words by Tom Jones, music by Harvey Schmidt; directed by
            Edward Gilbert

2975   MAJOR BARBARA
            by George Bernard Shaw; directed by Edward Gilbert

2976   OH! WHAT A LOVELY WAR
            by J. Littlewood and C. Chilton; directed by Eric House

2977   SGANARELLE
            by Moliere, English version by Miles Malleson; directed by
            Richard Digby Day. Performed the same evening as *Antigone*

2978   A THOUSAND CLOWNS
            by Herb Gardner; directed by Louis Criss

2979   THE THREE SISTERS
            by Anton Chekhov; directed by Edward Gilbert

1968-1969

2980   FIDDLER ON THE ROOF
            book by Joseph Stein, music by Jerry Bock, lyrics by Sheldon
            Harnick; directed by Jerome Robbins

2981   THE SCHOOL FOR WIVES
            by Moliere; directed by Keith Turnbull

1969-1970

2982   AFTER THE FALL
            by Arthur Miller; directed by Kurt Reis

2983   MAN OF LA MANCHA
            by Dale Wasserman, music by Mitch Leigh, lyrics by Joe Darian;
            directed by Kurt Reis

2984   MARAT/SADE
            by Peter Weiss, English version by Geoffrey Skelton, adapted
            by Adrian Mitchell, music by Richard Peaslee; directed by
            Edward Gilbert

1970-1971

2985   HOBSON'S CHOICE
         by Harold Brighouse; directed by Malcolm Black. Performed at
         the Playhouse Theatre, Vancouver

2986   A MAN'S A MAN
         by Bertolt Brecht; directed by John Hirsch

2987   WAR AND PEACE
         (adapted from the novel by Leo Tolstoy) adapted by Alfred
         Neumann, Erwin Piscator, and Guntram Prufer, English version
         by Robert David MacDonald; directed by Edward Gilbert

1971-1972

2988   THE HOMECOMING
         by Harold Pinter; directed by Michael Mawson

2989   LADY FREDERICK
         by W. Somerset Maugham; directed by Leslie Lawton

2990   THE SUN AND THE MOON
         by James Reaney; directed by Keith Turnbull

2991   WHAT THE BUTLER SAW
         by Joe Orton; directed by John Hirsch

1972-1973

2992   EN PIECES DETACHEES
         by Michel Tremblay, translated by Allan Van Meer; directed by
         Andre Brassard

2993   GUYS AND DOLLS
         (based on stories by Damon Runyon) book by Jo Swerling and
         Abe Burrows, music and lyrics by Frank Loesser; directed by
         John Hirsch

2994   HAMLET
         by William Shakespeare; directed by Edward Gilbert

2995   HEDDA GABLER
         by Henrik Ibsen; directed by Edward Gilbert

2996   JACQUES BREL IS ALIVE AND WELL AND LIVING IN PARIS
         (based on Brel's lyrics and commentary) production conception,
         English lyrics, and additional material by Eric Blau and Mort
         Shuman; directed by Richard Ouzounian

2997   THE PROMISE
         by Aleksei Arbuzov; directed by Tibor Feheregyhazi

2998   ROSENCRANTZ AND GUILDENSTERN ARE DEAD
         by Tom Stoppard; directed by Douglas Rain

2999   SLEUTH
        by Anthony Shaffer; directed by David Giles

3000   A STREETCAR NAMED DESIRE
        by Tennessee Williams; directed by Edward Gilbert

3001   A THURBER CARNIVAL
        by James Thurber; directed by Biff McGuire

3002   WEDDING IN WHITE
        by William Fruet; directed by Alan Dobie

3003   WOMEN'S LIBBY
        by Libby Morris and Leslie Lawton; directed by Leslie Lawton

3004   YOU NEVER CAN TELL
        by George Bernard Shaw; directed by Edward Gilbert

                        1973-1974

3005   BLACK COMEDY
        by Peter Shaffer; directed by Malcolm Black. Performed the
        same evening as *Indian*

3006   THE DYBBUK
        by S. Ansky, adapted by John Hirsch; directed by John Hirsch

3007   ESKER MIKE AND HIS WIFE AGILUK
        by Herschel Hardin; directed by Howard Dallin

3008   GODSPELL
        (a musical based upon the Gospel according to *St. Matthew*)
        conceived by John-Michael Tebelak, music and lyrics by Stephen
        Schwartz; directed by Dean Regan

3009   INDIAN
        by George Ryga; directed by Malcolm Black. Performed the same
        evening as *Black Comedy*

3010   JOE EGG
        by Peter Nichols; directed by Edward Gilbert

3011   JUBALAY
        by Patrick Rose and Merv Campone; directed by Edward Gilbert

3012   THE PLOUGH AND THE STARS
        by Sean O'Casey; directed by Edward Gilbert

3013   YOU'RE GONNA BE ALRIGHT, JAMIE-BOY
        by David Freeman; directed by Bill Glassco

                        1974-1975

3014   THE BOY FRIEND
        by Sandy Wilson; directed by Alan Lund

3015   THE CHERRY ORCHARD
            by Anton Chekhov, translated by David Magarshack; directed by
            Edward Gilbert

3016   FORGET-ME-NOT LANE
            by Peter Nichols; directed by Arif Hasnain

3017   RED EMMA, QUEEN OF THE ANARCHISTS
            by Carol Bolt; directed by Edward Gilbert

3018   THE SUNSHINE BOYS
            by Neil Simon; directed by John Going

3019   TRELAWNY OF THE "WELLS"
            by Sir Arthur Wing Pinero; directed by Leon Major

TITLE INDEX

DRAMATIST INDEX

DIRECTOR INDEX

TRANSLATOR INDEX

ADAPTOR INDEX

COMPOSER-LYRICIST-
MUSICAL DIRECTOR INDEX

THEATRE INDEX